Between the Rhine
and the Bosporus

Also by Moses A. Shulvass

The Jews in Wuerzburg During the Middle Ages
(Die Juden in Wuerzburg waehrend des Mittelalters)

Rome and Jerusalem
(Roma Viyerushalayim)

Chapters from the Life of Samuel David Luzzatto
(Pirqei Hayim)

Jewish Life in Renaissance Italy
(Hayei Hayehudim Beitalyah Bithequfath Harenaissance)

In the Grip of Centuries
(Bitsevath Hadoroth)

BETWEEN THE RHINE
AND
THE BOSPORUS

Studies and Essays in European Jewish History

by

Moses A. Shulvass

The College of Jewish Studies Press

5724   Chicago   1964

Between the Rhine and the Bosporus:
Studies and Essays in European Jewish History
Copyright © 1964 by Moses A. Shulvass

Library of Congress catalog card number: 64-20613

Printed in the United States of America

CONTENTS

PREFACE

Ever since I became a student of Jewish history more than a quarter of a century ago, I became increasingly impressed by the vitality and the geographical expansion of Ashkenazic Jewry. In the course of my researches I came to recognize that Ashkenazic Jewry as an historical phenomenon is the substance of what should be called the *European period* in the history of the Jewish people. The expansion of Ashkenazic Jewry deep into Eastern Europe during the Middle Ages is a matter of common knowledge, but the impact of Ashkenazic immigration upon Italian Jewry is not so well known. My detailed studies in Italian Jewish history and the source material that I gathered on Ashkenazic penetration into Byzantium-Turkey prior to the arrival of the Sephardim, both contributed to my concept of the "identity" of Ashkenazic Jewry and the European period in Jewish history. Although the studies presented here do not give a comprehensive description of the European period in Jewish history, they will convey to the reader a view of the period as a whole and of major aspects of its social, religious, and cultural life.

The first two studies permit a glimpse into the life of the individual Jew and the community in the cradle of Ashkenazic Jewry's history, medieval Western Europe. The period was one of extraordinary tension; difficult conditions began to make the thought of *emigration* loom ever larger in the mind of the Ashkenazic Jew. The following two essays, comprising almost half of the volume, describe how Ashkenazic Jewry created in Eastern Europe, the main area of its colonization, the largest Jewish community that has ever existed; how it forged a magnificent expansion of Jewish religio-cultural life, perhaps never equalled in the dimensions of its "democratization" — its penetration into the teeming masses of a community of many millions. The latter studies and essays describe the more "limited" success of Ashkenazic expansion into Italy and the Balkans. It is my sincere hope that this volume will help the contemporary Jewish reader to comprehend the magnitude of the historical phenomenon of Ashkenazic Jewry, which at the outbreak of the Second World War comprised over ninety per cent of the Jewish people.

The phenomena described in this volume may also contain an element of guidance to the problems of Jewish life today. Historic Ashkenazic Jewry became what it was after making a grandiose migratory movement to new homes in Eastern Europe. In more recent times Ashkenazic Jewry built, again by means of migration, the new Jewish community in the Western Hemisphere. This new community now faces problems of communal reorganization and acculturation similar to those encountered by the Ashkenazic Jews when they established a new life in Eastern Europe, in Italy, and on the Balkan peninsula. The studies "The Knowledge of Antiquity among the Italian Jews of the Renaissance," and "Rome — Europe's Oldest Jewish Community," both describe how Italian Jewry willingly accepted the non-Jewish culture of the Renaissance and at the same time succeeded in retaining its full Jewish identity. A closer acquaintance with the destiny of these ancestors may perhaps help this generation to cope with the perplexities encountered on the threshold of a new and still veiled historical future.

I regret that quotations from Hebrew literature could not be reprinted in Hebrew script. As a rule, the system of transliteration suggested in the "Instructions for Composition" of the Hebrew Union College Annual was used. In studies previously published in scholarly periodicals, the original transliterations were retained; biblical names are spelled in their commonly accepted form.

In this work, much more than in my former books, I want to acknowledge the wholehearted collaboration of my wife, Celia, who shared with me all the trials which confront the author in the preparation of his manuscript. Without her devoted and never failing support this book would not be the book it is. The following organizations, societies, and friends have helped in various ways in the publication of the volume:

The Alumni Association of the College of Jewish Studies, the Chicago Chapter of Hadassah, the Chicago Rabbinical Council, and the Women's Division of the Board of Jewish Education and the College of Jewish Studies; Rabbi Ralph Simon, Mrs. Maxwell Abbell, Mr. Joseph J. Abbell, Mr. Arthur Shechter, Dr. Max J. Tepper, and Mr. Myron Weinstein. My friend Robert L. Aronson has given me valuable advice as to the printing and binding arrangements and my colleague and friend Dr. William Weintraub assisted me in reading the proofs. At the initiative of Dr. David Weinstein, President of the College of Jewish Studies, this book appears as the first publication of the newly established College of Jewish Studies Press.

Moses A. Shulvass

The College of Jewish Studies
Chicago, April, 1964

I

CRUSADES, MARTYRDOM, AND THE MARRANOS OF ASHKENAZ

Originally published in Hebrew in "Hadoar Jubilee Volume," New York 1957, pp. 71-76. Translated by E. I. K.

To the sacred memory
of my uncle
Rabbi Abraham Nathan Elberg

a

Virtually to the moment that the crusaders began mobilizing, Jews and Christians in Germany lived peacefully side by side without serious clashes. To be sure, periodic anti-Jewish eruptions did result in casualties and some Jewish apostasy. These were, however, passing events that left no permanent mark on the life of the Jewish community and its relations with Christian society.

In 1084, several years before the First Crusade, the Bishop of Speyer cordially invited Jews to settle in one of the cities of his realm and granted them broad rights. In 1090 Emperor Henry IV visited this new settlement and confirmed all its privileges. This was not an isolated incident in demonstrating real friendship between the two segments of the population. Further testimony is the fact that in the eleventh century, Jews sincerely mourned the death of bishops who ruled important cities like Magdeburg, Metz, Mayence, and Cologne.

Even when news began to reach Germany from France about anti-Jewish sentiments manifested by the crusaders, the German

1

Jews still did not sense the danger that lay ahead. They proclaimed days of fasting and prayer in sympathy with their kinsmen in France. At the same time they wrote them: "We are deeply concerned for you, but we ourselves do not have much to fear." There was indeed, a solid basis to this sense of security. The emperor was their friend, and the high church authorities, too, who exercised political suzerainty in the Rhine cities, generally did all in their power to prevent outbursts against the Jews. Had the emperor not been abroad at that time, events may not have been so grave and tragic.

At the first look it seems difficult to explain this basic reversal in the Christian population's attitude toward the Jews; how almost overnight mutual friendship turned into open and implacable enmity. As in every important social or historical phenomenon, this change was caused by various forces active under the surface that came into the open during the preparations for the crusades. Most of these factors were related to the religious situation that preoccupied medieval man above all else. As a result, anti-Jewish violence at the time of the First Crusade had a decisive influence on the entire relationship between Jews and Christians in the following periods. The crusades created a dangerous cleavage between the two parts of Western Europe's population. In fact, the break continued to widen resulting in even more tragic upheavals during the next few centuries.

Until the beginning of the eleventh century the two centers of the Christian Church, Rome and Constantinople, were engaged in christianizing Northern Europe. The process of divesting the Germans and Slavs of the pagan national religions and their adoption of Christianity lasted hundreds of years. The Poles and Russians did not accept Christianity until close to the year 1000. Moreover, even among those peoples that had accepted Christianity hundreds of years earlier, the masses still clung secretly to the beliefs and practices of their pagan past. Thus the Church was engaged both in the spread of Christianity and in the battle to extirpate idolatrous vestiges from Christian nations. Hence, until about the year 1000 the Jews were not the only

2

non-Christian community in Europe. When account is also taken of their small numbers it becomes apparent why they did not pose a special problem for Christians.

However, the situation was undergoing a change. One after another the peoples of Europe forsook their ancient religions to become absorbed by the Christian Church. The "inner" missionary activity of the church also bore fruit and resistant idolatrous practices began to recede slowly. During the eleventh century the position of the pope as head of the Western church became stronger and the Cluny movement produced a more dedicated and aggressive type of Catholic priest.

At that time the Jewish population in Western Europe also increased. Until the second half of the tenth century the number of Jews in Germany and Northern France was unquestionably very small. They were remnants of the Jewish community that inhabited the Rhine area at the time of Roman domination. Apparently, most of this Jewish population was destroyed when the empire fell, and very few remained. When, however, Germany and Italy were united in the ninth century, Jews from the South started to cross the Alps and to augment the Jewish population in southwest Germany and northern France. An even larger number of Jews began to immigrate to Western Europe from the Orient. The decline of the oriental Jewish communities, marked by the end of the Gaonate and the Exilarchate drove many emigrants westward. These Jews brought a knowledge of the Talmud, and aided by favorable conditions, established the base for Torah study that produced Rashi and the other great luminaries of the early Ashkenazic period.

All these factors, the obliteration of idolatry in Europe and the strengthening of Christian feeling, coupled with the growth of the Jewish community and its intensified Jewish character, made the Jewish group loom ever larger as the only non-Christian community stubbornly resisting the religion that had become virtually universal. These anti-Jewish sentiments, accumulated over the generations, erupted violently during the preparations for the First Crusade as a result of *propaganda* that suddenly became a decisive factor. In order to arouse sufficient enthusiasm among the masses to participate in a distant and dangerous military venture, the Church had to use effective propaganda devices. The primary aim of the crusaders was the redemption of Jesus' tomb from the hands of the non-believers. It is natural that in this connection a new awareness of the act of crucifixion took hold of the masses. Fiery orators and receptive masses thus became aware of the many Jews roundabout, the very Jews who for more than one thousand years have been carrying on their shoulders the guilt of the crucifixion. All anti-Jewish feelings which were aroused yearly during the Easter week became a staple of such propaganda. This is why the Jews of the Rhineland were "discovering" "ancient" Hebrew gravestones that "proved" their communities to antedate the crucifixion. Western European Jews sorely needed this "alibi" to counter the recurrent accusation that they crucified Jesus. The propaganda achieved its objective. Many Christians joined the crusades. However, the propaganda also achieved a secondary goal: The Jew was singled out before his Christian neighbor as a stubborn heretic guilty of the Redeemer's death. Thus a dangerous rift opened between the Jews and the Christians, and its result was the destruction of the oldest Jewish communities in Western Europe.

b

What was the reaction of the Jews to this sudden attack? They were terribly bewildered. They could not understand why God should bring down upon them such a grave calamity. "And no prophet or seer, or man of wisdom and understanding could conceive that the sin of the community was that grievous . . . ", complains one of the chroniclers of the time.

They, of course, tried to protect themselves as best as possible. Emissaries were sent to the emperor who was in Italy at the time. They even defended themselves with arms against the crusaders. However, it soon became apparent that the wrath of the mob had reached its boiling point and the protective

4

devices of the local bishops would not suffice. It became clear to them that only one path remained for themselves, their wives and their children — to die for the sanctification of the Holy Name. The overwhelming majority then decided not to die at the hands of their enemies. They chose the way of mass suicide, which became the most widely followed pattern of sanctification of the Holy Name in Germany in that and many subsequent generations.

The martyrdom of the First Crusade was not the first mass suicide in our annals. Nine hundred and sixty Jews, men, women and children, who retreated to Masadah when the Second Temple was destroyed, killed themselves in the year 73 C.E. when they saw no possibility of continuing their defense against the Romans. Josephus recounts this unusual event at length in chapters eight and nine of the seventh book of his *History of the Jewish War*. Following Josephus, the Hebrew *Yosifon* (chapter 97) also gives a vividly dramatic description of the event. The plea of Eleazar, the leader at Masadah, that the people slaughter themselves rather than fall into Roman hands, is deeply moving. The concept of sanctification of God's Name by self immolation occupies an important place in *Yosifon*. We do not know whether *Yosifon* was written in Germany, Italy or some other land. We do, however, know that this folk book was well known in the Rhineland at that time and was the chief source of Rashi's historical knowledge. And as we read the speeches of the martyrs encouraging one another to slaughter their wives and children and then themselves, as recorded in the chronicles written about the time of the First Crusade, a strong impression emerges that the views of the anonymous author of *Yosifon* were one of the sources that nurtured the zeal of the martyrs.

Another factor in this unusual phenomenon of mass self-destruction is rooted in the inner life of medieval man. The Dutch historian Johann Huizinga describes in the first chapter of *The Waning of the Middle Ages*, how medieval man lived in a state of constant tension that periodically led him to violence

5

toward himself and others. The number of violent acts by Jews against others was negligible. However, the fearful stress under which Jews lived during the Middle Ages may, perhaps, have been a factor that led to self-destruction. A case when Jewish women drowned themselves when their husbands were murdered by Christians is recorded even prior to the crusades.

Moreover, the fact that medieval man also believed himself to be an inveterate sinner, contributed to his readiness to die a martyr's death. Even early in the chronology of the events when the Jews of the Rhineland in their bewilderment speculated on the extent of their sin that provoked such punishment, they concluded in astonishing haste that they were indeed laden with iniquity and that God is just and His judgement true. It then became apparent to the martyrs that public sanctification of the Name was the only opportunity of expiating their sinfulness. The astonishing yearning of Rabbi Amnon of Mayence, to whom the prayer "Unethaneh Toqef" is ascribed, to sanctify the Name as atonement for considering conversion, is a striking example of Jewish feeling at the time.

All these factors together evoked in the medieval Jew a constant readiness to offer his life as a martyr. When the *Sefer Hasidim (Book of the Pious)* suggests to the Jew how to subdue evil inclinations it argues: Imagine if you were called upon to offer your life for the sanctification of the Name, you would doubtless find the necessary courage! In comparison, the conquest of the evil inclination is a simple matter! From this advice we note that the author of *Sefer Hasidim* assumed that most Jews of that period were ever ready to die a martyr's death. Contemporary Christian writers, especially those who witnessed the mass martyrdom of Jews at the time of the Black Death, recorded that the martyrs approached death joyfully as though going to greet a bride and groom. Many of the Jews who fell into the hands of the crusaders courageously vilified Christianity in their last moments, knowing well that it would result in fearsome torture prior to death. Accounts of this sort are so numerous, it appears to be one of the characteristic lines in this terrifying drama.

6

c

The Jew's courage in the face of death despite the agonizing torments it involved was bolstered by the Hebrew literature of the epoch. We have indicated above the role of *Yosifon*. Rashi, too, who witnessed the mass martyrdom at first hand, extols the martyrs. On the verse "The princes of the peoples are gathered together, the people of the God of Abraham" (Psalm 47:10) he comments "who gave themselves to slaughter and death for the sanctification of His Name." *Sefer Hasidim* contains many stories that were intended to strengthen a Jew's preparedness for martyrdom. The moral of one of the stories (Wistinetzki edition, p. 428) is that it is meritorious to lie and induce martyrdom in order to prevent the conversion of a community. Rabbi Moses Taqu, author of *Ketav Tamim*, whose greatness is apparent despite our inadequate knowledge of his biography, tells his contemporaries that the world is destined to revert to primordial chaos and that it "was originally created as a vestibule to the world to come to test man whether he is for God or against Him." These words contain the essentials of Jewish propaganda in behalf of martyrdom: The conviction that the Jew must testify in this world to his dedication to God in body and soul; and the widespread belief, common also among Christians, that the world will revert to chaos and it was not worth selling the birthright of martyrdom for the pot of lentils of a few more years on earth. Rabbi Jacob Baal Haturim, who prior to leaving Germany witnessed the frightful slaughter of the Jews in 1298, argued that there is no comparison between these torments and "the delights after death." Rabbi Jacob was at least aware of the martyr's anguish at the time of death. But certain contemporaries of Maharam of Rothenburg quoted him as saying that as soon as a man decides to die a martyr he no longer feels any pain. Maharam argues: It is well known that a person cannot avoid crying out when even his small finger touches flame. However, many submit themselves to flame and slaughter for

7

the sanctification of the Name of God, blessed be He, and utter no outcry. It is also generally maintained — adds Rabenu Perets of Corbeil — that when the martyr utters the Name of God, he withstands the ordeal painlessly.

This propaganda advocating sanctification of the Name of God, conducted by religious literature, was a necessity. First, despite their remarkable preparedness for sanctified death, the martyrs needed strong bolstering to carry through the terrifying act of slaughtering their wives and children. This is attested by speeches which, according to the chroniclers, the leadership addressed to the martyrs during their preparations for the terrible act. There are also allusions that not all who assembled to sanctify the Name of God, especially the youth, met their bitter fate joyfully. The youngster in Mayence who tried to elude his mother's grasp when she sought to slaughter him, was certainly not the only child who quailed before death. Surely, the lads who marched toward death expressed the emotions of their contemporaries when they lamented, "woe to our youth that we will not see our progeny nor attain old age."

The people of that age exulted in their fate: "And this generation is chosen by Him . . . for we had the strength to stand in His temple . . . and to sanctify His great Name in His world . . . " Rabbi Isaac of Vienna, author of *Or Zarua*, rules in accordance with *Sefer Hamiqtsooth* (in the opinion of many scholars also written in Germany), that in the case of a Jew who dies a martyr all Jews must eulogize him in the synagogues and his widow should never remarry "for his glory and the glory of Heaven." An interesting story is related in *Sefer Hasidim* (p. 375) about a community threatened with destruction whose members decided upon martyrdom. Some of the would-be martyrs started to destroy themselves, but lacked the courage to complete the act and remained alive and recovered. With the passage of time, when these semi-martyrs died, one of the villagers dreamed that their entry into Paradise was barred by those who had completed their martyrdom. The obvious moral is that a Jew must be courageous and go the entire bitter length

8

of self-destruction for the sanctification of the Name.

It became natural for the martyrs, faced with their cruel ordeal, to identify themselves with Isaac who was bound to the altar at God's command. Compared to their lot, however, where parents in the hundreds slaughtered their children and then themselves, the binding of Isaac lost its greatness. For although Abraham was prepared to sacrifice his son, he slaughtered in reality the ram. But in Mayence alone the martyrs of the crusades sacrificed eleven hundred in one day. " . . . Who has ever heard or seen such a thing, has there ever been such a sacrifice in all the generations from Adam. Are eleven hundred sacrifices in one day comparable to the binding of Isaac? The world trembled over one who was bound on Mount Moriah . . . Why have not the skies darkened nor the stars lost their glitter . . . over the slaughter in one day of eleven hundred sainted souls, so many infants and sucklings who have not sinned and the souls of so many poor innocents." Isaac's binding became pale and meaningless in comparison to what was taking place, and they began to tell themselves in the contemporary liturgical poetry that Abraham actually did slaughter Isaac, but the Holy One, blessed be He, covered him with dew from the Garden of Eden and restored him to life. The frightful reality of the crusades period provoked an interpretation of the binding of Isaac counter to the Biblical version. It is obvious that all the martyrological historiography of that period felt obligated to transmit the record of their courage in the style of the Aqedah.

And indeed, later generations treasured the memory of the supreme heroism of German Jewry from the start of the crusades until the days of the Black Death in the middle of the fourteenth century. A Nuremberg rabbi, eyewitnessing events, attests: "We see that the majority of Jews, even the wicked, submit to martyrdom and not one in a thousand defaults." The chronicle *Shevet Yehudah*, written two centuries after the Black Death, recounts that German Jews withstood the ordeal and suffered martyrdom during the years of the fearsome plague with greater courage than those of other lands.

d

And yet, both forced and voluntary converts were in this community of martyrs and saints. Non-Jewish sources reveal that in the first half of the twelfth century a strong missionary campaign was successfully conducted among the Jews of Germany. Rabenu Tam recounts that in France he personally knew of more than twenty cases of conversion. *Sefer Hasidim* records that rebellious sons threatened their parents with conversion. The community, naturally, disdained and isolated voluntary converts or those who were forcibly converted and did not revert to Judaism when given an opportunity. Their charitable gifts were not deemed acceptable, and *Sefer Hasidim* suggests that converts be labeled with derogatory names, of which a complete roster is provided by Rabenu Tam. However, when a convert did revert to Judaism every effort was made to erase the memory of his act. A reverted kohen was permitted to ascend the pulpit and offer the priestly benediction and would also be privileged to be called first to the Torah. Rabenu Gershom who encouraged this conciliatory attitude towards penitents argued that to do otherwise would stifle their resolve to recant. Rabenu Gershom himself experienced the deep tragedy of having a convert in the family, when his son was forcibly converted to Christianity. Apparently, the son never managed to revert and died a Christian.

Much sympathy was extended to those Jews who, during riots underwent forcible conversion in self-preservation. It is clear that despite the events described above and the pro-martyrdom propaganda waged by the Jewish literature, not every Jew died a martyr's death. There were Jews who accepted conversion to save themselves, and the chronicles reveal a sizable number of such converts. For example, the entire community of Regensburg accepted Christianity in 1096, and the same was true of most Jews in Metz. Small numbers of converts existed in virtually every community.

Practically all of these converts returned to Judaism. Both Jewish and Christian chroniclers recount that the moment that the crusaders left a city, the converts returned openly to Judaism. Emperor Henry IV, a friend of the Jews, in 1097 officially granted the right to Jews who had been forcibly converted to revert to their faith. This was a daring act by the emperor who perpetually was under papal attack. While the Church did not officially support a movement to forcibly convert the Jews, it did not concede the right of a convert to return to Judaism.

The emperor's edict and information from other sources demonstrate that virtually all forcible converts re-accepted Judaism. We have a curious story from Second Crusade days about a Christian priest who helped forcibly converted Jews to escape from Germany to France that they might openly declare themselves as Jews. And, adds the chronicler, "he accepted no money for it." The extent of Jewish loyalty by such converts can be seen from an event in the life of one of the community leaders in York (England). He came to London in 1189 as part of a Jewish delegation to bring greetings to King Richard the Lionhearted on the occasion of his coronation. At that time severe pogroms against the Jews broke forth and many were slain. Several Jews underwent forcible conversion to Christianity, among whom was Benedict (Barukh? Berekhyah?), the leader from York. When, on the morrow, the priests presented this convert to the king, to their amazement he unflinchingly introduced himself as: "I am Benedict, a *Jew* from York." Benedict remained a Jew and died shortly thereafter of wounds sustained on the day of the massacre.

And yet, a serious problem arose within the Jewish community in regard to forced converts who reverted to Judaism. We recall the story in *Sefer Hasidim* about Jews who were forbidden entry into Paradise because they were merely wounded and did not actually expire for the sanctification of God's Name. More hostility even was shown toward those who made no attempt at all to undergo martyrdom. In fact, the sources know of many people who scornfully reminded reverted converts of their temporary weakness. There was also a sizable number of Jews who refused to marry returnees to the fold.

Jewish leadership vigorously fought this hostile attitude. Ninety years before the First Crusade Rabenu Gershom, himself sorely wounded by his son's forced conversion, threatened to excommunicate those who derided the penitents. The records describing the events of the First Crusade try to defend the converts. They reiterate that their principle reason for converting was to be in a position to give Jewish burial to the thousands of martyrs. One chronicler reproduces a consolatory message sent by the leaders of a community to the converts: "Do not fear nor be concerned over what you have done." Another chronicler goes to the point of pronouncing that insulting them (the marranos) is like speaking against God. The rabbis decreed that returnees to Judaism are valid witnesses, and even *Sefer Hasidim,* saturated as it is with enthusiastic pro-martyrdom propaganda, advises to accept a contribution for the purchase of a Torah scroll from a convert who has not as yet had the opportunity to return publicly to Judaism. This indicates that the community leaders were convinced that forced converts strove to return to Judaism. Rabbis at the end of the thirteenth century tell of converts who endangered their lives in order to return to Judaism. Rabbi Isaac ben Moses of Vienna speaks with compassion of women who were forced into apostasy: "And the chaste young women were forcibly converted, yet their hearts turned to God; it is forbidden to speak derogatorily of them and one should tell their praise.

e

A comparison of the attitude of the German rabbis and pietists to forced converts in the age of the crusades, and the attitude of the Spanish religious leaders toward the marranos in Spain, reveals a deep and striking difference. The German pietists who never ceased advocating martyrdom, sympathized with the personal tragedy of forced converts and defended them. Whereas, in Spain only few defended the converts or understood the tragedy of their bizarre existence. On the contrary, Rabbi Solomon Alami, the great moralist who lived at the time of the

12

agonizing events of 1391 and the disputation at Tortosa, castigated the marranos and the strata of Jewish society that produced them. In a similar vein a later moralist, Rabbi Joseph Yaavets, who witnessed the Expulsion of 1492, had only words of contempt for the Jews who chose to practice their religion clandestinely instead of going into exile.

This divergent approach toward forced converts in the two branches of our moralistic literature did not arise over the question of why Jews should submit to conversion. This was obvious: Not every Jew had the spiritual stamina, nor was he prepared to accept death and torture if they could possibly be avoided. The emphasis was, rather, on whether or not a forced convert returned to Judaism at the earliest opportunity. And without discussing why the number of Spanish converts was disproportionately greater than that of the German converts, one fact is indisputably obvious: Virtually all German converts reverted to Judaism, while very few Spanish converts left their homeland in order to return to open Jewish practice.

The major factor in this difference is rooted in the deep disparity between the Jewish character of German and French Jewry and that of the Jews of Spain. The spiritual life of Spanish Jewry was riven with cleavages, with many perplexed Jews who sought philosophical rationales diametrically opposed to the fundamentals of Judaism. Since the Golden Age a strong secularistic current emphasizing temporal values dominated large segments of the Jewish population. Thus, when the calamity of 1391 befell Spanish Jewry, the base of Judaism speedily disintegrated and many passed over to Christianity. In these circumstances the men of learning instead of encouraging the masses to cling to Judaism at all costs, as did the German pietists, produced several of the most dangerous foes of Judaism, who during the dark days of the Tortosa disputation used their knowledge of Jewish lore to undermine the faith of their fathers.

Preachers and great moralists such as Rabbi Solomon Alami and Joseph Yaavets were well aware of this. Alami complained in bitter anguish against the intellectuals and aristocrats whose conduct and false teaching, according to him, provoked the great tragedy that befell Spanish Jewry. Following the expulsion, Rabbi Joseph Yaavets repeatedly emphasized in his book *Or Hahayim* that during the ordeal the common people and the poor withstood the test for Judaism far more courageously than did the intellectuals.

The situation in Germany was totally different. No spiritual cleavages prevailed in the Jewish community. From its establishment in the times of Rabenu Gershom until its decimation at the time of the Black Death, a period of three hundred and fifty years — the Franco-German Jewry was uniformly wholesome spiritually. The German Jew was mainly preoccupied with the study of Torah, possessed a deep and simple faith in God, and needed no philosophical speculation to resolve his doubts. German Jewry had virtually no intellectual types akin to those that were common in Spain's Jewish community. It was therefore apparent to all that forced conversion resulted from external compulsion and human weakness. True, the general guilt feeling of medieval man impelled the Franco-German Jew to rationalize that "his sins" were responsible for all travails. However, this was a mere repetition of an old fixed and general formula. It was far removed from the specific accusations that the Spanish moralists hurled at their brethren regarding their deep spiritual erring and evil practices. If such corruption existed in Germany as well, it was too rare to constitute a rationale for events. The crusades and other afflictions were disasters for which perhaps God's justifications could be found, but for which, in the ultimate analysis, the Jew could not be blamed. This was Rabenu Gershom's position at the turn of the millenium, and this remained the attitude of the rabbis in the middle of the fourteenth century. For the Jewish contemporary of Rabenu Gershom and his descendant ten generations later was the same humble simple believer, complete in his faith in his God.

II

ONE HUNDRED YEARS IN THE HISTORY OF THE JEWISH COMMUNITY OF WUERZBURG (1250-1350)

Originally published in Yivo Annual of Jewish Social Studies,
vol. 12 (1958-59) , pp. 196-210.

The Bavarian city of Würzburg is situated in a beautiful part of Franconia, on the banks of the Main River. The city was founded in the 7th century, and as early as 741 it became the see of a bishop. Its importance was constantly rising and it attracted the special interest of Charlemagne. In later years the city frequently played an important political role. Several of the German diets met there during the Middle Ages.

Initially Würzburg was an imperial city. But the power of the bishop was in the ascendancy and the city and its vicinity became a feudal state, one of those which sprang up rapidly in Germany at that time. The bishop came to be regarded as the duke of Eastern Franconia and assumed the title duke bishop. The Würzburg bishopric-state underwent many metamorphoses until it was secularized at the time of the Napoleonic wars. The Congress of Vienna ultimately denied the status of a state to the bishopric and it became a part of the province of Bavaria.

a

A Jewish community in Würzburg is mentioned for the first time in 1147. At the beginning of the second crusade the local populace together with a group of crusaders attacked the Jews

15

and killed several score of them.[1] Undoubtedly, however, the Jewish settlement in Würzburg is considerably older. It dates probably from the first years of the 12th century.[2] With the passage of the storm, there began a period of rapid advance for the Jews of Würzburg and in the second half of that century and in the first half of the following the community was one of the most prominent and apparently also most numerous in Germany.[3]

Around 1250 the Jewish section was in the center of the city, in the vicinity of the town hall, near Lake Rigol, which was gradually drying out. At least two streets in this area were known as Jews' Streets[4] and were in all likelihood settled by Jews exclusively. Nevertheless medieval Würzburg never had a Jewish ghetto in the true sense of the word. Non-Jews resided in the immediate neighborhood of the Jews' Streets and even had a monastery and a hospital there.[5]

To be sure, the Jewish section was not noted for its cleanliness. Lake Rigol was gradually turning into a swamp, into which the neighboring sewers emptied. It had, however, its advantages. It was in the center of the city. The non-Jewish population was apparently annoyed by the fact that the Jews occupied an area so close to the town hall and to several Christian religious institutions. A Frankfurt chronicle[6] narrates that the reason the Flagellants in 1349 attacked the Jews[7] was their resentment of Jewish occupation of the center of the city.

---

[1] Habermann, A. M., *Gezerot ashkenaz vezarfat* (Jerusalem 5706) p. 119; Salfeld, S., *Das Martyrologium des Nürnberger Memorbuches* (Berlin 1898) pp. 119, 371.

[2] Shulvass (Szulwas), Moses A., *Die Juden in Würzburg während des Mittelalters* (Berlin 1934) p. 9.

[3] The history of this period is given in detail in Shulvass, *op. cit.,* pp. 13-22.

[4] A document published in *Monumenta Boica* (cited herein as *MB*), XLII, p. 111, speaks of Jews' streets in the plural.

[5] Shulvass, *op. cit.,* p. 15, and the sources cited there.

[6] Hoffmann, Hermann, "Die Würzburger Judenverfolgungen von 1349," *Mainfränkisches Jahrbuch,* V, p. 113; Schudt, J. J., *Jüdische Merkwürdigkeiten* (Berlin 1922) II, p. 43, ascribed the same cause to the attack of the Flagellants on the Jews of Frankfurt. He erred, however, in the date, which he gave as 1346.

[7] Or were preparing to attack. See further.

Nevertheless the Jews remained in residence in their section near Lake Rigol. But, around the middle of the 13th century, the non-Jews apparently succeeded in setting a limit to the further expansion of the Jewish section. Whereas purchases of land near the Rigol by Jews in the period between 1147 and 1250 were frequently recorded, there is no mention of such activity later on.[8] There is no explanation in the sources for the cessation of this activity and we may assume that it reflected an effort by the non-Jews to dislodge the Jews from the center of the city.

The tension arising from the proximity of the Jewish quarter to Christian religious institutions found an outlet in constant disputes between the two sides. A permanent bone of contention was the question of payment for cleaning out the Rigol swamp. At last a settlement was reached: the Jews had to pay three-fourths of the expenses.[9] Although this is by no means certain, it may be assumed that this proportion of the expenditures would indicate that Jewish land holdings near Lake Rigol considerably exceeded those of the non-Jews.

There are no data on the size of the Jewish community in Würzburg in th 12th century. Too large, apparently, it was not, for it was only in 1147 that it acquired a cemetery.[10] Thereafter its growth was rapid. Toward the end of the 13th century Würzburg was considered among the large Jewish communities. In the Rindfleisch massacres in 1298 no less than 800 Würzburg Jewish residents perished.[11] The rise in the Jewish population was apparently the result of a large natural increase. There is no indication of any immigration of Jews to Würzburg on a considerable scale in the second half of the 13th century. To be sure, a small number of Jews from other towns undoubtedly did immigrate, for the Jews of Würzburg enjoyed then a period of comparative tranquility. This immigration was limited, however, by the size of the Jewish quarter, as indicated above. An analysis of

8 Shulvass, *op. cit.*, p. 29.
9 *MB*, XXXIX, pp. X ff.; *Regesta Boica* (cited herein as *RB*) , VII, p. 21, VIII, p. 109.
10 Habermann, *op. cit.*, pp. 119-120.
11 Salfeld, *op. cit.*, pp. 43 ff.; 192 ff.

the detailed lists of the victims of the Rindfleisch massacres shows that the average Jewish family consisted of four or five children and there were many families with eight children.[12] This natural increase was undoubtedly the result of the political stability and economic well-being of the Jewish community, as will be indicated later. Incidentally, the lists of the victims show that a large number of men had Germanic (Yiddish?) given names. The others had Hebrew names. Among the women Hebrew given names were rare.

Entirely different was the constituency of the Würzburg Jews in the first half of the 14th century. The laments written to commemorate the events of 1298[13] undoubtedly exaggerated when they stated that not a single Jew survived in Würzburg,[14] the fact nevertheless remains that thereafter a considerable part of the Jewish community consisted of new arrivals from other cities. At least ten cities in various parts of Germany, some of them quite distant, were represented in the rebuilt Jewish community.[15]

b

In the course of that one century, from 1250 to 1350, the Jews of Würzburg passed through an important stage in the development of their political status. The Jews of Würzburg, as well as those of other German cities, were in theory subjects of the central (imperial or royal) government, not of the local feudal lords. They were considered as "servi camerae,"[16] and the imperial government was responsible for the protection of the Jews, which responsibility it actually discharged from time to time. However, general developments were in the direction of weakening the central authority and of strengthening the local feudal rulers. In line with this course the Jews in many places were removed from imperial authority and placed under the

12 *Ibid.*
13 Habermann, *op. cit.*, pp. 216, 221, 227.
14 Shulvass, *op. cit.*, p. 39
15 *MB*, XXXIX, pp. X ff. and pp. 41, 68 ff.; *RB*, VII, p. 21.
16 Dubnow, S., *Velt-geshikhte fun yidishn folk*, V, pp. 133-136.

18

rule of the local powers.[17]

The earliest document extant in which the Jews of Würzburg are designated as "servi camerae" dates from 1322.[18] However, they were undoubtedly under imperial authority prior to that date, and from time to time they were actually given protection by this authority.[19] Nevertheless the Jews of Würzburg had to reckon with the local power—the bishop. Toward the end of the 12th century, although under no specific obligation, they began paying taxes to him.[20]

On the eve of the century herein described, the Reich took the first step to hand over the Jews of Würzburg to the bishop formally. In 1247 King Henry Raspe pledged the Jews of Würzburg to Bishop Hermann I of Lobdeburg as surety for a loan of 2,300 mark. According to the agreement, the Jews had to pay their taxes henceforth to the bishop and he in turn was obligated to protect them.[21] Although the agreement was presumably part of the loan transaction, in reality it constituted a gift from the king to the bishop. It was an expression of gratitude for the support given him by the bishop at the time of the royal elections in 1246. The agreement provided that in case of redemption of the pledge by the Reich the bishop was not required to refund to the Reich the taxes paid in by the Jews. The most important feature of the agreement was the bishop's responsibility for the protection of the Jews. This made him the virtual lord over the Jews: to him they paid their taxes and from him they expected protection in times of need.

To be sure, the agreement was provisional. But it gradually passed into a state of permanency and ultimately led to the total dependence of the Jews upon the local bishop. The Würzburg bishops were fully aware of the fact that the Reich could redeem

[17] Stobbe, Otto, *Die Juden in Deutschland* . . . (Braunschweig 1866) pp. 20 ff.

[18] *MB*, **XXXIX**, p. 218.

[19] Shulvass, *op. cit.*, pp. 18 ff.; Caro, G., *Sozial-und Wirtschaftsgeschichte der Juden* . . . I (Leipzig 1908) p. 403; Aronius, J., *Regesten zur Geschichte der Juden* . . . (Berlin 1902) no. 466.

[20] *MB*, **XLVI**, p. 17; Shulvass, *op. cit.*, p. 19.

[21] *Ibid.*, **XXXa**, pp. 303 ff.; Aronius, *op. cit.*, no. 564.

the pledge at will. They concluded formal treaties with the Jews for the continued payment of their taxes to them in return for which they would fight any renewed demand on the part of the Reich that the Jews pay their taxes into the royal exchequer.[22] Jewish consent to such treaties need elicit little surprise. The Jews well knew the weakness of the central government and realized that their safety depended upon the local authority, such as the bishop.

That the bishop was the stronger party with reference to the *Juden Regal* (royal privileges concerning the Jews) was made amply manifest in the case of Rudolf von Hapsburg's attempt to force the Würzburg Jews to resume payment of their taxes to the royal treasury. To be sure, the bishop did not succeed in fully rejecting the royal demand but had to resort to a compromise. Under its terms, the annual tax of the Würzburg Jews, amounting to 1,000 pounds of heller, was divided between the bishop and the emperor, with the former receiving 60 per cent.[23]

The Jews of Würzburg were in a peculiar situation: they were dual subjects. Their virtual lord and protector was the bishop, to whom they paid the major share of their taxes. And although the emperor agreed to a lesser share of the taxes, he continued to consider the Jews as his subjects from whom he extorted additional annual taxes of large or small sums. In 1322 an imperial official afforded protection to the Würzburg Jews. On this occasion the Jews were designated as "servi camerae."[24] But the bishops did not relent. After each annual payment by the Jews of 400 pounds of heller to the emperor, the bishop would issue a declaration that this practice was provisional and would cease with the death of the emperor in question. One of the bishops went so far as to declare that the emperor was extorting this sum from the Jews illegally.[25]

---

[22] Such a treaty of 1281 is extant. See *MB*, XXXVII, p. 526. The sum that the Jews paid in taxes at this time was 1,200 pounds of heller. In the next ten years the Jews paid only 1,000 pounds of heller a year.

[23] Shulvass, *op. cit.*, pp. 35 ff.

[24] *MB*, XXXIX, p. 218.

[25] *Ibid.*, p. 200; Wiener, M., *Regesten zur Geschichte der Juden in Deutschland während des Mittelalters,* I (Hannover 1862) p. 110.

These utterances may be taken as the natural exaggerations of a party to a dispute. Undoubtedly, the official imperial sanction of the division of the taxes, of 1334, with the bishop receiving 60 per cent, represented a great victory for the bishop. Emperor Ludwig then assured the bishop that the Reich would never demand of the Jews more than 400 pounds of heller a year.[26]

The end of the process that transferred the Jews from the authority of the Reich to the authority of the bishop came in 1349. In that year practically the entire Jewish community of Würzburg underwent martyrdom and Emperor Charles IV bequeathed their possessions to the bishop.[27] This bequest was on the basis of the theory that the sole heir of the property of the Würzburg Jews was the emperor. Although no formal "release" of the Würzburg Jews from the authority of the Reich was ever proclaimed, the Reich thenceforth no longer intervened in the affairs of these Jews and the annual taxes were paid to the bishop only.[28]

This development, which placed the Jews under the rule of the bishop, brought about a conflict between the Jews and the burghers, who were engaged in a long and bitter struggle with the bishop.[29] In the 1250's the burghers began to plot against the Würzburg Jews under the pretext of avenging the five children whom the Jews had allegedly slain in Fulda in 1235, the first blood accusation in Germany. In the beginning the Jews succeeded in enlisting the aid of Pope Innocent IV. In a papal epistle written in 1253 he confirmed the privileges conferred upon the Würzburg Jews by Bishop Hermann I, promising them protection of life and goods as well as of their community property.[30] The papal epistle was of little avail. The relations between the

[26] MB, XXXIX, p. 526.

[27] Ibid., XLI, pp. 389, 408.

[28] Shulvass, op. cit., pp. 61 ff.

[29] Füsslein, W., Zwei Jahrzehnte Würzburgischer Stifts-, Stadt- und Landesgeschichte (1254-1275) (Meiningen 1926) pp. 33 ff.

[30] Aronius, op. cit., no. 592 and 593. The papal letter was published in Grayzel, S., The Church and the Jews in the Thirteenth Century (Philadelphia 1933) pp. 292-95.

Jews and the burghers remained tense and continued to depend entirely upon the relations between the bishops and the burghers. In 1261 Bishop Irring concluded an agreement with the citizenry in which the latter agreed not to demand taxes from the Jews without the consent of the bishop. Latent in this agreement was the threat that sooner or later the Jews would have to pay taxes also to the municipal authorities. Nevertheless, the stipulation that such demands could not be made without the consent of the bishop was of some value. At least once, in 1281, the Jews of Würzburg with the aid of the bishop succeeded in nullifying the demand for taxes by the municipal authorities.[31] But finally the Jews had to yield. Just as they had to pay taxes to the bishop despite the fact that they were "subjects" of the Reich, simply because the former was a significant power factor on the spot, they now had to reckon with the rising power of the citizenry. The first direct taxes to the municipality were paid in 1288. The sum was considerable—1,500 silver mark. In return the municipality pledged to give protection to the Jews.[32]

Later on, in the course of the first half of the 14th century, there is no further mention of a direct Jewish tax to the municipality. The Jews, however, contributed to a number of communal expenditures for the protection of the city. In 1333 the Jews contributed liberally to the construction of a new wall with towers.[33]

Beside paying taxes to the municipality, the Jews were exposed to various forms of vexation because they were considered as subjects of the bishop. In 1265 relations between the bishop and the municipality deteriorated badly and the latter expelled from the city a number of the bishop's adherents, among them several Jews. A reconciliation was soon effected and the exiles were permitted to return.[34]

[31] *MB*, XXXVII, p. 526. For the interpretation of this document see Shulvass, *op. cit.*, p. 34.
[32] *Historische Zeitschrift*, XXXIV, pp. 282 ff.
[33] *RB*, VI, p. 149; Fries, L., *Würzburger Chronik*, Bonitas-Bauer, ed. (1924) p. 390.
[34] *MB*, XXXVII, p. 429.

Gradually there was an improvement in the relations among the Jews, the municipality and the bishop. In 1337 the municipality came to the defense of the Jews and decreed that anyone harming them would be banished from the city. This was probably a reaction to the anti-Jewish disorders of the previous year, which the municipal council combatted.[35] In 1344 full understanding concerning the Jews was practically reached between the bishop and the municipality. The city council at last recognized the bishop's rights over the Jews and promised its help in the protection of the Jews.[36]

Notwithstanding all the agreements that the Jews of Würzburg concluded with the bishop and the municipality, they were thrice subject to frightful massacres in the period under consideration. In 1298, when the community was fairly prosperous and constantly growing, came the Rindfleisch massacres. The Jews of Röttingen, Franconia, were accused of desecrating the host. Rindfleisch, a local nobelman placed himself at the head of a mob and fell upon that community, exterminating it completely. He continued to rage in the neighboring communities and some hundred and fifty of them became his victims.[37] Würzburg was particularly hard hit, so that it came to be referred to in contemporary Hebrew writings as "Würzburg, the bloody city." [38] The slaughter began on July 23, 1298, and about 900 Jews perished, 800 from Würzburg and about 100 from the neighboring communities, who sought safety there. Entire families, occasionally numbering ten or even twelve people, were wiped out.[39] It is difficult to say whether they were the victims of the Rindfleisch hordes or committed suicide, as was the case in other cities. The expression "dragged to the slaughter," which occurs in one of the Hebrew elegies,[40] may possibly indicate that the Würzburg Jews

35 *Ibid.*, XL, p. 145. For further interpretation of this document see Hoffmann, *op. cit.*, p. 91.
36 Hoffmann, *op. cit.*, p. 92. The sources are indicated there in n. 7.
37 A detailed description is given in Dubnow, *op. cit.*, V. pp. 152 ff.
38 The responsa *Zikhron Yehuda*, by Judah the son of the ROSH (Berlin 5606) p. 46a.
39 See the lists of the victims in Salfeld, *op. cit.*, pp. 43 ff. and 192 ff.
40 *Ibid.*, p. 342. The elegy is also published in Habermann, *op. cit.*, pp. 230 ff.

fell at the hands of the murderers. The tragic event in Würzburg found eloquent expression in contemporary Hebrew poetry.[41]

In the summer of 1336 anti-Jewish disorders occured again.[42] The mob attacked and killed Jews in several towns in Franconia, in the vicinity of the Main River. A mob gathered in Kitzingen, near Würzburg, and decided to march on Würzburg to attack the Jews there. Upon arrival in that city, the mob discovered that the local populace had preceded it and had fallen upon the Jews. These disorders, which had their rise among the lower strata of the population, were greatly and energetically combatted by the city council. The citizenry became alarmed over the possibility of the spread of these disorders to its own detriment. The armed forces of the municipality were called out and several score rioters were taken prisoners. Possibly, the agreement calling for the protection of the Jews concluded between the Jews and the municipality in 1337 (see above) was the result of the events of the previous year.

And even this agreement was of little avail twelve years later, at the time of the massacres of the Black Death. The terror that seized the population of practically the entire world upon the approach of the dreadful epidemic led to renewed massacres of Jews in many European countries. The Jews were suspected of poisoning the wells. Conditions were aggravated by the rise of the Flagellants, who hoped by their public self-castigation to atone for the sins of the generation. Social conflicts added oil to the conflagration which enveloped the house of Israel.[43]

In Germany the anti-Jewish movement began prior to the coming of the Black Death. The Jewish communities there were destroyed through slaughter or self-immolation. In isolated instances the city councils attempted to protect the Jews, or at any rate showed some reluctance to hand the Jews over to the

41 Habermann, *op. cit.*, pp. 213-32; *Kovez al yad*, III. p. 18.
42 The source of these events is the aforementioned chronicle of L. Fries. Details are given in Hoffmann, *op cit.*, p. 91. Hoffmann is of the opinion that the treaty concluded with the municipality in 1337 was the result of the events of the previous year, which demonstrated the need of Jewish protection by the city authorities.
43 For a detailed description see Dubnow, *op. cit.*, V, pp. 258 ff.

bloodthirsty mob. The Würzburg city council which twelve years before had threatened with expulsion anyone harming the Jews, now decided not to act hastily and proceeded to inquire of the other cities how they had dealth with their Jews.[44] The bishop did less. Mainly he was interested in securing the property of the Jews slain in case of massacres.[45]

The inquiry of the city council brought forth a number of responses. Copies of the responses of the following city councils are extant: Breisach, Frankfurt, Freiburg, Fulda, Heilbronn and Obernheim. They tell of apprehending Jews who poisoned wells or committed other great offenses and the punishment meted out to them. Only the city councils of Erfurt and Strasbourg answered that the Jews were not guilty of wrongdoing and that they would continue to protect them.

Exactly what happened then in Würzburg is unknown. Apparently the Jews realized that their situation was hopeless, particularly when the Flagellants approached the city.[46] They therefore decided to die for the Sanctification of the Name. On April 21, 1349, they locked themselves in their houses and set fire to them.[47] A Würzburg chronicle of the 16th century tells that the Jews buried their treasures prior to their self-immolation.[48] But the bishop got his share of the Jewish property. Several months later Emperor Charles IV made the bishop the sole heir of the communal property of the Würzburg Jews.[49]

Undoubtedly the vast majority of Würzburg Jews perished on that fateful day. A small number saved themselves by escaping from the city. Shortly thereafter Würzburg Jews are recorded in Erfurt, Frankfurt, Mainz and Nuremberg.[50] The irony of the

---

[44] Shulvass, *op. cit.*, p. 48. The text of the inquiry is unknown. In the manuscript M-ch-f-140, in the Library of the University of Würzburg, the answers from eight cities are found on pp. 275-77. They were published by Hoffmann, *op. cit.*, pp. 98-103.

[45] *MB*, XLI, p. 389.

[46] Hoffmann, *op. cit.*, p. 111.

[47] The date of Jewish self-immolation was up to recent times set as of April 20. Hoffmann, however, is right in his insistence on April 21.

[48] Hoffmann, *op. cit.*, pp. 93 ff.

[49] *MB*, XLI, p. 408.

[50] See the sources in Shulvass, *op. cit.*, p. 49, n. 188.

situation was that the Black Death did not come to Würzburg at all.

c

It is impossible to state exactly on what basis the Jewish communal organization in Würzburg was established between 1250 an 1350. However, the existence of a Jewish communal organization is certain. Contemporary documents refer frequently to a Universitas Judeorum Herbipolensium—the community of the Jews of Würzburg. In 1298 the Jewish community was represented by a group of twelve people, among whom was one of the rabbis.[51] This group made commitments in the name of the community and guaranteed them with the Jewish land holdings in the city. Still it is hard to say whether this was a permanent community organization or an ad hoc body for a specific communal transaction. Another record points to the possibility of "daughter communities" of the Würzburg community. These were in the towns of Kitzingen and Iphofen.[52]

As in previous years, similarly in the period under consideration, the Jewish community was recognized as a juridical entity owning various communal institutions. In the year 1289 there were in Würzburg at least two synagogues, and even after the great fire and the self-immolation of the community in 1349 one of the synagogues remained intact.[53] Whether the community had a shelter for transients or the Hospitium Judaicum, mentioned in contemporary documents, was merely a house owned collectively by a number of Jews, is difficult to ascertain.[54]

Included in the property of the Jewish community that in 1349 passed into the possession of the bishop was the cemetery.[55] Several years ago two old tombstones were found in Würzburg

[51] *MB*, XXXVIII, p. 13.
[52] Possible proof may be the facts that in 1243 the Jews of Kitzingen buried their dead on the Jewish cemetery of Würzburg (Aronius, *op. cit.*, no. 539) and that one of the Jewish community leaders of Würzburg resided in Iphofen (*MB*, XXXIX, pp. X ff:; *RB*, VII, p. 21).
[53] *MB*, XLII, p. 111; Shulvass, *op. cit.*, p. 50.
[54] *RB*, VII, p. 21; Shulvass, *op. cit.*, p. 46, n. 175.
[55] *MB*, XLII, p. 111.

on Augustine Street, in the vicinity of the old city hall. One of the tombstones dated from 1306 (the young man R. Jacob son of the martyr R. Mordecai) and the other from 1339 (the elder R. Jacob son of R. Moses). According to the reports of the men working on that street, many fragments of Jewish tombstones were found there. Some were discarded and others were immured in the walls of a building, which a butcher by the name Fischer was erecting.[56]

d

Little is known of the economic conditions of the Würzburg Jews in that period. Earlier, Jews possessed vineyards. There is a record of a Jewish family cultivating a vineyard in 1329.[57]

Similarly little is known of the commercial activities of the Würzburg Jews. In 1341 they were forbidden to buy fish on Friday and on Catholic fast days, when fish are eaten instead of meat. Possibly this measure was aimed at preventing Jews from dealing in certain products on the days when Christians needed them most.[58]

Considerably more is known of Jewish banking transactions. Loans made by Würzburg Jews are recorded in the beginning of our period. These transactions are constantly on the increase and in the first half of the 14th century they occupy a prominent position among economic activities. Significant is the fact that practically all borrowers were noblemen and the clergy, including the Würzburg bishop. In 1336 Bishop Otto von Wolfskehl was so heavily indebted to the Jews that he appealed to Pope Benedict XII for aid. And although the pope had no juridical basis for his intervention, he cancelled the bishop's debt to the Jews.[59]

[56] Bernstein, Mordecai W., *Nisht-derbrente shaytn* (Buenos Aires 1956) pp. 306-307, cites the texts of the tombstones and relates the details.
[57] Wiener, *op. cit.*, p. 117.
[58] Details are found in Hoffmann, *op. cit.*, p. 92.
[59] Aronius, *op. cit.*, no. 707; *MB*, XXXVII, pp. 456 ff.; XL, p. 36; *Historische Zeitschrift*, XXXIV, p. 302; Bendel, F. J., *Urkundenbuch der Benediktinerabtei St. Stephan in Würzburg*, I (Leipzig 1912) pp. 410, 435 ff.

27

These business activities apparently brought opulence to many members of the community. A Hebrew source of the 13th century records that among the Würzburg Jews "the customary dowry and supplementary dowry amounted to 100 pounds, each pound valued at two mark."[60] Thus the majority of the Jews belonged to the middle class. Toward the end of the 13th century some Würzburg Jews employed private teachers for their children. Others kept servants. One, Joseph son of Shmaryah Halevi, kept both a servant and a private teacher.[61]

Besides the aforementioned fact, nothing is known about elementary Jewish education in Würzburg. But the general cultural level of the community was very high. Prior to the catastrophe of 1349 there was a Yeshiva in Würzburg, presided over by Rabbi Moses Hadarshan. Rabbi Moses perished with the rest of the community.[62] The city must have counted a considerable number of Jewish scholars, for the expression "our teachers of Würzburg" occurs several times in the contemporary literature.[63] Rabbi Meir of Rothenburg advises a correspondent, who inquires about a law governing inheritance, that "if you are in doubt about the Law, inquire of our teachers in the community of Würzburg."[64] Even laymen must have had a considerable Jewish education. The lists of the victims of the Rindfleisch massacres contain many names with the title *haber* affixed to them.[65] This was the title of scholars who were not rabbis.

On the whole, however, little is known of the Würzburg rabbis of the second half of the 13th century. Some of them, as Rabbi Elijah son of Samuel, Rabbi Ephraim son of Abraham, Rabbi Isaac son of Nathan, Rabbi Hillel son of Azriel and Rabbi Menahem son of David figure either as martyrs of the massacres of 1298 or as the authors of questions to which Rabbi Meir of

60 *Tashbez katan,* par. 455.

61 Salfeld, *op. cit.,* pp. 46, 196.

62 Landshuth, E. L., *Amude Haavoda* (Berlin 5617) supplement p. IV; *Hamazkir,* IX, p. 24.

63 The commentary *Mordekhai* on *Baba mezia,* cited from Agus, Irving A., *Rabbi Meir of Rothenburg,* I (Philadelphia 1947) p. 21, n. 38.

64 *Sheelot uteshuvot MaHaRaM,* Prague-Budapest, par. 934.

65 Salfeld, *op. cit.,* pp. 43 ff.; 192 ff.

Rothenburg wrote responsa.[66] Another Würzburg scholar, R. Hezekiah, is known to have left for Spain, where he studied in the Yeshiva of the RaSHBA in Barcelona.[67]

Only about two Würzburg rabbis of that period is there slightly more information available. One of them was Rabbi Eliezer son of Moses Hadarshan. A great-grandson of Rabbi Judah the Pious, he was a kabbalist and a liturgical poet. He wrote a commentary on the *Sefer Yezirah,* a mystic cosmogony, and a commentary on the Pentateuch called *Sefer Hagimatriaot.* His method was to interpret the Scripture by means of *gimatria,* a system based on the numerical value of the word. There is also extant a poem by him—*Zion Ateret Zevi.* The year of his death is unknown. His widow, Shone, and his son, Meir, perished in 1298. Another son, Moses, was then rabbi in Erfurt.[68]

The other one was Rabbi Menahem son of Natronai, called Rabbi Koblin of Würzburg. He was a relative of Rabbi Meir of Rothenburg and possibly a teacher of Rabbi Hayim Or Zarua. Rabbi Menahem was also a prominent communal figure and occasionally acted as the community representative to the bishop. In the Latin documents of the period he figures as *Kobelinus magister universitatis Judeorum Herbipolensium.* Apparently, he is the Rabbi Menahem of Würzburg who participated in the conference that met in Mainz between the years 1286 and 1291 to discuss the problem of the heavy tax levied on the German Jews by King Rudolph of Hapsburg. Rabbi Menahem son of Natronai is mentioned in several contemporary Hebrew works. His expositions of certain passages in the Bible were cited in *Paaneah Raza,*

---

[66] *Ibid.,* pp. 44, 47, 193, 198; *Sheelot uteshuvot R. Hayim Or Zarua,* par. 299; *Sheelot uteshuvot MaHaRaM,* Berlin, p. 218, par. 177, p. 131, par. 93; *op. cit.,* Prague-Budapest, par. 92, 143; *ibid.,* par. 28: "your popil Menahem, son of R. David, may he be remembered for life eternal"; Agus, *op. cit.,* pp. 462, 670; *Sheelot uteshuvot MaHaRaM,* Lwow (cf. Agus, *op. cit.,* p. 504) ; the commentary *Mordekhai* on *Baba batra,* ch. 9, par 614. I cite from Back, S., *R. Meir ben Baruch aus Rothenburg* (Frankfurt 1895) p. 19, no. 2.

[67] For futher data on him see A. Freimann's monograph on the ROSH in *JJLG,* XII, p. 279. R. Hezekiah is also mentioned in *Sheelot uteshuvot lharav rabenu Asher,* ch. 73, par. 12.

[68] Shulvass, *op. cit.,* p. 25 and "Letoldot hayahas bemishpahat R. Yehuda Hehasid," *Aluma* (Jerusalem 1936) pp. 152 ff.

by Rabbi Isaac son of Judah Halevi.[69]

Apparently, most of the Jewish sages of Würzburg of the second half of the 13th century died before the massacres of 1298, the other met their death then. Thus the close of the 13th century marked also the end of the golden period of the Würzburg rabbis. In the first half of the 14th century Würzburg is no longer as frequently mentioned in rabbinic literature as heretofore.

At that time there lived in Würzburg an interesting Jewish personality, referred to in the documents as Michelman. A confidant of the bishop, who entrusted him with a special mission, Michelman had travelled extensively and had acquired a large fund of practical knowledge which he applied skillfully. Bishop Manegold decided in 1293 to convert the village of Iphofen, which was always very loyal to him, into a fortified town. He entrusted this enterprise to Michelman, who was exempted from taxes for a period of four years. He was also given the privilege of leaving the new town at will.[70] How Michelman succeeded in the building of the town and his fate beyond this period is entirely unknown.

Similarly, little is known about the Würzburg rabbis of the first half of the 14th century. One of them was Rabbi Shlomo son of Meir, who died in 1342.[71] In addition, there have come down to us the names of three rabbis who died a martyr's death in 1349: Rabbi Goldknop, who is referred to in contemporary

[69] *Sheelot uteshuvot R. Hayim Or Zarua,* par. 110. There mention was merely made of the fact that the Mainz conference there was present "the rabbi R. Menahem of Würzburg." The name of his father was not indicated. However, it may be safely assumed that he was R. Menahem, son of Natronai, and not R. Menahem, son of David, for the former figures as a communal leader also in other sources (*Sheelot uteshuvot MaHaRaM,* Prague-Budapest, par. 34). In the commentary *Mordekhai* on *Baba batra,* ch. 9, par. 614 (cited from Agus, *op cit.*), he is called: "R. Menahem, son of R. Natronai, known as R. Koblin of Würzburg"; *MB,* XXXVII, p. 526, XXXVIII, p. 13. See also *Sheelot uteshuvot MaHaRaM,* Prague-Budapest, pars. 987 and 988 and the note of the editor Moses Aryeh Bloch, to par. 987; Zunz, I., *Zur Geschichte und Literatur* (Berlin 1919) p. 94, n. b.

Concerning the date of the Mainz conference see Baron, Salo W., *The Jewish Community* (Philadelphia 1948) III, p. 76.

[70] *MB,* XXXVIII, pp. 48 ff.

[71] Shulvass, *op. cit.,* p. 47.

elegies as Rabbi *kaftor zahav* (golden button), Rabbi David Ha-kohen and the aforementioned Rabbi Moses Hadarshan, the only head of the Yeshiva in Würzburg at that time whose name has come down to us.[72] Otherwise we know nothing about these men.

The events of 1349 put an end to the Jewish community of Würzburg. It took a while before Jews returned to the city, even in small numbers. Gradually, the community resumed its growth and regained its prominence. It boasted anew of several distinguished rabbis.[73] The later community, however, was developing along more individualistic lines. The zenith of Jewish communal life in Würzburg was between 1250 and 1350.

[72] Salfeld, *op. cit.,* pp. 28, 248, 281; Landshuth, E. L., *Amude Haavoda, loc. cit.; Hamazkir, loc. cit.* The possibility is not to be excluded that this Rabbi Goldknop is identical with the one to whom Rabbi Jacob, author of the *Turim,* wrote his famous letter in 1329 suggesting flight from Germany and settlement in Spain (see *Hasoker,* II, pp. 37 and 38).

[73] Shulvass, *op. cit.,* pp. 50 ff.

III

JEWISH DESTINY IN EASTERN EUROPE — A HISTORICAL PANORAMA

To Emanuel Congregation of Chicago,
where I served as Albert Mecklenburger
scholar-in-residence in the year 1963-64.

a

The oldest echoes reaching us from Jews in East Europe come from a little-known corner in the South, the *Crimean peninsula*. In the first century, only a few years after the destruction of the Second Temple, there were Jews living in various colonies founded by the ancient Greeks on the northern shores of the Black Sea. The information available to us tells of a Jewish settlement that lived peacefully and enjoyed a certain degree of organized religious life. Information about Jews in those regions — namely, in what is known today as Southern Ukraine — also reaches us from the period of the early Dark Ages.

This Jewish settlement of southern Russia began to expand more and more when a part of the people of the Khozars, who then established in those regions a strong commonwealth, were converted to Judaism. This was some time during the eighth century. The persecution of the Jews in the neighboring Byzantine empire no doubt induced many of them to emigrate to the friendly, partly Jewish, Khozaria. Then more Jews arrived in Khozaria from the teeming Jewish centers in western

32

Asia over the mountains of the Caucasus and through the Gate of Nations. A legend tells us that the Jews even tried to convince Duke Vladimir of Kiev (980-1015) to accept the Jewish religion. Vladimir, as is known, did not become a Jew, but instead introduced Christianity into Russia. This earned him in the Church the status of a saint. The Jewish settlement nevertheless kept on growing, and it is probable that when the Khozarian kingdom was destroyed, a number of the Jewish Khozarians were absorbed within the Jewish community of South Russia. The Jewish community of the capital city of Kiev attained some degree of importance — with its Jewish streets and relatively high level of culture. But it seems that Southern Ukraine's Jewish population, together with the remnants of the Jewish Khozarians, were obliterated by the terrible invasions of the Tartars during the first part of the thirteenth century. In the decades following the Tartar invasions no Jewish settlements are known to have existed in the Ukraine.

Whereas the oldest Jewish community of Russia was thus the result of immigration from the South and the Orient, the Jewish settlement of Poland emerged, as all signs indicate, as a result of the immigration of Jews from Germany. The incredible slaughter of Jews in Western Europe preparatory to the first two Crusades (1096, 1147), it seems, initiated the tremendous historic process which transferred within several hundred years great numbers of Jews from Germany to Poland, and gave to the Jewish people in Eastern Europe its specific Western character.

b

The history of the great development of the Jewish community in Eastern Europe is henceforth closely tied in with the destiny of Poland. The kingdom of Poland appeared on the arena of world history about the year 1000. At the beginning it was a weak kingdom that still had to overcome the painful process of being broken up for a long period into a mosaic of small principalities. In 1241 a considerable part of

33

the country was totally devastated by an invasion of Tartars. Little by little, however, the country began to take on strength and to become an important factor in Eastern Europe. During the second part of the thirteenth century many immigrants arrived from Germany, and from other parts of Western Europe, to settle the desolate land, to build cities, and to develop commerce. At the same time the State began to expand in a southeastern direction, and what was later known as Galicia became part of its territory. Before the fourteenth century was concluded, the greatest event in the history of Poland took place — its unification with the principality of Lithuania. Through this union Poland acquired a considerable part of the Baltic Sea Coast and a vast territory in the Ukraine. Poland was now a great power and its influence reached "from sea to sea" — from the Baltic in the North to the Black Sea in the South. Poland's significance grew rapidly also in the realm of international trade. Great markets opened in Western Europe for products from the Polish fields and forests. A golden epoch began in the history of the Polish State and it lasted until the end of the sixteenth century.

The developments just described prepared the ground for large-scale immigration of Jews from Germany. In their German homeland the Jews had been experiencing a process of degradation politically, socially, and economically. The Crusades, the anti-Jewish legislation of both the State and the Church, and the repeated blood accusations, followed by bloody pogroms, convinced the Jews more and more that there was no future for them in Germany. They began to designate the country in which they had lived for more than a thousand years the "land of calamity" (erets gezeirah). Not only did the number of Jews who escaped the country grow rapidly, but the leaders of the Jewish community were actively agitating their co-religionists to leave the land soaked with Jewish blood.

The Jewish refugees from Germany escaped in different directions. Some of them went to Southern France and from there to Spain; larger groups went to Italy and even further

34

into the Balkan peninsula. But the simplest course was to go to Poland. The country was devastated by the Tartars and thirsty for immigrants. The backwardness of Poland's economy in the thirteenth century presented great opportunities for the many experienced merchants and moneylenders among the Jewish immigrants from Germany. In addition, the Polish kings and princes gave them a friendly reception. The tendency of the government to promote the founding of new cities also helped to create good conditions for the immigration of Jews, all of them former city dwellers. In addition, there was not even the necessity to learn the language of the new country. The Polish cities of the thirteenth century, overflowing with immigrants from Germany, were, in fact, German settlements in which German remained the spoken language for a very long time.

Small wonder that the Jews of Germany, in search of a new home, moved in large masses eastward into Poland. It is probable that shortly after the First Crusade small groups of Jews from Germany and from Bohemia reached Poland. However, the earliest documentary evidence about Jews in Poland dates from the end of the twelfth century. Quite naturally the first Jewish settlements in Poland appeared in the western provinces, close to the German border. In the fourteenth century, however, we find Jews and Jewish communities scattered over all parts of the country.

The rapid expansion of the Jews in their new homeland was to a great extent the result of the friendly attitude of the rulers toward Jewish immigrants. One of them, Duke Boleslaw of Kalisz, granted them in 1264 a charter which became the legal foundation for their stay in the land. This charter was modeled after a constitution granted them a few decades earlier in Austria and in Bohemia and was quite favorable to them. It became the Magna Charta of medieval Polish Jewry.

Of utmost importance for the development of the Jewish community in Poland was the fact that when the greatest wave of Jewish immigrants from Germany arrived — they were the refugees who escaped the terrible persecutions in the times of the "Black Death" — Poland was ruled by the famous King Casimir the Great (1333-1370), who was their devoted friend. In 1334 he granted to all the Jews of his kingdom the charter obtained by the Jews of Kalisz in 1264. Also later he granted them many favors. The historian Jan Dlugosz, who wrote his *History of Poland* about one hundred years later, tells us that the great king fell in love with the Jewess Esterka, the daughter of a tailor from a small town. In this fashion later generations tried to explain the remarkable friendship of the great king for his Jewish subjects.

The Jewish community of Poland kept on growing also after Casimir's death. When Lithuania entered a union with Poland in 1386, there existed in her Ukrainian regions several Jewish communities. It is hard to determine whether these were remnants of the Jews of Southern Ukraine and of Khozaria from before the Tartar invasions. Or, were they perhaps also German Jews who penetrated that far eastward? During the fifteenth century new immigrants arrived from Germany in large numbers. A series of local expulsions threw into Poland whole Jewish communities, including their rabbis and other communal functionaries. When at the turn of the century the Jews were expelled from Spain, a certain number of them also came to Poland. As a result of all these migrations, the number of Jewish communities in fifteenth-century Poland was six times as large as it was one hundred years earlier. In 1421 we find for the first time Jews in Warsaw, the city that was destined to become the capital two hundred years later. Nine years later the city had a Jewish street. Obviously, the number of Jews was rapidly growing. At that time the Jews did not live any more solely in the big cities where also the Gentiles spoke German. They were now scattered in many cities and little towns, and it is estimated that they numbered thirty thousand.

c

The Jews from Germany who settled in Poland entered

various fields of economic endeavor. Many of them had had much experience in the field of banking and money exchange. And we find during the thirteenth century Jews who became farmers of state mints. During the whole of the fourteenth century and the first half of the fiifteenth, money lending became a source of income to a considerable number of Jews. However, during the second part of this period money lending began to lose ground among them. Trade, local as well as international, began to attract them more and more. A certain number of them, in Poland as well as in Lithuania, earned their livelihood in the various branches of agriculture. It is also worth noting that there was a number of Jewish physicians, some of them immigrants from Spain.

During the fifteenth century we find all over Poland fairly well organized Jewish *communal institutions*. The high level of communal organization in this young settlement should, of course, be attributed to the fact that the immigrants brought with them old, solid forms of communal life. The most important aspect of the communal organization was the fact that within the framework of medieval society, the *Kehillah* was a religious as well as an administrative body whose duty it was to care for the safety and welfare of the "Jewish Street." It also wielded considerable judicial power. Within this communal framework an important process began to take shape; many small communities located in suburbs or villages, which until then were under the control of the neighboring large Kehillahs, began to throw off their yoke and to establish themselves as independent communal organizations.

d

The rapid growth of the Jewish population, its penetration into all provinces of the country, and its influence in economic life evoked considerable resentment among the clergy and the burgesses. The clergy looked ascance at the friendly attitude of the State toward the Jews; the burgesses saw in them, typical city dwellers as they were, dangerous competitors in the economic struggle.

37

By the middle of the fourteenth century, when the clergy became aware of the remarkable friendship of Casimir the Great toward the Jews, they began to incite the populace against them. This anti-Jewish propaganda resulted in a number of riotous outbreaks against the Jews. The outbreaks of this type even increased in number during the fifteenth century. In 1399 the first trial took place in Poland in which a Jew was accused of stealing and defiling the holy wafer — an accusation which was quite common in Western Europe. The fight of the Polish clergy against the Jews was in general conducted by methods similar to those practiced in Western Europe. However, the outbreaks against the Jews in Poland were by far not so dreadful as those in Western Europe. In their plight the Jews found help among the magnates and the lesser gentry, who derived from the Jews many profits. In addition, many of the nobility were well educated men, full of zeal for the ideals of the Renaissance and Humanism. They were by far the most liberal part of the Polish population. On the side of the clergy, however, were, as already mentioned, the burgesses. They conducted an energetic as well as systematic fight against the commerce of the Jews, and here and there they succeeded in curtailing the right of the Jews to do business. The immediate result was that Jews began to abandon commerce and became craftsmen and artisans. These occupations later became a major factor in the economic life of the Jews.

The burgesses, not being content with partial success in their fight against the Jews, began to call louder and louder for their expulsion. When the news of the many local expulsions in Germany reached Poland, it whetted the appetite of the burgesses to act likewise. In 1453 the famous preacher John Capistrano visited Poland and he "became frightened" when he saw the large number of Jews living in the capital city of Cracow. He, therefore, preached vigorously against them and demanded that they be expelled. This demand erupted again in 1492 under the impact of the gigantic expulsion of the Jews from

Spain. Increased propaganda of the Polish anti-Semites caused then a new wave of pogroms. In a number of cities the dream of the burgesses became true and the Jews were expelled. A number of cities even obtained from the king the doubtful privilege "de non tolerandis Judeis," the right not to tolerate Jews within their limits. In 1495 Duke Alexander of Lithuania, who later ascended the Polish throne, expelled all the Jews from his territory. He hoped that the confiscation of their property would save his shaky finances. He quickly realized, however, that the expulsion of the Jews was a mistake; they were recalled and their communal property was returned to them.

In spite of all their troubles, the partial expulsions, and their eternal struggle for the right to earn a living, the Jews found Poland and Lithuania a paradise in comparison with Germany. Jews from Germany, therefore, continued coming. When Poland became in the sixteenth century one of the powerful and prosperous countries in Europe, its Jewish settlement, too, became the leading Jewish community. The golden age of Poland became also the golden age for the Jewish people in Eastern Europe, who surpassed other Jewish communities in economic and cultural importance.

e

The political rise of the Polish commonwealth lasted all through the sixteenth century. The union with Lithuania increased immensely its territory. The vast areas of South Ukraine, which lay waste for hundreds of years following the Tartar invasions, began now to be colonized. Poland's export was increasing; the r i c h e s t countries in Western Europe — England and Holland and the Scandinavian countries in the North — bought the products of its agriculture and forestry. Humanism and Reformation evoked a mighty response and vigorously stimulated all cultural endeavors.

No wonder that Poland still was an attraction to Jews of other lands. From Germany new Jewish immigrants arrived, and they continued to come all through the sixteenth century and even in the first part of the seventeenth, when unmistakable signs began to indicate that Poland with its Jewish community was entering upon an era of economic and political decline. During the sixteenth century many Jews also arrived from Bohemia. Their number in Cracow became so large that they even were able to establish a communal organization of their own, recognized by the authorities. And even from Italy, where the Jews lived during the period of the Renaissance fairly peacefully, some came to settle in Poland.

As a result of all these great migratory currents — and thanks to the economic prosperity of the country — Poland's Jewish community increased immensely in size. It has been estimated that about the year 1550 the Jewish community of Poland numbered between 70,000 and 100,000 and was outnumbered only by its sister community in Turkey. One hundred years later, on the eve of the "Great Catastrophe," the Polish Jewish community numbered between 300,000 and half a million and represented the largest territorial concentration of Jews in the world. About one quarter of them lived in the territory of the Duchy of Lithuania.

The main occupation of the Jews during the sixteenth century was still commerce in all its forms. This was true especially of the western and central provinces of the Commonwealth. However, the number of Jewish craftsmen was constantly on the increase. In the then newly colonized areas of the Ukraine the main occupation of the Jews was the farming of tolls and taxes and the leasing of estates. They became a well-to-do class. Most of the Jewish sections in the cities had beautiful stone houses; many wealthy men built beautiful synagogues, often designed by famous architects. The Jewish sections in many cities and towns expanded considerably in area, and a network of specifically Jewish settlements sprang up outside the cities which refused to admit them.

The growth of the Jewish population, its economic success, and the influence which Jewish magnates exerted in the royal palace, provoked, as had happened two hundred years before, a bitter attack from the clergy and other anti-Semitic circles. The struggle of the Catholic clergy against the various Protestant groups was accompanied by an intensification of the fight against the Jewish "heretics." And when the counter-Reformation achieved a decisive victory over the Protestants, it was followed by a deterioration of the position of the Jews. The anti-Semites now began to fight the Jews also with literary means. The country was virtually flooded with anti-Jewish pamphlets, satires, and caricatures. Special books were written to discredit the Jewish physicians in the eyes of the Christian population. The number of the blood libel trials was on the increase, especially during the first part of the seventeenth century. At the same time the accusations against Jews for allegedly defiling the holy wafer also increased. More and more cities won the privilege "de non tolerandis Judeis." Ironically, the Jews, too, obtained similar privileges, the right "de non tolerandis Christianis." The Jewish sections of various cities and all the Jewish communities of Lithuania had the right not to admit Christians, because they were overcrowded. In spite of all this, the Jew lived generally in fairly friendly relations with his Christian neighbor, with whom he traded and for whom he worked as a craftsman. It is worth noting that in the Lithuanian provinces of the Commonwealth, where the burgesses were fewer and weaker as a group, anti-Semitic riots were much rarer and the familiar tension between Jew and Gentile was less intensive.

The growing anti-Semitism was the direct cause of two major processes which developed among the Jews of Poland around the turn of the century. Ever-growing numbers of Jews began to leave the big cities and to settle on the private territories of the magnates. At the same time many began to leave the western provinces of the Commonwealth altogether and to migrate southeast to the areas of the new colonization in the Ukraine. As a result of these movements many villages and towns sprang up, totally inhabited by Jews. The magnates received the Jews in a friendly fashion, similar to that mani-

41

fested by the kings of Poland a quarter of a millenium earlier. The Jews contributed greatly to the economic development of the vast waste areas controlled by the noble families; they introduced trade and commerce and brought wealth into the land. In 1539 the king formally gave up his jurisdiction over the Jews living on the territories of the noblemen. This change in the legal status of a considerable part of the Jewish population contained a great potential danger. The Jews now lost completely the protection of the central government and were exposed to the good or ill will of individuals. And, as we shall see, much trouble later developed from the new situation with the advent of the eighteenth century.

Of mighty dimensions was the second process which the Polish Jewry experienced — the migration of great masses from the western provinces eastward and southward. Jews who became tired of the enmity of the populace in the cities of the West and victims of the economic attack of the burgesses and other groups, as well as individuals who had conflicts with the leadership of the Jewish communities, began streaming into the Ukraine. Here was a "frontier" country, and the Jews who settled there were true pioneers, bringing with them material and spiritual culture. The economic opportunities were virtually unlimited. Constituting the most civilized part of the population of this wild and waste land, they cooperated closely with the big Polish landlords, who developed the country, and were an important factor in the tremendous effort to colonize it. Their main occupation was in the area of management. They were the leading farmers of customs and other categories of taxation; they rented distilleries, breweries, inns, and similar enterprises. And as the opportunities were great, the wave of Jews going to the Ukraine rolled on uninterruptedly till the very year of the "Great Catastrophe" (1648). Even from Germany and Italy Jews came directly to the Ukraine. During the second part of the sixteenth century many completely new communities came into being. In the immediate neighborhood of Kiev and Bratslav there were as many as fifty densely populated Jewish towns.

The only annoying aspect of the Jewish developments in the Ukraine was the one-sidedness of the Jewish occupations. As managers and lessees of enterprises owned either by the Polish government or by Polish noblemen, they were considered oppressors by the Ukrainian, Greek-Catholic peasant population, or at least representatives of the Polish Roman-Catholic oppressors. The hatred shown toward the Polish noblemen in the Ukraine and their Jewish agents on social, religious, and ethnic grounds grew steadily; so that in 1648 when the great revolt erupted, led by Bohdan Khmelnitsky, it brought with it a terrible calamity to the Jewish population of the Ukraine and of the Polish Commonwealth at large.

f

With the growth of the Jewish population and the expansion of its economic endeavors, its communal organization, the Kehillah, increased in importance. This was an epoch of great cultural aspirations and the Kehillah was called upon to satisfy these needs. The growing tension between Jews and Gentiles imposed on it additional responsibilities. The activities of the Kehillah were, therefore, steadily expanding and becoming more and more ramified. Besides the official Kehillah, an impressive number of voluntary societies sprang up to care for the various religious, social, and cultural needs. Special communal trustees ("gabbaim") were appointed to ransom Jewish captives and to collect alms for the needy in the Holy Land. Various communal officials cared for the sanitation of the Jewish streets, and supervised prices, weights, and measures. The ban or excommunication was a mighty and often cruel instrument at the disposal of the Kehillah to impose its control. The court of the Kehillah had even the authority to sentence Jewish criminals to bodily punishment. The importance of the Kehillah manifested itself in the title given to its head in official documents: Burgomaster of the Jewish Community. The Kehillah was usually controlled by a handful of rich aristocratic families. More than once their

43

dictatorial rule caused great damage to the Jewish masses. Already in the sixteenth century the first attempts at revolt against the rule of the aristocrats were made. It seems that the major complaints were directed against the misuse by the Kehillah of its right to impose the ban (herem). In the middle of the seventeenth century, therefore, some limitations on this right were enacted.

A major development in the communal organization of the Jews was the establishment of the *Council of the Four Lands.* The idea of a central Jewish communal organization was born simultaneously among the Jewish leaders and in government circles. The Polish Treasury believed that a national Kehillah would simplify the collection of the taxes from the Jews. In those times the Treasury did not have at its disposal a well organized tax-collecting machine, and it resorted to the system of imposing taxes in lump sums on different social and professional groups. It was then the duty of the groups to collect the taxes from their members and deliver the lump sums to the Treasury. Each local Kehillah thus had to serve as collector of taxes for the government. With the spectacular increase in the number of the Jewish communities throughout the Commonwealth and their spread over vast areas, it became increasingly difficult for the Treasury to negotiate separately with each local Kehillah. Consequently, the government became inclined to force the Jewish communities of the various provinces to unite on a regional basis.

Simultaneously, as mentioned before, the idea of creating a central communal organization became more and more popular also within the Jewish community. The struggle against the growing anti-Semitism among the burgesses and the clergy became more involved. To deal with such tragic phenomena as blood accusations was far beyond the capabilities of small local Kehillahs. The necessity for enacting important economic legislation also demonstrated the need for centralized communal organs.

The first step towards a central organization of Polish

44

Jewry was the establishment of Regional councils (Vaadim Geliliim) in various provinces of the Commonwealth during the first decades of the sixteenth century. The next step was the creation of a central rabbinic court. Many Jewish merchants from all over the country met regularly at the famous Fairs in Lublin and Jaroslav, and because of their business transactions the need for a Jewish Fair-Court became evident. With the establishment of this court the first truly central organ of Polish Jewry became a fact. In 1581 the Treasury decided to change the system of collecting taxes from the Jews. From then on more and more often one lump sum was imposed annually on all the Jews of the Commonwealth. The task of justly partitioning this sum among hundreds of communities and of collecting their contributions was a major effort, and the establishment of the "Council of the Four Lands" — (Vaad Arba Aratzoth), that is to say, of the four provinces of Jewish settlement in Poland — became inevitable. To be sure, the primary task of the Council was to serve as a tax agent of the Treasury. However, from the very first moment of its inception the Council began also to consider and take effective action on all great Jewish religious and communal issues. It met twice annually, in Lublin and in Jaroslav, during the great Fairs held there. Consequently, the already established Jewish Fair-Court turned automatically into a sort of Jewish supreme court with seven leading rabbis as justices. The institution served as a court of appeals from local Kehillah courts. It also acted as a mediator in litigations among Kehillahs, Jewish regional councils, and other Jewish public agencies. The Council elected a permanent executive committee to implement its decisions and to act in emergency cases occurring between sessions.

Among the regional councils, that of the Lithuanian province was the most important. It enjoyed autonomous status and held joint sessions with the Council of the Four Lands to discuss issues affecting the Jews in both parts of the Commonwealth. The importance of the central organ of Polish Jewry was considerable, and official documents termed it the *Parliament of the Jews of Poland.*

g

The general situation of the Jews in Poland, which was better than that in any other country in Europe, began to deteriorate shortly after 1600. The reason for this was the change in the policy of the government toward the Jews. Between 1588 and 1632 the Commonwealth was governed by King Sigismund III, a Swedish prince who was converted to the Catholic faith in order to become eligible for the Polish throne. He became a very devout Catholic and was virtually a captive in the hands of the clergy. He was generally known as the "king of the Jesuits." Needless to say, Sigismund lent his ear to the anti-Semitic propaganda of the clergy much more than his predecessors. Apart from the deterioration in the situation of the Jews, the Polish Commonwealth in general began to go down the road to political anarchy and economic decline. Especially dangerous became the situation in the Ukraine which had become by then the home of a considerable part of the Jewish population. The progress of the Polish colonization began to meet with stiffer opposition on the part of the Ukrainian peasants. Dangerous social, religious, and ethnic tensions increased rapidly.

All these tensions came to a head in 1648 when Bohdan Khmelnitsky raised the banner of a bloody Cossack revolt against the Polish magnates. Khmelnitsky defeated several Polish armies and occupied large parts of the Ukraine. His victories turned everywhere into a cruel slaughter of Poles and Jews. Within a short period practically all Jewish towns and settlements lay in ruins. Not fewer than 100,000 Jews lost their lives and the survivors escaped penniless to the more western provinces of the Commonwealth and to foreign countries — even as far as the Netherlands. The size of the catastrophe was horrifying, and Polish Jewry never completely recovered from it.

The revolt of the Cossacks was followed by another calamity. Before the Ukraine quieted down and the destitute survivors

46

could return to their ruined homes, Poland was again flooded by alien armies. The Muscovites invaded the Duchy of Lithuania and the Swedes occupied Western Poland. The invading armies, especially the Muscovites, murdered and pillaged the Jewish population mercilessly. And when the Poles arose to resist the "Flood," again the Jews were penalized under the accusation that they betrayed the country to the enemy.

The net result of ten years of war and revolt was that about half of the Jewish population of the Commonwealth had perished. The Polish army itself destroyed sixty Jewish communities in Western Poland to avenge the alleged treason of the Jews. Then when the wars were over a wave of pogroms fell upon the Jews, especially in the big cities. These were accompanied by an ever-growing number of blood accusations. The blood accusations plagued the Jewish communities in short intervals, and more than once sent the whole Jewish population of many a town fleeing after leaving behind all of their belongings. The Council of the Four Lands saw itself even compelled to send a special messenger to Rome to ask for the protection of the Pope against the terrible, senseless accusations.

At the same time also the legal status of the Jews in the Commonwealth began to deteriorate. The Parliament (Sejm) vigorously supported the burgesses in their fight against the Jews. Even among the magnates, who until then had been staunch protectors of the Jews, anti-Jewish feelings could be noticed. The hatred of the clergy towards the Jews was still on the increase and the bishops usurped illegally the right to permit or prohibit the erection of new synagogues. Some respite was given to the Jews only during the two decades of the reign of John III Sobieski (1674-1696). After his death the friends of the Jews in government circles became very few, indeed. A new uprising of the Cossacks in 1768 again ruined countless Jewish communities in the Ukraine. All of the eighteenth century down to the time of Poland's partition presents one long epoch of pogroms, blood libel trials, and other forms of oppression.

h

When the Ukraine calmed down and the "Flood" was over, thousands of refugees began to return to their homes. After all, it was easier for them to earn a livelihood and find a home in those provinces of the Commonwealth where the Polish, Roman-Catholic elements were not too numerous. About 1750 again a half of Polish Jewry lived in those parts of the country. The exodus of the Jews from the big cities also continued uninterruptedly. Most of the migrants now settled in villages rather than in towns. By the middle of the eighteenth century a third of Poland's Jewry lived in villages. The Jewish settlements on the private territories of the noblemen kept on multiplying, and here and there also a large city inhabited solely by Jews sprang up. Such a community, for instance, was Brody, which was founded during the last years of the seventeenth century and eighty years later was the largest Jewish community in the Commonwealth. A census conducted in 1764 revealed that the total number of Jews who lived in the united Commonwealth of Poland and Lithuania was 600,000.

The economic position of the Jews grew weaker. About a quarter of the Jewish population were craftsmen and a third were small inn-keepers. A majority of the Jewish population thus belonged to the poorest social classes. But even Jews who still belonged to the higher economic strata were steadily plagued by the bitter attacks of their Polish competitors. The more the Commonwealth was losing its leading position in East Central Europe, the more its general economic situation was deteriorating and the more stubborn was becoming the effort of the Polish merchants to force their Jewish competitors from their positions. As a result, about ten per cent of the Jewish population were declassés, and their number kept on growing. When in 1772 Poland was partitioned and some of its western provinces were annexed by Prussia, King Frederick the Great was shocked by the large number of Jewish paupers in the newly acquired land. The enlightened great king then forced tens of thousands of them to enter into what remained of Poland. The large ranks of Jewish paupers in the crippled Commonwealth thus swelled considerably. After the First Partition a certain revival of economic activity occurred and the first steps were taken towards the establishment of a local industry. A certain number of Jews participated in the new economic effort; but the large masses of the Jewish population lived all through the eighteenth century in want or total lack of an occupation.

In these hard times, when a strongly organized Kehillah could act to alleviate the sufferings of the people, this once important institution was losing its position. The weakened economy after 1600 drastically reduced the financial means at the disposal of the Kehillah. And to make things worse the needs of the local Kehillah, as well as of the Council of the Four Lands, kept on growing. The result was that about 1640 the Kehillahs found themselves deeply in debt. After the calamity of 1648 and the "Flood," the Council of the Four Lands was still strong enough to mobilize help on a major scale. However, the successive developments drove the Council into such immense debt that it could not free itself of it until its dissolution in 1764. The enormous debt accumulated not only because of the pauperization of the Jewish population and the ensuing curtailment of the income of the Council, but it also grew because the annual head-tax, which the Jews paid to the government, was in the eighteenth century four times as high as a century earlier. The Council also had to borrow considerable amounts at high interest rates to pay for expensive blood libel trials, to finance efforts to combat anti-Jewish laws and ordinances, and to bribe a host of government officials and other influential people in whose hands the fate of the Jews rested. In view of this situation there is little wonder that the debt of the Council reached the sum of two and a half million Guilders. The leaders of the Council had to borrow money again and again, from Jews and Gentiles alike, in Poland and even in other countries. More than 90% of the Council's income went to the government as head-tax and to the debtors as interest. All of this tended to increase the pressure of the Kehillah on its individual members while its positive achievements were diminishing. The once communally active Regional Councils were now mere agencies for the collection of taxes. In addition, as always in similar situations, corruption began to raise its head in the different departments of the Kehillahs.

When the broad masses became aware of this situation, they began to rebel more vigorously against the aristocracy which ruled the Kehillahs on the basis of a constitution that granted voting rights only to the rich and the learned. To be sure, the success of the fight for the democratization of the Kehillah was insignificant; it only undermined what still remained of the prestige of the Kehillah. The Council of the Four Lands did not meet now as frequently as before, and the sessions of the Regional Council of the Lithuanian Jews met only occasionally.

The sad position of the Kehillahs and of the Council of the Four Lands did not escape the attention of the Polish government. Circles hostile to the Jews began, therefore, to agitate for the abolition of the Jewish autonomous, communal organs. This was in the late seventeenth century. The Council, however, could continue in its agony until 1764, when a royal decree put it out of existence. What remained was an enormous debt which continued to plague the Jewish community for a long time.

Aside from the question of the Council of the Four Lands, the Jewish problem as a whole became a matter of discussion within the Polish society. The Polish Commonwealth, as mentioned above, was rapidly losing its strength at a time when its neighbors — Russia, Prussia, and Austria — were well on the way to becoming great Powers. Their interference with domestic issues of the Commonwealth became more frequent and more arrogant. It was quite evident that they were preparing to divide it among themselves. Serious patriotic circles, therefore, began to discuss programs of reforms which would strengthen the country and help it out of its predicament. The broad discussion of the issues of government and society produced some interesting ideas on the status of the Jewish community. The urge for reform became especially strong after the First Partition of the Commonwealth in 1772, when large areas were cut off from it and annexed by neighbors. Of especial importance were a number of projects in favor of the Jews that were discussed by the so-called "Great Sejm," the Parliament of 1788-1792, which worked on a new constitution for the Commonwealth. Some of these projects even envisaged a non-negligible measure of political and social equality for the Jews. None of these projects, however, was approved by the Sejm because the enemies of the Jews were numerous. Nevertheless, a certain change in the attitude of Polish society towards the Jews could be noticed. In the army which fought in 1794 under General Kosciuszko for the liberation of the country, a Jewish unit under the Jewish Colonel Berek Joselewicz gained a heroic record. But these were already the last minutes in the agony of the dismembered country. One year later the remnants of the once mighty Commonwealth were divided between her neighbors, and the name of Poland vanished from the map. The once solid and homogeneous Polish Jewry now was started on a new and a different historical course. It was now divided into three groups of different political and social interest and of different and rapidly changing cultural patterns.

i

During the first decades of the nineteenth century the territories of the partitioned Polish Commonwealth and their Jewish communities passed a stormy epoch of great upheavals caused by the Napoleonic Wars. When the congress of Vienna (1814-1815) adjourned after stabilizing the situation in Europe for a long period, Poland remained divided among its mighty neighbors. Poland's Jewry had, therefore, to continue its new historical course as set by the First Partition in 1772.

The Jews who lived in the western provinces, now annexed by Prussia, were first treated as citizens of a lower rank. Many of them were forced, as mentioned above, to cross the border back into Poland. However, little by little their situation began to improve. Already in 1802 they were permitted to settle in all parts of Prussia and some of their legal disabilities were abolished. To be sure, when the Jews of Prussia attained full equality in 1812, this did not apply to the inhabitants of the former Polish provinces. All the barriers were finally removed in 1848 when Prussia obtained a liberal constitution, and full equality was granted to all its Jews. In those decades a great exodus began among the Jews of the Polish provinces of the kingdom to its more western parts, and especially to the capital city of Berlin. This was accompanied by a vigorous process of Germanization. And yet, these German Jews of Polish origin did not lose their East-European character altogether. They continued to worship according to the order of prayer followed in Poland, and the tradition of Torah learning survived among them almost down to our own times. Moreover, until the middle of the nineteenth century this part of Germany even retained the character of an important center of Jewish learning.

Somewhat different was the historical course of the Jews in southern Poland which was annexed by Austria under the name of Galicia. It is true that under Emperor Joseph II (1780-1790) their civil and social conditions slightly improved. However, they still had to pay, till the end of the century, a series of insulting, specifically Jewish taxes. There were still in those days a number of cities in Galicia in which Jews were not tolerated. There, too, the situation of the Jews greatly improved in the year of the "Spring of Nations" (1848). The new imperial constitution of Austria-Hungary, of 1867, finally granted to all the Jews of the Empire, including those in Galicia, full equality.

All through this time the Jewish population grew impressively. From about 200,000 in 1772 it increased to almost 900,000 by 1910. The natural process of Germanization affected them to a considerably lesser degree than the Jews in the Prussian part of Poland. The Jews of Galicia even developed an independent political activity in the city councils, in the regional parliament, and in the federal parliament in Vienna. In the 1870's the Jews had controlling majorities in about fifty city councils, and a number of them elected Jewish burgomasters. The efforts of Joseph II to force upon the Jews of Galicia German culture in effect failed. Even the forcible dissolution of the Jewish communal organization during his reign could not break up Jewish society. Galician Jewry in its entirety remained a consciously Jewish group. Galicia was a great center of Jewish culture in all its ramifications and developed great Jewish social movements.

j

Of an entirely different character was the historical course of the major part of Polish Jewry that became the Russian Jewry of the nineteenth century, the "Mother of the Diaspora."

When it annexed the eastern part of Poland, Russia found there about three quarters of a million Jews living in compact masses. The main concern of the government was to prevent the Jews from Poland from moving into the inner Russian provinces, which were practically "Judenrein." To achieve this goal the notorious "Pale of Settlement" was established which remained in existence until the downfall of the Czarist government in 1917. In the Pale the Jewish population lived squeezed together under unbearable economic and social conditions. Nevertheless, Russian Jewry increased by six hundred per cent during the nineteenth century. At the turn of the century the five million Jews that lived in Russia were the greatest Jewish territorial aggregation in the world. Already beginning with 1850, Russian Jewry comprised at least a half of all the Jewish people. The hard economic and political conditions caused great masses of them to emigrate to America and other countries. Nevertheless, Russian Jewry remained a community of millions. Moreover, in spite of the rigid laws, about a million succeeded in penetrating into Russia proper and settling beyond the Pale of Settlement. Simultaneously many Jews, especially from Lithuania, went to live in the purely Polish regions of the

Russian Empire, where the political and economic situation was somewhat more favorable. Also in this part of the empire the Jewish population grew rapidly. Here two magnificent communities sprang up in Warsaw and in Lodz, the Polish "Manchester," with hundreds of thousands of Jewish inhabitants.

During the first decades of the nineteenth century Czar Alexander I showed an interest in the improvement of the situation of the Jews. However, nothing tangible was done. When Nicholas I became czar in 1825 the situation of the Jews deteriorated drastically and reached such a tragic point that Nicholas began to be considered one of the greatest oppressors of the Jewish people in all history. He abolished the Jewish communal institutions. Under the disguise of bringing modern culture to the Jews he initiated a system of forced assimilation and conversion. The culmination of his anti-Jewish policy was the introduction of the cruel system of kidnapping twelve-year old boys for "military service," the true task of which was to bring about their conversion to Christianity. This whole issue of the *Cantonists,* as these unhappy children were called, ruined countless Jewish families and spread demoralization throughout Jewish society. The extent to which the cruel system was employed is shown by the fact that solely during the last three years of Nicholas's reign more than thirteen thousand Jewish boys were kidnapped for full twenty-five years of military service that only a handful survived. The system was practiced for almost thirty years (1827-1856) and produced not only indescribable suffering but also countless acts of great Jewish heroism. Many of the unhappy children opposed courageously the attempts of the czarist officials to convert them. They lived their Jewish life clandestinely in the homes of Russian peasants or in military schools in which they were placed, far away from their unhappy parents. The degree of suffering to which the Jewish population was exposed under Nicholas I is sufficiently shown by the more than six hundred special anti-Jewish laws enacted during his reign, besides another several hundred anti-Jewish orders issued by the government in secret.

JEWISH DESTINY IN EASTERN EUROPE

During the reign of Czar Alexander II (1855-1881) the Jews began to breathe more freely. When the revolutionary movements started, however, the situation of the Jews deteriorated again. The czarist secret police reasoned that the best way to combat the anger of the masses against the abuses of the regime was to incite them against the Jews. This was the true background of the waves of pogroms which plagued Russian Jewry during the last two decades of the nineteenth century. The riots were organized everywhere by the police, and their result was the recurring murder and pillage in scores of towns and cities densely populated by Jews. Czarist Russia thus earned the doubtful distinction of being the first government to use anti-Semitism as means of preserving its regime.

The Jews tried to defend themselves as much as they could. A number of great Jewish leaders appeared on the horizon who tried to intercede in behalf of their co-religionists wherever they could. Jewish leaders in Western Europe and in the United States organized public opinion into a stormy protest against the czarist government because of its outrageous persecution of its Jewish subjects. From time to time prominent Jewish leaders from the Western countries came to Russia in order to intervene personally in favor of their brethren. For almost a hundred years many legends were circulating among the people about the visit in 1846 of the wondrous Jewish philanthropist, Sir Moses Montefiore of England, to the court of the oppressor of his co-religionists, Nicholas I. Sir Moses again visited Russia in 1872 in order to help his brethren when the policy of Alexander II towards them began to be less liberal. In thousands of Jewish homes in Russia and in Poland the portrait of the great benefactor was hanging in expression of gratitude for his efforts. Many legends also surrounded the visit of Theodore Herzl in Russia in 1903, when the founder of the Zionist movement implored the ministers of the czar to let the Jews live more peacefully and to lift the ban on Zionist activities.

Little by little Russian Jewry itself awoke to struggle for the betterment of its lot. Great Jewish political movements came into being with dynamic programs designed to attain equality. They organized the Jewish masses in times of elections, and Jewish representatives fought valiantly for the full emancipation of the people. When at the turn of the century new waves of pogroms started, Jewish groups for self-defense began to resist the attacks of the hooligans. A Jewish press sprang up in Hebrew, Yiddish, Russian, and Polish that fought courageously for Jewish equality and could not be silenced by the czarist censors. Also the Haskalah, the Jewish Enlightenment movement, helped to awaken the social will of the Jewish masses in Russia and to "straighten their backs." On its fertile grounds a wondrous literature grew up in Hebrew and in Yiddish. The modern Yiddish theater with its high artistic level also had its roots in the Haskalah. The Jewish people continued to maintain their communal institutions on a voluntary basis after the Kehillah was forcibly abolished in 1821 in the Polish provinces and in 1844 in the rest of the Pale of Settlement. A countless number of religious and philanthropic societies and fraternities organized themselves voluntarily to fill the vacuum created by the abolition of the Kehillah. The movement of the Lovers of Zion (Hibbat Zion) and later political Zionism flourished here more than in any other place in the world. In 1903 Russia counted not fewer than 1,572 Zionist groups. All of this gave much courage to the Jewish man and enabled him to live with human dignity although he remained until 1917 a citizen of second rank.

Another way open to the individual Jew was to emigrate to the Western countries where the climate for the Jew was friendly. The West began to attract Eastern European Jews as early as the middle of the seventeenth century. The emigrants went to Germany, to the Netherlands, and to England. A few of them even reached the American shores. The migration of the Jews from Russia, and especially from its Lithuanian regions, gained momentum about 1870 following a terrible famine. It became a real mass movement, however, about a decade later with the start of the so-called "New Immigration."

The movement was greatly accelerated by the pogroms. But it is worth noting that also from Galicia, where pogroms were Russia, Lithuania, and Poland. The migratory movements of the Eastern European Jews thus kept on growing until during the three decades between 1880 and 1910 a third of the Jewish people were on the road to new and better homes. The migratory movements finally produced the multi-million Jewish community of the United States, the flourishing Jewish settlements in England, in Latin America, in South Africa, and to a large degree also the Jewish community of the State of Israel.

The large-scale exodus from Eastern Europe did not seriously weaken Russia's Jewish community. In 1900 it still comprised a half of the Jewish people, and it vigorously continued its fight for equality and human dignity. In those times, at the turn of the century, the million and a quarter Jews who lived in the Polish provinces of the Empire were forced into a grave struggle for economic survival. The czarist government tried hard to uproot the language and culture of the Poles; its pressure on their Jewish neighbors, therefore, lessened. But then the Poles began to persecute their Jewish neighbors. It was of no avail that many Jews fought together with the Poles during their two uprisings against the Russians in 1830-1831 and in 1863. The Polish political parties and the Catholic clergy kept on inciting the population against the Jews, calling for an economic and social boycott against them. The last years before the outbreak of the First World War thus were times of suffering and disappointment to Eastern Europe's great Jewish community. Pogroms, boycotts, and persecution by officials were a daily event. During the month of June, 1914, on the eve of the World War, Nicholas II, the last of the czars, managed to issue more than fifty laws directed against his Jewish subjects. . . .

The grave political persecution and the economic pressure thus kept the large masses of the Jewish population at a permanent disadvantage. Jews strove vigorously for wider economic activity. But only a very few succeeded in freeing themselves unknown, Jews streamed to the American shores in almost the same proportion as their brethren from the Ukraine, White from their tight position. Those few lucky ones established new industries, built highways and railroads, founded banks, and developed Russian export to foreign countries. Some of them became incredibly rich. Warsaw had its rich Jews, Lodz had a Jewish plutocracy, and in the Ukraine, in Volhynia, and in Podolia, the number of wealthy Jews was non-negligible. All this Jewish "aristocracy," however, comprised a very thin layer of the Jewish population. The overwhelming majority of the Jewish population in Eastern Europe on the eve of the First World War was a large, poverty-stricken, and gravely oppressed mass of hungry people deprived of their rights.

k

As soon as the war was declared, hundreds of thousands of Jews in all parts of Russia were mobilized into the army. They fought valiantly on the various fronts. In spite of the anti-Semitic attitude of the czarist government, a wave of sincere patriotism encompassed the Jewish population, and many Jews distinguished themselves in the various areas of the war effort. However, again the Jews were the first victims of the events. The Russian generals suffered one defeat after another and needed a scapegoat to blame for their failures. Rumors, therefore, began to spread to the effect that the Jews betrayed "Mother Russia" to the German invaders. The rumors were followed by a cruel expulsion of the Jewish inhabitants from areas close to the front. The hostilities had hardly started when hosts of Jewish refugees began to show up on the roads, most of them old people, women, and children, whose sons, husbands, and fathers were mobilized for service at the front. The expulsions became more and more cruel and the metropolitan Jewish communities were flooded with refugees for whom they had to care under the hard conditions of the war.

Especially ruthless was the expulsion from Lithuania, where probably a majority of the Jewish population were evacuated from their homes. From the province of Kovno 160,000 Jews were driven deep into Russia. Jewish aid societies tried to bring help to their homeless brethren, but often were not allowed to do so. Simultaneously mobs began to attack the few Jews who were permitted to stay in their homes. Hard was also the lot of the Jews in Galicia when the Russian army appeared there. Whoever did not flee in time southward to Austria or Hungary was exposed to grave persecutions on the part of the Russian occupational armies.

In view of this situation it can be easily understood why the Jews of Poland and Lithuania greeted the victorious German armies as liberators. And, indeed, the Germans tried during all the time of their occupational rule in Poland and in Lithuania (1914-1918) to treat the Jews with full equality. For the first time Jewish citizens were elected as burgomasters in towns that had a Jewish majority. Many Jews were appointed to government offices. Even the police force had many Jewish members. The Jews thus lived in Poland and in Lithuania under the rule of the German occupants fairly peacefully, although they were, like the rest of the population, subject to the general hard conditions of the war. In comparison with the czarist anti-Semitic dictatorship, the German occupation brought with it a definite improvement in the situation of the Jews.

Soon the hopes of the Jews for a better future reached a climax. Under the impact of the Russian defeats, Czar Nicholas II abdicated and a new democratic government took his place. One of its first acts was to revoke all the laws limiting the rights of the Jews and to give them full equality. But, alas, Jewish equality in Russia lasted only a short half-year. In October, 1917, the Communists revolted against the legal democratic government and proclaimed the establishment of the Soviet State. On that day Russia's great Jewish community entered upon one of the most tragic epochs in its history, which has been lasting now for more than forty years, and during which its religious, social, and cultural life has almost come to an end.

Jewish suffering reached a terrible climax during 1919-1921

59

when civil war raged in Russia. The "white" armies that fought against the Red Army, the nationalistic Ukrainian military units that fought for the separation of their homeland from Russia, and often also the Red Army, attacked the defenseless Jewish population and plundered their property, especially in small towns. But hardest hit were the Jews by the Ukrainian Cossack units. A wave of bloody pogroms flooded the country. And although the Jews organized armed groups for self-defense that fought courageously, more than sixty thousand Jews lost their lives in a series of more than one thousand pogroms in five hundred towns. The most terrible of the massacres took place in Proskurov, where 1,200 Jews were murdered in one single day. Thousands from among the survivors of the pogroms died as a result of their wounds, and together with those who perished as a result of epidemics, the war victims of the civilian Jewish population in the Ukraine reached 200,000.

1

At the time when the civil war came to an end and the Soviet government established itself firmly, Russia had a Jewish population of more than three million. The majority of the Jews who until 1914 were Russian subjects now became citizens of a series of newly created states, such as Poland, Lithuania, Latvia, Estonia and Finland. Many others fled from the Soviet regime to the Western countries.

The official approach of the Soviets to the Jewish question was that the Jews should enjoy full equality, but should assimilate themselves culturally. The Pale of Settlement was, of course, abolished and large numbers of Jews began to settle in regions where they were formerly not permitted to live. The economic decline of the small towns, generally inhabited by Jews, also caused many of them to move to metropolitan areas. In the capital city of Moscow, for example, where under the czars Jews were not permitted to live, a Jewish community of about half a million people came into being.

During the first years of the Soviet regime the government

fought against anti-Semitism and its manifestations became rare. However, when considerable numbers of Jews appeared in regions that were formerly closed to them, the Gentile population began to show resentment. Anti-Semitic feelings rose sharply in the thirties, when a group of leading Communists, who were Jews, were sentenced to death in the famous trials instituted by Stalin for the purpose of purging the old leadership of the Communist Party. At the same time high Jewish officials began to be quietly dismissed from their positions. The agreement concluded between the Soviets and Hitler in 1939 also strengthened the anti-Semitic feelings of the Russian people. When the Nazis finally invaded Russia in 1941, they occupied the western provinces of the country where a major portion of the Jewish population lived. The Soviet government knew quite well that the Germans would exterminate the Jewish population. Nevertheless, only a few of the Jews were evacuated before the arrival of the Germans. Some of the Russian guerillas who fought th Germans from their bases in the forests treated with hostility the handful of Jews who tried to save themselves by joining them. Many of the Jewish refugees were banished to Siberia. Some 400,000 refugee Jews from Poland were transferred to labor camps located deep in Russia where they worked for the Russian war effort. Of these many died of epidemics and exhaustion. The result was that of the four and a half million Jews who lived at the beginning of 1941 in Soviet Russia, including the annexed provinces of East Poland and the Baltic countries, only two million were still alive when the war was over. And this happened at a time when 700,000 Jewish soldiers fought in the Red Army against Germany and numerous groups of Jewish guerillas conducted a heroic war behind the German lines.

The economic lot of the Jews in Soviet Russia was very hard at the beginning. Most of them belonged to the middle class and were, therefore, hardest hit by the Soviets' socialized economy. During the first years of militant Communism, about one and a half million Jews became wretched declassés who were

61

literally starving. The situation was somewhat eased during 1921-1926, when the Soviets gave in and introduced the so-called New Economic Policy (NEP). The peasants again began to sell their produce and the Jewish retailer could again be in business.

During all these years great economic changes took place among the Jews. Growing numbers of them, especially young people, were integrated as workers in the factories and as officials in the government service. Many Jews also switched to agriculture, and a number of kolkhoz settlements with exclusively Jewish memberships were organized. The government encouraged the transition of Jews to agriculture. It even began to show interest in the establishment of exclusively Jewish agricultural regions. At first, steps were taken to concentrate the Jewish colonists in a certain part of the Crimea. However, the land which was alotted to them turned out to be of poor quality, and the project was abandoned. Quite similar was the fate of the Jewish autonomous region in Biro-Bijan, in the Far East. Although at a certain time the Soviet government gave its full support to the project, less than two per cent of Russia's Jewish population settled there. In the last few years all has been quiet around Biro-Bijan. Both the Crimean and Biro-Bijan projects cost a fortune, of which about three quarters was contributed by Jews of the free Western countries, mainly American Jews. Both projects ended in a failure, mainly because of the poor quality of the land given to the Jews and because the Soviet government revoked its support before any noticeable results could be attained.

m

When Poland regained its independence, and the three parts into which it was partitioned at the end of the eighteenth century became reunited, a new, very large Jewish community came into being. To be sure, in the province of Posen Jews were but few. Almost all of them in this part of Poland during the nineteenth century underwent a process of Germanization and became an integral part of modern German Jewry. When

62

the area was separated from Germany after the First World War, most of its Jewish inhabitants moved to Berlin and to other parts of Germany. Galicia, however, which now became part of Poland, was inhabited by a numerous Jewish community with a strong ethnic and religious consciousness. Thus, the three million Jews of the new Polish republic were able to develop, in spite of their hard political and economic conditions, a very intensive and rich political, social, and religio-cultural life.

The kind of treatment the Jews could expect in the new republic became evident during the first days of the liberation: the national independence was celebrated by the Poles by beating and plundering the Jews. Of an especially tragic character was the pogrom in Lemberg on November 22, 1918, during which regular Polish army units murdered seventy-two defenseless Jews, among them old people, women, and children. The Congress of Versailles forced the new Polish republic to sign a special treaty according to the terms of which Poland was obliged to extend to its minorities, including the Jews, broadest political equality and full national-cultural autonomy. During the two decades of its existence Poland not only did not fulfill its obligations under the treaty, but instead consistently and stubbornly discriminated against its Jewish citizens and turned their life into one long chain of political, cultural, and economic oppression.

During all this time a venomous anti-Jewish propaganda was conducted in which the Catholic clergy had a leading part. The representatives of the Jews in the Polish Parliament (Sejm) fought heroically for Jewish rights, but the results were negligible. In the latter years of the Republic the election laws became so discriminatory that the Jews, who comprised thirteen per cent of the population, remained practically without parliamentary representation. The universities discriminated against Jewish students in an unbelievable manner. In the thirties segregated seating was introduced for the Jewish students in the universities. Consequently, they **stood** during their classes because they refused to accept a ghetto in the institutions of learning. In the last few years before the Second World War, bloody anti-Jewish pogroms took place in a number of cities.

The political oppression was accompanied by an economic and fiscal policy almost openly pledged to bring about the ruin of the Jews. At the time of Poland's liberation 67% of the Jewish population were engaged in business, trade, and industry. About 62% of Poland's commerce and a considerable part of its industry, notably the light industry and the textile industry in Lodz and in Bialystok, were owned by Jews. To begin with, almost immediately the position of commerce and industry began to deteriorate because the vast Russian markets, for which they formerly produced, did not exist any more. In addition, masses of Polish peasants began to stream into towns and cities and to enter urban occupations. These new Christian merchants and artisans enjoyed the full support of the government and quite easily displaced Jews from hitherto occupied positions. But the greatest blow to the Jewish middle class was the fiscal policy of the government, which beginning with 1924, imposed on the Jewish population a ruthlessly disproportionate burden of taxes and a compulsory stoppage of business on Sundays. Among the more than three million Jews only a very negligible number opened their stores on the Jewish Sabbath, Saturday. Nevertheless, the Jews were compelled to close their businesses on Sundays and on all Catholic religious holidays. The Jewish citizen, therefore, could earn a livelihood only about 235 days a year, while his Gentile competitor was occupied or employed about 300 days a year. At the same time a fierce propaganda was conducted among the Christian population to boycott Jewish stores, and Gentiles who would normally buy from Jews were afraid to do so. Above all this, Jews were totally excluded from the Civil Service and from municipal offices where several million citizens earned their livelihood.

The Jews tried to defend themselves in various ways. A vigorous campaign was conducted to stimulate productivity among the Jewish masses. An impressive network of cooperative societies helped the oppressed Jewish merchant and artisan with badly needed credit. Of great importance was the helping hand extended by the American Joint Distribution Committee to the Polish Jews in their bitter struggle for existence. These acts of self-aid were a unique phenomenon in Jewish history in modern Europe. But they could not stop the anti-Jewish economic policy followed by the Polish government. Consequently, on the eve of the Second World War Poland had more than a million Jews who had no permanent occupation or employment. Everybody was anxious to emigrate to the Holy Land or to the United States. However, the rigid immigration laws of the two countries made large-scale emigration impossible, and only a handful of the Jews of Poland escaped the "Great Catastrophe" through emigration.

II

Besides Poland, four other states were liberated in 1917 from the Russian yoke: Lithuania, Latvia, Estonia, and Finland. The Jewish communities of Finland and Estonia were always very small. Lithuania and Latvia, however, both had a Jewish population of considerable numbers who were very conscious of their Jewishness.

The efforts to establish an independent Lithuanian state received effective support from Jewish leaders, and, consequently, the situation of the Jews in the new state was favorable. Jewish citizens held high government offices and a special Ministry for Jewish Affairs was organized. At the beginning the Lithuanian government honored its obligations under the Treaty on Minorities. When in the summer of 1920 about 100,000 Jews of those evacuated five years earlier by the Russian generals returned to Lithuania, action was taken to set up the Jewish national-cultural autonomy envisaged by the Treaty on Minorities. However, already in 1923 a change for the worse took place. A census revealed that the Jewish population in Lithuania totaled only 150,000. They began, therefore, to be considered as a factor of minor importance on the political scene, and the government moved to abolish the Jewish autonomy. In addition, discriminatory laws against the Jews were enacted, including a prohibition to do business on Sunday. When in 1926 a Fascist government took over, the situation of the Jew deteriorated even more. At the beginning of the Second World War Lithuania was annexed by Soviet Russia, and the few Jews who survived the Nazi occupation shared now the fate of Soviet Russia's Jewry.

The Jewish population of Latvia totaled about 100,000, one half of whom lived in the capital city of Riga. In Latvia, too, the government at the beginning was friendly to the Jews and granted them educational autonomy. The club of Jewish Representatives in the Latvian Parliament was an important factor in the country's political life. Equally important was the share the Jews had in commerce, industry, and banking.

In Latvia, too, the situation of the Jews deteriorated when the new Fascist government began to be influenced by Nazi Germany. The Jews then began to emigrate in considerable numbers. Like all the Baltic countries, Latvia became a part of Russia. A certain number of Jews returned after the war to Riga, and they, too, shared the lot of Soviet Russia's Jewry.

o

At the time of the Soviet Revolution (October, 1917) Russian Jewry was well on the way to organizing its much-needed communal institutions. Also Jewish cultural life in all its aspects began to blossom under the newly-found freedom. However, as soon as the Soviet government became more firmly established, it began to systematically liquidate the Jewish communal institutions. Jewish political parties were forcibly dissolved, Zionists began to be terribly persecuted, and the democratically elected Kehillahs were abolished. At first, a special department for Jewish affairs was functioning, allegedly for the purpose of caring for the social needs of the Jewish population. However, in 1923 also this last remnant of Jewish autonomy disappeared from the scene. The major factor in Jewish life now was the "Yevsektsya," the Jewish section of the Communist

Party. The Yevsektsya considered the fight against the Jewish religion as its most important task. Thousands of large synagogues and smaller houses of worship (Batei Midrash) were transformed into clubs. Simultaneously, the government prohibited the teaching of Jewish religious subjects. For some time many Jewish religious schools (Hadarim) were maintained clandestinely by devoted idealists, but the mounting difficulties later caused their gradual disappearance.

It was the avowed policy of the Soviet government to discourage the cultivation of the Hebrew language and its literature among the Jews. Even the famous Hebrew theater **Habima** was compelled to leave Russia early in 1926. But the government still openly supported Jewish secular culture in the Yiddish language. A wide network of Yiddish schools was founded, and besides them an impressive number of Yiddish state theaters and publishing houses were established. Jewish sections were organized within the Research Academies of the Ukraine and White Russia, and scholarly periodicals in Yiddish were published by them. Ultimately, however, the Soviet government put an end to Jewish culture in Yiddish too. Of the eleven hundred Yiddish schools that were operating in 1931, not a single one functions today. The twenty Yiddish state theaters have been closed for many years, and not a single Yiddish daily paper remains of the many that were published before. During the years of the Second World War, the fight against the Jewish religion weakened. Recently a new, although limited, edition of the Jewish prayer-book was published. It had, indeed, become a rarity during the forty years that it had been forbidden to be printed. A yeshivah, a school for the training of rabbis and other religious functionaries, was established in Moscow several years ago. However, only a negligible number of students were permitted to register in its classes. In the large cities a number of synagogues are still open to worshippers. It is now quite obvious that decades of religious persecution did not achieve their goal and were not able to completely eradicate the religious spirit among the Jews of Russia.

P

The two decades between 1918 and 1939, which marked an almost total obliteration of Jewish communal and religious life in Russia, were for the Jews of Poland a period of unusual communal and cultural endeavor. The worse their political and economic position became, the stronger grew their effort to strengthen the communal framework of their life. A very wide network of Jewish schools served to promote the ideologies and philosophies of the various Jewish groups. A daily Jewish press of high quality guided the Jewish population. There were also a large number of political and literary magazines in Yiddish, Hebrew, and Polish. Many publishing houses brought to the market thousands of books of Jewish content.

Although the Polish State refused to grant the Jews the wide communal autonomy provided for by the Treaty on the Minorities, the Kehillah became an institution of utmost importance. It cared quite effectively for the religious life of the Jewish people and served as a central agency for Jewish social work and welfare. The country was full of talmudic academies, training schools for rabbis, cultural societies, and research institutions. Practically every town or city possessed a Jewish public library. The Zionist movement grew to tremendous dimensions. It appealed especially to the young people. Also the Jewish labor movement, with its various ramifications, occupied an important place on the "Jewish Street." A continuous stream of pioneer-emigrants (halutsim) was going to the Holy Land. This widely ramified and inspired communal and religio-cultural activity was carried on to a large degree even in the ghettos established in Poland by the Nazi invaders when Poland's great Jewry was thrown into convulsions of agony.

The course taken by Jewish communal and cultural life in Latvia and Lithuania was quite similar to that of the Jews of Poland. The Latvian government extended to the Jews full autonomy in the educational field. And as for Lithuania, as was pointed out above, its experiment in Jewish autonomy was implemented on a very broad scale. There was a special Ministry for Jewish Affairs. The Kehillah Councils were elected in a truly democratic manner and were, in addition, united in an association of Kehillahs headed by a Jewish National Council. Only a few weeks before a reactionary government moved to abolish Jewish autonomy, a democratically elected National Assembly of all Lithuanian Jewry convened in Kovno. The Fascist revolution, which swept Poland and the Baltic countries in the thirties, brought much trouble to the Jews in this region. But Jewish communal life kept on flourishing until the Nazis put the tragic end to all East European Jewry.

q

The tragic end of East European Jewry is well known to our generation. Like an avalanche, Hitler's hordes flooded Eastern Europe in the first days of the Second World War. Their first victims were the Jews. It was obvious that Hitler's diabolic plans in regard to the Jewish population of Europe were much more terrible then was anticipated even by the greatest pessimists. From the first moment of the Nazi invasion into Poland in the fall of 1939, and two years later into Soviet Russia and the Baltic countries, the German occupational forces began to liquidate the Jews — to simply exterminate them and put an end to the Jewish people. How the Nazi occupants forced the Jews into ghettos, confiscated their property, exploited them in labor camps in favor of the German war effort, and then exterminated them in gas chambers and in death camps is common knowledge. But perhaps not everybody knows how heroically this wondrous East-European Jewry lived during the last moments of its agony. Only later generations may be able to fully comprehend and describe the life of a community of millions in the shadow of death. Eastern European Jewry left the stage of history in the full vigor of life and at the peak of its creativity, never undergoing the process of decline. Its historic course came to an abrupt end in the death camps, and there the legend of East European Jewry was born.

IV

THE STORY OF TORAH LEARNING
IN EASTERN EUROPE

Originally published in Hebrew in "Beth Israel Bepolin," vol. 2,
Jerusalem 1953, pp. 13-35. Translated by Leonard Oschry.

To the sacred memory
of my grandfather
Rabbi Zevi Ezekiel Michelson

a

The information we possess concerning the medieval Jewish
community of the Polish Commonwealth tells mainly of its
struggle for political and economic survival. Its spiritual character is still hidden in obscurity. Here and there, however, in
the latter half of the period, a few signs are found of the growing
spiritual life of the community that was destined to become the
heir of medieval German Jewry. Here and there individual
scholars are mentioned who came from Poland to the Torah
centers of Western Europe. Rabbi Eliezer of Bohemia, a disciple
of Rabenu Tam, relates that "in most places in Poland, and in
Russia and Hungary, there are no students of the Torah.
That is so because of the poverty of the population. Hence they
hire for themselves from wherever they can find a person who
is capable, and he becomes their cantor, rabbi, and teacher of
their children." Rabbi Moses of Kiev, also a disciple of Rabenu
Tam, must surely have spread the teachings of his French
masters in the Ukraine. At that time, to be sure, Polish Torah
learning had not yet expressed itself in literary form; nor had

70

any specific Polish "school" of learning arisen. On the other hand the daily religious life became solidly formed within the mould of the minhag, the local custom. This "minhag Polin" later became the basis of the distinctive "Polish Torah School" as represented by Rabbi Moses Isserles (known as Rama) and his successors. The Jewish scholars of sixteenth century Poland considered the local minhag, a product of popular religious experience, as equal in importance to the *Shulhan Arukh,* which embodies the codified religious law as practiced by Sephardic Jewry. The fact that they could do so shows that already long before that time the religious life of Polish Jewry had become firmly rooted in Torah and Halakhah.

By the middle of the fifteenth century higher forms of Torah learning began to appear in Poland. The intellectuals among the immigrants from Germany and Bohemia brought to their new homeland a new method of Torah study known as *pilpul* or *hiluq,* developed at the time in Western Europe. By this they aroused among the Polish Jews a significant movement for Torah learning.

Cracow and Posen, the two main cities of western Poland, attracted many of the early immgirant-scholars. These cities thus became the first Torah centers in Poland. In the last quarter of the fifteenth century we find Rabbi Moses Minz, one of the outstanding rabbis of Germany, teaching Torah in Posen. Simultaneously Lemberg too, the large city of the Southeast, became known as "the home of the scholars, the fountain of wisdom, the cornerstone and foundation of faith." Several decades later the knowledge of Torah had increased so greatly that Rabbi Jacob Pollack was able to establish in Cracow a yeshivah, a school of higher Talmudic studies.

With Rabbi Jacob Pollack a great era began in the spiritual life of Polish Jewry. It lasted for many centuries. During that period the desire for Torah learning grew to such heights as were never seen before, unless we look back to the period of the Amoraim and Geonim in Babylon or the Tosafists in Western Europe. Innumerable yeshivoth sprang up in the cities and towns. The scholar was accorded a privileged social status and the Torah became the heritage of the masses.

b

Rabbi Jacob Pollack, the first of the great scholars of Poland, was born about 1460. He studied in the yeshivah of Nuremberg in Bavaria where Rabbi Jacob Margalioth was his teacher. From there he proceeded to Bohemia and later to Poland where he spent most of his active life. In his times he was one of the great exponents of the method of pilpul.

This method has persisted in various forms to our own days. Its avowed purpose was to sharpen the intellectual skill of the student to the point where he would be able, unaided, to deduce correct legal decisions from the discussions of the Talmud and the ancillary works of the early authorities (Rishonim). To this end the students were trained to use all the variegated Talmudic literature stored in their memory through years of assiduous study. True, this method produced a great extention of the boundaries of learning, and to a certain degree a liberation from excessive submission to the authorities of the past. However, while it was suited to the gifted few, the majority of students were very much likely to mistake the shadow for the reality. The fact that adverse criticism was levelled at the pilpul from its very introduction, proves sufficiently that it did more harm than good. And yet, the pilpul rapidly gained acceptance and became the recognized manner of study in most of the yeshivoth that were henceforth established in Eastern Europe. It captivated the interest of the students, and became even more widespread through the influence of Rabbi Jacob Pollack's disciple Rabbi Shalom Shakhna, the founder and first rosh-yeshivah of the famous Yeshivah of Lublin.

The few scraps of information we have concerning Rabbi Shalom Shakhna do not yield enough material to construct a biography. It is likely that he was born in Lublin where his father was one of the leaders of the community. About 1520 he was appointed rabbi of Lublin. There he founded its famous

72

yeshivah. For about forty years he headed this institution in which practically all the outstanding legal authorities of the sixteenth century were trained. One of his disciples was the greatest of all the jurists produced by Polish Jewry — Rabbi Moses Isserles. The latter testified of his master and father-in-law, "that he had sent forth pupils to the ends of the world so that all the rabbis and great scholars of the generation were his disciples." Similarly, Rabbi David Gans, author of the chronicle *Tsemah David,* related: "Rabbi Shakhna is the great rabbi, head of the whole Jewish diaspora, exalted above his generation — his fame extends from the East to the West."

The extraordinary success of Rabbi Shalom Shakhna's yeshivah was partly due to its location. Lublin at that time was a growing and expanding community. Rabbi Shakhna's family (his father was the well known tax farmer, Yosko) was very influential in the city because of its relations with the government, and also on account of its wealth. These factors certainly facilitated the growth of the yeshivah and maintained its financial stability. After the death of the founder (1558) his son Israel succeeded him as rosh-yeshivah.

Rabbi Shalom Shakhna continued to cultivate the method of pilpul which he had learned from Rabbi Jacob Pollack. Some say that in this he went even farther than his master. According to Rabbi Meir of Lublin, known as Maharam, "he often prolonged his pilpulistic inquiry of a halakhic subject to such an extent that it was impossible to follow him to the end." The opinion of others was, on the contrary, that Rabbi Shakhna did not indulge in the pilpulistic method as much as Rabbi Jacob Pollack. They felt, however, that he was too much inclined to rely upon his own judgements and self assurance in giving new interpretations to various Talmudic subjects. The greatest of his disciples, Rabbi Moses Isserles, expressed a somewhat different view. He considered Rabbi Shakhna the "Teacher of all Israel." His decisions could be relied on — but only to the extent that his pilpulistic discussions did not contradict the decisions of the earlier authorities. As rabbi of Lublin, Rabbi

73

Shakhna exerted his authority over the community and issued decisions in accordance with his best judgment. Nevertheless, he refrained from any attempt to impose his authority over the Jewish world as a whole. "As I live (wrote his son Israel), I and many others who studied under him urged him to compose a code of the Jewish law. His answer, prompted by his great piety and humility . . . was: 'I know that the rabbis would afterwards not render decisions contrary to what I have written, since the law always follows the last decision, and I have no desire that all should rely on me.' "

Rabbi Jacob Pollack and his great disciple left almost no literary work for posterity. Nevertheless, the memory of their endeavor for the diffusion of Torah learning in Poland lasted through many generations. When the period of Rabbi Shakhna came to its end, there was already in Poland a large group of learned men. The need was now to deepen the work of Talmudic research, and on the other hand to crystallize the social and religious forms of the large, expanding community. These tasks were performed by Rabbi Moses Isserles and Rabbi Solomon Luria.

c

Rabbi Moses Isserles, known as the Ramah, was a native of Cracow. He was born there in the early 1520's. His father, Isserl, was known as a learned man and was also one of the leaders of the community. Rabbi Moses lived and was active in Cracow, where he died at the age of about fifty. His broad intellectual interests included philosophy, astronomy, and history. His philosophical work *Torath Haolah,* though not distinguished by precise formulations, was the most important work produced in this area by a Polish Jew prior to modern times. His interest in history was more than the desire shared by many Talmudic scholars since the days of Rabbi Sherira Gaon to establish the line of the continuity of the oral tradition. His annotations printed in the Cracow edition of the *Sefer Yuhasin* (1581) and his influence on Rabbi David Gans,

74

author of the chronicle *Tsemah David,* reveal a definite inclination to historiography.

As a young man, and while his master was still alive, Rabbi Moses Isserles founded a yeshivah in Cracow. Students flocked to him from far and near. They were attracted by the fame of the founder that rapidly spread all over Poland and beyond its borders. In addition, Rabbi Moses was a wealthy man and was able to contribute lavishly towards the maintenance of the students. He was the first of the scholars of Poland whose correspondence dealing with Jewish legal problems, responsa, has been preserved and published. To this day they serve as an important source for all who study the Halakhah. His contacts reached as far as Italy and the Holy Land. He became hallowed by the masses more than any other Jewish scholar of Poland except, perhaps, the Gaon of Vilna. Till our own days, it was customary in Cracow to visit his grave on Lag-Baomer, the anniversary of his death.

The Rama's outstanding contribution was in the field of Halakhah. He lived at the time when in the Sephardic world a successful attempt was made to codify the Jewish law. Quite naturally Rama too, turned to this field. Indeed, tradition has it that he himself felt the need of a Code of Jewish law and planned to compile it. However, Rabbi Joseph Karo completed his *Shulhan Arukh* before Moses Isserles' plan could materialize. All that remained for Rama now was to comment on Karo's work on the basis of the material he (Rama) had collected.

At first Rabbi Joseph Karo had written his *Beth Yosef,* a collection of laws arranged in the form of a commentary on the *Tur* of Rabbi Jacob ben Asher. In his work Karo elaborated on the Talmudic sources of the laws, and in addition also gave the opinions of the Sephardic scholars who had preceded him. On the other hand, he did not, as a rule, take account of the Franco-German school, whose ideas were embodied in the commentary of Rashi on the Talmud, in the collective works of the Tosafists, and in the minhag. The Rama therefore arranged his work *Darkhei Mosheh* on the model of the work of Rabbi

75

Joseph Karo. It is also an independent commentary on the *Tur,* and contains comments and critical remarks on the opinions of the *Beth Yosef* as well. Rama based his opinions mainly on the teachings of the Franco-German Talmudic scholars, and on the customs (minhag) as practiced by Ashkenazic Jewry, even though his attitude to them was sometimes critical.

In the last years of his life Rama undertook the task of adding his glosses to the *Shulhan Arukh* which Rabbi Joseph Karo had published in the meantime. The latter work was in the form of a code and contained the essence of the matters discussed in *Beth Yosef.* Rama added his own glosses to almost every law in the *Shulhan Arukh.* He called his glosses *Mapah* — for he regarded them as a "cloth" to cover the "prepared table" *(Shulhan Arukh).*

The *Darkhei Mosheh* and the *Mapah* were accepted by Ashkenazic Jewry as an authoritative and binding code. Only as amended by these works did the *Shulhan Arukh* become the guide for their religious life. The *Darkhei Mosheh* became important enough to be provided with commentaries and additions. And as for the *Mapah,* it was "woven" into the text of the *Shulhan Arukh* and became an integral part of it.

While Rama represented the codifying tendencies of this generation, his relative and contemporary, Rabbi Solomon Luria, known as Maharshal, represented its inclination towards theoretical research in the Talmud. Rabbi Solomon ben Rabbi Yehiel Luria was born about the year 1510. During his youth he spent several years at the home of his maternal grandfather in Posen. Later he went to the eastern part of the country and lived in various Lithuanian and Volhynian communities till he succeeded his father-in-law Rabbi Kalman Haberkasten as rabbi in Ostrog. Here he also held the position of rosh-yeshivah. Late in his life he came to Lublin and was head of the yeshivah founded by Rabbi Shakhna. Soon conflicts arose between him and Rabbi Shakhna's son Israel. The reason of the conflict may have been Maharshal's opposition to the method of pilpul. He ultimately was compelled to leave the yeshivah and he opened a new independent school, where he was free to teach in his own way. Many great scholars were his pupils. Among them were some who later carried on his struggle against the pilpul.

As against the spread of pilpul and the proliferation of the codifying literature, Maharshal called for a return to the Talmud itself. He felt that the attempts at codification failed in their purpose since they distracted the main attention from the real source of the Halakhah, the Talmud. The magnum opus of Rabbi Solomon Luria was his work, *Yam Shel Shelomoh,* which embodies many explanations and novellae on those tractates of the Talmud considered most important. In the course of his discussion, based on the commentaries of Rashi and the Tosafists, he endeavored to deduce directly from the Talmud legal decisions through the exercise of keen and critical analysis. In the introduction he describes the tremendous amount of labor he devoted to this work: "I searched and inquired with sevenfold effort into every primary source of the law, working unsparingly and allowing myself only a minimum of sleep. In addition, I devoted much time to discussion with my colleagues and students. Sometimes I sat for a whole week poring over a single subject until I succeeded in discovering its source. Then I recorded it in my book."

In the course of his investigations of many problems in the Talmud, Rabbi Solomon Luria also made emendations in the text. These were based upon old manuscripts and quotations of Talmudic passages in the works of early authors. No one before him had taken the liberty of correcting the errors that the copyists had made. Most of the scholars of Poland of those days endeavored rather to seek pilpulistic solutions to the textual difficulties caused by these errors. Among the contemporaries only Moses Isserles had permitted himself to suggest textual emendations and even he had only done so very rarely and with extreme care. Maharshal, however, did this work on a large scale. The results were collected in the book *Hokhmath Shelomoh* which also contains notes on the Talmud and on the commentaries of Rashi and the Tosafists. Many of the emendations were accepted by later publishers and the text of some printed editions of the Talmud was corrected in accordance with them. Among the other works of Rabbi Solomon Luria we find a collection of critical notes to the commentaries of Rashi and Ibn Ezra on the Pentateuch. He died in Lublin in 1574.

d

The third generation of Torah scholars in Poland lived during the last decades of the sixteenth century. By then many yeshivoth had been existing in Poland and the country was teeming with Torah students. Among them three were outstanding, both as teachers and authors: Rabbi Mordecai Yafeh, Rabbi Joshua Falk Kohen, and Rabbi Meir ben Gedaliah of Lublin. They all were active and they died at almost the same time.

Rabbi Mordecai Yafeh came in his youth from his native Prague to Poland to study Torah in the yeshivoth of Rabbi Moses Isserles and Rabbi Solomon Luria. In the school of Rabbi Moses Isserles he learned the method of pilpul. Rabbi Solomon Luria and certain scholars of Italy, among whom Mordecai Yafeh spent ten years of his life, influenced him against it. In his youth he had toyed with the idea of compiling a book of laws for practical use. When the *Beth Yosef* appeared, Rabbi Mordecai Yafeh found it too long, and he began to prepare an abridged version of the work. Soon the news reached him that Rabbi Joseph Karo was doing just that and he decided to abandon his project. However, when the *Shulhan Arukh* was published, Rabbi Mordecai Yafeh found it too short and he resumed the work on his book. At that time he became aware of the fact that his teacher Moses Isserles was working on the annotations *(Mapah)* to the *Shulhan Arukh;* again Rabbi Mordecai Yafeh stopped. But even the *Shulhan Arukh* as amended by the *Mapah* did not satisfy him. He felt impelled to complete the work he had interrupted so many times.

Rabbi Mordecai Yafeh called all his main works by the

general name *Levush Malkhuth (The Royal Robe)*. Five of his works discuss halakhic subjects. They were written, as he explicitly states, for the Ashkenazic Jews: "I said to myself, the master (Rabbi Joseph Karo) had left room for my work. He has rendered most decisions in accordance with the opinions of Maimonides, for such is the custom in the Islamic countries, and he (the author of *Beth Yosef*, of blessed memory) was the leader and teacher of those Jewish communities. In our lands (i.e. the Ashkenazic communities) we do not do so. I therefore decided to resume my work and to write down and explain the laws followed in these countries, namely Germany, Bohemia, Poland, Ukraine, and their adjoining territories." From these remarks we learn that Rabbi Mordecai Yafeh regarded the minhag as a basis for deciding the laws. It seems that he went further than Rama, and he took account not only of the customs recognized by the legal authorities but even of the popular folkways. Similarly he injected a very noticeable measure of kabbalistic ideas into the body of the Halakhah. The growth of Jewish communal autonomy in Poland also induced Rabbi Mordecai Yafeh to devote special attention to Jewish civil law.

The arrangement of the laws in the *Levush* is very systematic. Its Hebrew style is lucid and fluent. For some time the *Levush* was very popular and was studied side by side with the *Tur* in many yeshivoth. Here and there the *Levush* was even preferred to the *Shulhan Arukh*. Later, however, the star of the *Levush* began to wane, even in those places where it had shone most brightly. Obviously, Polish Jewry was not willing to permanently replace the *Shulhan Arukh* by another code. And above all, Rabbi Moses Isserles had put his stamp of approval on the *Shulhan Arukh* by his annotations and had thereby given it a dominant position in Poland.

The second leading scholar of the generation, Rabbi Joshua Falk, was also a disciple of Rama and Maharshal. As we have indicated, also he devoted his attention to the area of the codes. Neither the *Shulhan Arukh* nor the *Levush* satisfied him. Nevertheless, he arranged his book of laws in the form of a commentary on the *Shulhan Arukh*. The commentary of Rabbi Joshua Falk was given the title *Sefer Meirath Ainayim,* and the author is known by the abbreviation of its title, "Sma." Rabbi Joshua was not able to complete his commentary to the entire *Shulhan Arukh*, and the *Sefer Meirath Ainayim* we possess only covers its civil law section *Hoshen Mishpat*. In this work he also endeavored to correct, by reference to a manuscript in his possession, many of the errors which had crept into the printed editions of Rabbi Moses Isserles' *Mapah*.

The other important work of Rabbi Joshua Falk was the dual work *Derishah Uferishah,* a commentary on all four sections of the *Tur*. The study of the *Tur* was widespread throughout the yeshivoth of Poland, yet there was no satisfactory commentary on it. The *Beth Yosef* can hardly be called a commentary; it is rather a collection of views and opinions bearing upon and related to the *Tur*. Rabbi Joshua Falk attempted to fill the need in a twofold manner. In the *Perishah* he gave a simple explanation of the contents of the *Tur* and the *Beth Yosef* as well as references to the sources of the laws. In the *Derishah* he elaborated upon the explanations he had given in the *Perishah,* and defended his own views on those questions where he had taken an independent stand.

The third great scholar of the generation and the youngest of the three was Rabbi Meir ben Gedaliah, known as Maharam of Lublin. He served as rabbi and rosh-yeshivah in the three leading communities of Poland, Cracow, Lublin, and Lemberg. His outstanding works were *Meir Ainei Hakhamim* and a collection of responsa. The *Meir Ainei Hakhamim* consists of novellae on, and explanations of, the Talmud, Rashi, and Tosafoth. These novellae were included in many printed editions of the Talmud and are consulted by most advanced students of the Jewish law. They are written in a concise and simple exegetical style. Maharam, unlike most of his contemporaries, did not regard the pilpul as the only method of Talmud study; he looked upon it as one of many ways in which to cultivate the mental powers of the students. He therefore used "to explain the halakhic subjects with keen and profound pil-pulistic analysis in the yeshivah," while in the novellae this method is nowhere in evidence. He too, like Maharshal, did not hesitate to emend the text of the Talmud. In line with this Maharam considered all attempts at codification as futile and even regarded them with comtempt. "It is neither my custom nor in my nature — he wrote — to occupy myself with the *Shulhan Arukh*. Still less would I base any legal decision upon the details of their obscure statements, for they are not the work of a single author. Instead they have been gathered and joined together from many diverse and separate works, many times without justification. It is not in my nature to base any rules for legal decisions on works which merely re-semble chapter-headings and are unintelligible. Many are led astray by these words. They permit what is really forbidden, declare the guilty innocent and vice-versa . . . " Maharam discerned the inner logic of the Talmud and wanted to use it to reach the true ruling. Similar tendences were revived in the nineteenth century by the scholars of Lithuania.

e

At the time Rabbi Mordecai Yafeh, Rabbi Joshua Falk, and Maharam of Lublin had passed away, a new younger generation of Torah scholars had emerged. There was a multi-tude of yeshivoth which by that time had produced an impres-sive number of rabbinic authors. And yet, only a few gave the period its significance in the field of Torah learning. The dominance of the pilpul in most of the yeshivoth had prevented many of the scholars from producing works of lasting value. The few truly great men of the period, however, had rejected the pilpulistic method either wholly or in part and were able to produce works of significance.

The two outstanding authors of the period, Rabbi Samuel Edels and Rabbi Joel Serkes, both developed a new approach to Talmudic research by emphasizing the simple interpretation of the Talmud, devoid of any pilpulistic exercises. This new approach is clearly discernible in the systematic commentary on the Talmud composed by Rabbi Samuel Edels, and in the new code of religious practice arranged by Rabbi Joel Serkes.

Rabbi Samuel Edels was born in Cracow about the year 1560. By the time the seventeenth century had begun, he was already counted among the famous scholars of Poland. He was the son-in-law of Edel Ashkenazi of Posen and thus he became known by the name of Samuel Edels or Maharsha. Edel was a wealthy woman and generously supported the yeshivah established by her son-in-law. After her death Maharsha left Posen to accept the position of the rabbi of Chelm. When Maharam died, Rabbi Samuel Edels was called to occupy the posts of rabbi and rosh-yeshivah of Lublin. Maharsha spent his last years in Ostrog as head of a yeshivah, the fame of which remained undimmed for centuries.

Maharsha opposed the pilpul with severe criticism. "True — he wrote — the scholars of the Holy Land found difficulties in the Talmud and tried to reconcile them . . . They examined and set everything right, and the Halakhah was clarified by their pilpul . . . But the scholars of Babylon did otherwise; possibly they conducted their pilpulistic discussions much like the hiluq of our generation . . . with worthless pilpul . . . and each one merely tried to refute the statements of another . . . Such pilpul distracts one from the truth and one does not attain the desired end." Maharsha's research was mainly directed towards an explanation of obscure passages in the Talmud and in the great commentaries of Rashi and the Tosafists. His great work *Hidushei Halakhah Waagadah* is a penetrating commentary rather than a collection of novellae. He exercised meticulous care before suggesting any textual emendations of the Talmud. His interest extended to the Agadah as well. He studied the writings of medieval Jewish philosophers and used them in his own works. Nor was he unfamiliar with the Kabbalah, although he was opposed to excessive preoccupation with the teachings of the mystics. Maharsha adopted a critical attitude, to a great extent, even towards the words of the Rabbis, of Rashi, and of the Tosafists. The work of Maharsha which was a result of his discussions and debates with pupils, achieved very great popularity among students of the Talmud. In recent times it has been printed in almost every edition of the Talmud. One of the great scholars instructed his sons before his death to study intensively Maharsha's writings "for their brevity and profound truth."

Such universal recognition was not accorded to the new method of research in the religious practice adopted by his contemporary, Rabbi Joel Serkes. Rabbi Joel Yafeh, called Serkes after the name of his mother, Serke, was also known as Bah, the abbreviation of the title of his main work, *Bayith Hadash*. He was born in Lublin in 1561. He served as rabbi in various communities, as was customary in those days. In 1618 he was called to Cracow as rabbi and rosh-yeshivah. There he served for more than twenty years until his death. In each community where Rabbi Joel Serkes lived he established a yeshivah and trained many disciples.

The literary work of Rabbi Joel Serkes had a direct bearing upon the problem of the *Shulhan Arukh,* to which the reaction of the Torah world of Poland was very sensitive. While most of the opponents of Rabbi Joseph Karo found fault with the *Shulhan Arukh* mainly because of its brevity, Rabbi Joel Serkes was antagonistic to the *Beth Yosef* itself. It was as if the very name of his book, *Bayith Hadash (New* House) suggested that it was meant to supersede the *Beth Yosef (House of Joseph)*. *Bayith Hadash* is a commentary on the Tur. Its aim, like that of *Sefer Meirath Ainayim* of the previous generation, was to restore the *Tur* to its former power and significance. In the *Derishah Uferishah* the *Tur* is explained by reference to the *Beth Yosef*. Here, however, a pronounced tendency to contradict the views expressed in the *Beth Yosef* is clearly evident. Rabbi Joel Serkes carried on his work in a completely independent manner and developed a systematic critical approach to the *Beth Yosef*. This led him to challenge the unqualified authority enjoyed by Rama as well. He considered such authority harmful to original research in the field of Halakhah. He himself proceeded to analyze the laws included in the *Tur* in the light of their Talmudic sources, and was led to conclude that many accepted prohibitions had no Talmudic basis. Rabbi Joel Serkes also wrote responsa. He made emendations in the text of the Talmud. He was categorically opposed to the pilpul and demanded that books employing that method should not be printed any more since they were most harmful.

At this point some of the other scholars of the early seventeenth century should be mentioned. Rabbi Isaiah Horowits, known as Sh'lah, and Rabbi Ephraim Solomon Lunchits spent their early years in Poland. Both were sharply opposed to the pilpul. Sh'lah was a kabbalist; he was the first to open the Halakhah to a broad influx of kabbalistic ideas. His main work, *Shenei Luhoth Haberith (The Two Tables of the Covenant)* is an anthology of laws, customs, and theological subjects, presented by reference to kabbalistic ideas. Rabbi Ephraim Lunchits was a famous preacher who endeavored to popularize the Agadah of the Talmud among the masses. His commentary on the Pentateuch *Keli Yaqar* was reprinted many times and was universally studied in Poland with almost the same veneration as that of Rashi. These two works have remained popular in the hasidic circles to our own times.

f

Lithuania at that time was a part of the Polish Commonwealth. This, of course, strengthened the ties between the Jewries of the two countries in the areas of communal life and Torah learning. Nevertheless, their development was not uniform. At first Lithuanian Jewry lagged behind. In Poland Torah learning was flourishing and its scholars were becoming famous throughout the Jewish world. In Lithuania, however, only a few had left their mark. A radical change took place in the seventeenth century. The massacres of the years 1648 and 1649 and the persecutions resulting from the Muscovite-Swedish invasion had devastated the Torah centers of Poland. From

84

that time onward the hegemony passed to Lithuania and there it remained until the destruction of East European Jewry during the Second World War.

We have little information about the spread of Torah study in Lithuania before the last quarter of the fifteenth century. However, about fifty years later, both Rabbi Moses Isserles and Rabbi Solomon Luria mentioned in their writings the "scholars of Brest Litovsk." Obviously, not only was Brest Litovsk in those days the most important community in the Duchy of Lithuania, but it was also an important center of study. The first rabbi of Brest Litovsk known to us by name was Rabbi Yehiel Luria, an ancestor of Maharshal. He served there as rabbi about the year 1470. No details concerning him or his colleagues in other communities of Lithuania are known. In 1495 the Jews were expelled from Lithuania. When they returned in 1503, Jewish life began to prosper and with it the level of Torah learning rose as well. We have seen above that Maharshal spent a number of years in various parts of Lithuania. Indeed, both his style and method of study resemble the concept "Lithuanian Torah" as it has been understood in the Jewish world beginning with the days of the Gaon of Vilna. During the second half of the sixteenth century numerous yeshivoth were functioning in Lithuania. Among them the yeshivah of Brest Litovsk seems to have gained the greatest prominence.

The first native Lithuanian scholar was Rabbi Joshua ben Joseph who was known as Harif. Born in Vilna about the year 1580, he received his Torah training there and in various yeshivoth in the eastern part of the Commonwealth. Rabbi Joshua Falk and Maharam of Lublin were among his teachers. After having occupied rabbinic positions in Tykocin, Grodno, Przemysl, and Lemberg, he was called in 1639 to Cracow to head its great yeshivah. Rabbi Joshua achieved fame as a teacher and had many disciples.

In the history of rabbinic literature Rabbi Joshua occupies a prominent place as the author of *Meginei Shelomoh,* a collection of novellae on several tractates of the Talmud. The avowed purpose of the work as indicated in the title, was to defend Rashi against the criticisms of the Tosafists. His work achieved much popularity among advanced researchers of the Talmud and was reprinted several times. *Penei Yehoshua,* a collection of his responsa, is an equally important work. Rabbi Joshua did not follow the method of the pilpul. He was also opposed to the *Shulhan Arukh* because he believed that the codes closed the door to independent research in the field of Halakhah. In his opinion the *Shulhan Arukh* also gave too much authority to the early scholars.

g

The opposition to the *Shulhan Arukh* continued for about eighty years in Poland. We have seen it assume various forms during that time. Some scholars were opposed in principle to any form of codification and some recognized the need of a code and tried to produce their own formulations. Still others contented themselves with "amending" the *Shulhan Arukh* in the way indicated by Rabbi Moses Isserles. Rabbi Joel Serkes was the last of the radical opponents of the work of Rabbi Joseph Karo. After his death in 1640, the opposition to the *Shulhan Arukh* was gradually weakening. No one any longer declared all forms of codification harmful. No more did anyone brush aside the views of Rabbi Joseph Karo or those of the outstanding Sephardic jurists. From that time onward, the scholars began to write *systematic commentaries* to the *Shulhan Arukh*. The *Shulhan Arukh* thus assumed the form in which it has been ever since accepted in the Ashkenazic world. This form was given to it by four great jurists who lived and taught during the seventeenth century: Rabbi David ben Samuel, author of *Turei Zahav* (called *Taz),* Rabbi Moses Lehma, author of *Helqath Mehoqeq,* Rabbi Shabethai ben Meir, author of *Sifthei Kohen (Shakh),* and Rabbi Abraham ben Hayim of Gombin, author of *Magen Avraham.*

Rabbi David ben Samuel was born late in the sixteenth century, when most of the luminaries of the preceeding generation were still alive. One of them, Rabbi Joel Serkes, was his teacher and father-in-law. After having occupied rabbinic positions in various towns and cities, Rabbi David was called to the important rabbinate of Ostrog. At the outbreak of the Cossack riots in 1648 he fled abroad. When he returned to Poland he became rabbi of Lemberg, where he died in 1667.

Rabbi Moses Lehma was a disciple of Rabbi Joshua Harif. He first served as rabbi of Slonim and subsequently became head of the rabbinic court of Vilna. He was famous as a jurist both in Poland and abroad, and his legal opinions carried great weight. Shabethai Kohen, a native of Vilna, was another pupil of Rabbi Joshua Harif. When Rabbi Joshua was appointed rosh-yeshivah and head of the court of Cracow, young Shabethai followed him there. After some time the young scholar returned to his hometown to become a member of its rabbinic court. When the Muscovites approached Vilna in 1655, Rabbi Shabethai escaped to Moravia where he died in 1663.

Rabbi Abraham Gombiner, author of *Magen Avraham,* was born in 1637. His parents perished during the massacres. He spent most of his life in Kalish, first as a teacher (melamed) and later as a member of the rabbinic court. His contemporaries described him as a very humble man who lived all his life in poverty. He wrote several books but achieved his fame mainly through the work *Magen Avraham.*

Rabbi David, who was known as Taz, compiled a comprehensive commentary on all four sections of the *Shulhan Arukh,* while the other three produced their commentaries only on parts of the code. Rabbi Moses Lehma wrote his commentary on the *Even Haezer* section, which contains the Jewish marriage law. The contribution of Rabbi Shabethai Kohen (Shakh) was a commentary on the sections *Yoreh Deah* (describing "the things forbidden and permitted") and *Hoshen Mishpat* (the civil law and the procedure in courts of justice). The youngest of the four commentators, Rabbi Abraham Gombiner, wrote the definitive commentary on the section *Orah Hayim,* describing the daily religious duties of the Jew. Only fragments have remained of his planned commentary to *Even Haezer*.

The *Taz* and *Shakh* commentaries on the *Yoreh Deah* section were both published in the year 1646. The *Taz* achieved immediate recognition as a reliable authority, while the *Shakh* was hardly noticed, even though the *Shakh* is superior to the *Taz* in analysis and style. The author of *Taz* brushed aside the *Shakh* completely, without condescending to engage in controversy. The author of the *Shakh*, however, upon reading the *Taz* composed a major work called *Nequdoth Hakesef* in which he refuted one by one the decisions contained in the *Taz*. The standing of *Taz* in the world of Halakhah was thus challenged. Some time later Rabbi Joel ben Gad, a grandson of the author of *Taz*, published a work called, because of its purpose, *Meginei Zahav, Defender of the (Turei) Zahav*. In this work he made an effort to refute the criticisms of the *Taz* contained in *Nequdoth Hakesef*. The book was published with the official approval of a group of leading men in the Polish rabbinate, which was tantamount to a declaration that the decisions of the *Taz* should be considered as binding. Nevertheless, it became customary to print the *Yoreh Deah* section of the *Shulhan Arukh* with the two commentaries *Taz* and *Shakh* side by side. This remained the practice till this very day even in the textbook editions printed for the yeshivoth. With regard to the laws where the two commentators differed, each rabbi felt free to decide according to his own understanding and preference.

In like manner, a conflict arose over the commentaries *Taz* and *Magen Avraham* on the *Orah Hayim*. A long time after both authors had died, however, the publishers began to print both commentaries side by side. In these editions the *Taz* commentary is named *Magen David*, while that of Rabbi Abraham Gombiner is called *Magen Avraham*. Both commentaries came to be recognized as being ancillary to the *Orah Hayim* and equal in importance and authority. Nevertheless the practice in rendering legal decisions has been to give preference to the *Magen Avraham*. This commentary was written with extreme conciseness and the reader is expected to be completely familiar with the widely ramified rabbinic literature. Consequently, many books were compiled to explain the *Magen Avraham*. Their main purpose was to further elaborate on what had only been hinted at in this work.

The commentary of Rabbi Shabethai Kohen on the *Hoshen Mishpat* section of the *Shulhan Arukh* attained great, compelling and decisive status. He wrote it during the last years of his life while he was rabbi in Holleschau. Rabbi Shabethai displayed in this work his great analytical talents when he discussed the intricate matters of the civil law. In contrast, Rabbi David ben Samuel clearly revealed in his commentary on *Hoshen Mishpat* his predilection for synthesis and his endeavor to effect a reconciliation whenever the views of the leading scholars were contradictory.

Of the four sections of the *Shulhan Arukh,* the *Even Haezer* had the greatest practical significance. The Jewish marriage law never lost its validity, and appeal to the general courts of the country in matters of matrimony was very rare. A reliable, authoritative commentary on the *Even Haezer* was therefore a vital necessity. This need was filled by the *Helqath Mehoqeq* of Rabbi Moses Lehma. His work found quick and ready acceptance in the entire Jewish Diaspora. In the course of time the authority of the commentary became equal to that of the *Even Haezer*. Even in our generation it is still possible to hear a student of Jewish law state that he studies *Helqath Mehoqeq,* which in his words means that he is studying the *Even Haezer* together with this commentary.

In the lifetime of the four great commentators of the *Shulhan Arukh* Jewish scholarship in Poland reached its peak. Among the many other scholars of that period, Rabbi Heshel ben Jacob and Rabbi Yom-Tov Lippman Heller were the most outstanding. "The Rebbe Reb Heshel," about whom many legends were told, was rabbi and rosh-yeshivah in such leading communities as Lublin and Cracow. He had a host of disciples. He wrote novellae on several tractates of the Talmud, as well as annotations on the *Sefer Mitsvoth Gadol,* an important thirteenth century work on the precepts by Rabbi Moses of Coucy. Most of Rabbi Heshel's works, however, have been lost. Rabbi Yom-Tov Lippman Heller was a native of Wallerstein in Bavaria. To be sure, he spent most of his life as rabbi in Bohemia and Austria. But the years that he spent in various communities in Poland late in his life had a great impact on Poland's flourishing Torah world. Rabbi Yom-Tov was one of the most prolific rabbinic authors in his time. The greatest of his works is his systematic commentary on the Mishnah, *Tosfoth Yom-Tov.* It is included in many of the latest printed editions of the Mishnah side by side with the classical commentary of Rabbi Obadiah of Bertinoro.

h

The first part of the seventeenth century witnessed a great expansion of Torah learning in Lithuania too. The cultural center of Lithuanian Jewry had now shifted from Brest Litovsk to Vilna. We have seen that two of the four great commentators of the *Shulhan Arukh,* Rabbi Moses Lehma and Rabbi Shabethai Kohen lived in this city. Besides them, three other Lithuanian scholars attained great fame: Rabbi Moses Rivkes, Rabbi Ephraim ben Jacob, and Rabbi Aaron Samuel Kaidanover. They all left the country at the time of the Muscovite invasion and went to Germany, Bohemia, and Hungary.

Rabbi Moses Rivkes, a native of Prague, came to Vilna early in his life. During the war he left the city for Germany, but returned after some time. He died there in 1671. As a scholar Rabbi Moses manifested a strong inclination to independent research. In line with this he was always reluctant to ascribe undue importance to the later scholars. Consequently, he attempted to trace each law to its primary source. This aim is clearly visible in all his books. Among his works we find a study on the principles of codification and a commentary on the Mishnah. His magnum opus, however, is *B'eir Hagoleh,* an index of the sources of the laws codified in the *Shulhan Arukh.* This work became a very important aid in the field of Halakhah and was printed in many editions of the *Shulhan Arukh*.

Rabbi Ephraim ben Jacob was famous for his Talmudic erudition. At the age of twenty years he was appointed a member of the rabbinic court headed by Rabbi Moses Lehma. In 1655 he fled Vilna because of the war, and went to Moravia. Later he was appointed rabbi in Budapest, where he founded a yeshivah. The school was very famous and attracted many Sephardic students from the Balkan countries. The fame of Rabbi Ephraim spread to the Orient and he was invited to occupy the position of a rabbi in Jerusalem. He accepted the position, but died in an epidemic in 1678 while preparing for the journey to the Holy Land. Rabbi Ephraim owes his literary fame to his work *Shaar Ephraim*. The book consists of about one hundred and fifty responsa, arranged according to the order of the *Shulhan Arukh*. His homiletical work on the Pentateuch as well as most of his novellae on the Talmud have been lost.

A prolific author and a popular teacher was Rabbi Aaron Samuel Kaidanover, of Kaidanov in the vicinity of Minsk. During the war he migrated to Austria where he became rabbi of a community of Polish refugees in a small town. Afterwards he served as a rabbi in Fuerth in Bavaria. He returned to Poland to serve as rabbi in Rzeszow and later in Glogau in Silesia. He ultimately was appointed rabbi in Cracow. He died in 1676 in Chmielnik while participating in a regional communal conference. In the field of Halakhah Rabbi Aaron Samuel was reluctant to rely on the later authorities, and he advised his students to turn to the original sources. From far and near questions of law were directed to him. His book *Birkath Shemuel* is a collection of homilies on the Pentateuch. Another book, *Tifereth Shemuel,* contains novellae on the Talmud and on the codes. However, his work *Birkath Hazevah* attained special distinction. It is a commentary on the tractates of the Talmud which discuss the laws of the sacrificial service.

i

Among the important factors which advanced the study of

Torah in its manifold forms and the development of rabbinic literature, were the communal institutions of Polish Jewry: the local Kehilloth, the Provincial Councils, and the Council of the Four Lands. The concern for education on all levels manifested by these institutions, and the large degree of legal autonomy enjoyed by Polish Jewry, were a source of great encouragement to Torah study in that country.

The basic responsibility for education and for the study of Torah rested with the local communal authorities. It was their duty to care for the support of a proper number of students in the local yeshivah. The rabbis steadily strove to attract large numbers of students to their yeshivoth so as to spread Torah learning and in the same time to enhance their own position in the world of Jewish scholarship. Maharshal accused with bitterness some of the rabbis of trying to attract masses of students "after the manner of princes who hire servants to run before them." It happened, indeed, that some communities could not afford to support the large numbers of students attracted by their yeshivah or rabbi. The Council of the Four Lands therefore introduced a system of allotting to each Kehillah a student quota in accordance with the number of its families. The Council also encouraged the printing of textbooks for the yeshivoth by making it the obligation of each community to buy a certain number of copies.

The curriculum followed in the yeshivoth was based on a uniform program of studies. All yeshivoth studied one and the same tractate of the Talmud each semester. The academic year was divided into two "Zemanim" or semesters. The winter semester began on the first day of Heshvan and ended in the middle of Shevat; the summer semester began on the first day of Iyar and ended in the middle of the month of Av. During the first half of each semester the classes would concentrate on the text of the Talmud with the commentaries of Rashi and Tosafoth. The rosh-yeshivah would lecture on the theme of the daily assignment and engage in discussion with the class. The second half of the semester was devoted to the study of the codes, such as *Tur, Alfasi,* and *Shulhan Arukh,* and their main commentaries. During the periods between the semesters no regular classes were held, but study continued uninterruptedly.

The rosh-yeshivah was highly respected in the community. Many learned laymen of the city would come to attend his daily lectures. At times the rosh-yeshivah would ask outstanding students to lead the discussion in the class. In this way he trained them in the art of teaching. The older students were given the task of tutoring their younger schoolmates and introducing them to higher levels of study. Generally, a close relationship existed between rosh-yeshivah and students. He would advise them about their careers, and his interest in them would often continue beyond their stay in the yeshivah. Of course, not all yeshivah students became rabbis or teachers. Also those who chose other occupations did not abandon study altogether. Consequently, each and every city had many learned laymen who held the degrees of Haver or Moreinu. This class wielded considerable influence in the community.

The yeshivah students were granted a weekly stipend by the community to cover their living expenses. In addition, many of the residents would give them board on Sabbaths and even on weekdays. By and large the yeshivoth relied upon the communities for their budgets. However, funds were also established by private donors for these purposes. Some of the yeshivoth were maintained by wealthy relatives of the rosh-yeshivah, as was the case with the schools of Rabbi Shakhna, Rabbi Moses Isserles, and Rabbi Samuel Edels.

The high standard of Torah learning in Poland became known throughout the Jewish world. From many lands — from Germany, Bohemia, Holland, and Italy — students flocked to the Polish yeshivoth. A letter written in 1619 by a Jew of Prague is quite characteristic. The writer wished to persuade his son to return and study Torah at home. This would be considered, he wrote, "as if you had gone to Poland to study . . . "

The leaders of the local communities and the Provincial Councils took even greater care of elementary education. Their rules fixed the maximum number of pupils allowed in a class, the hours of instruction, and the salaries of teachers. Poor children were usually given free education until they reached the age of thirteen years. In the larger communities the responsibility for the education of the young was entrusted to the "Talmud Torah Societies." Once a week, either on Thursday or Friday, examinations were held in the various schools. The curriculum was more or less similar to that of a heder. The pupils would begin with the commentary of Rashi, or *B'eir Mosheh* of Moses Sertels. This was followed by instruction in Mishnah and Talmud. Since the study of Talmud was considered of major importance, the study of the Prophets and of the Hagiographa, as well as that of the Hebrew language was often neglected. Many scholars protested against this lack of balance — but generally speaking, the situation remained unchanged.

During the entire period of two hundred years since the first immigrant-scholars had arrived, Jewish scholarship in Eastern Europe was constantly on the rise. "Matters that are well known need no proof — wrote Nathan Hanover at the close of that period — for throughout the dispersions of Israel there was nowhere so much learning as in the Kingdom of Poland . . . " His distress at the destruction of Polish Jewry caused him to see the past in greater glory. Nevertheless, his remarks in this respect were not too exaggerated. Indeed, the massacres had their effect on the Torah centers. Heads of many yeshivoth and leading rabbis were among the refugees who fled to Germany, Austria, Hungary, Holland, and Italy. Many Polish communities were devastated and were unable to support Torah learning as heretofore. Only gradually some of the refugee-scholars began to return to Poland and to reopen their yeshivoth. Once again Jewish youth of other lands began to flock to Poland, to the centers of Torah learning. An effort was made to revive the glorious conditions of the past. We read in one of the sources that a society of scholars was formed in Kalish for the purpose of studying Torah in the manner practiced in the yeshivah of Lublin. Programs such as this brought about a partial restoration of Torah learning. Rabbi Abraham Gombiner, author of *Magen Avraham*, may serve as an example. He was but a young boy at the time of the massacres. Yet he grew up to be one of the four great commentators of the *Shulhan Arukh*.

j

Major changes took place in the cultural life of Polish Jewry during the eighteenth century. The political and social conditions in the Polish Commonwealth were deteriorating. As a result, the economic conditions of Polish Jewry were steadily worsening. Similarly, the Jewish communal autonomy was losing much of its strength and vitality. The troubles caused by the renegade sect of the Frankists, and the conflicts with rising Hasidism, further weakened the Jewish communal organization. Under such conditions the study of Torah was, of course, curtailed. The number of yeshivoth decreased; there were fewer scholars. There was a direct connection between this decline, and the avowed aim of early Hasidism to deprive the scholar of his privileged status. This was also one of the factors which caused the center of Torah learning to move from Poland to Lithuania. Hasidism developed mainly in the Ukraine, Galicia, and central Poland. In Lithuania its position was rather weak. Even after the struggle against Hasidism had subsided, the movement did not spread in the same degree in Lithuania as elsewhere. Consequently, a much broader base for the continuation of Torah study existed in Lithuania. Moreover, even Hasidism had to adapt itself to local conditions, and to manifest a more friendly attitude to scholarship.

All these processes were unfolding throughout the entire century, and their results did not become fully apparent until the beginning of the nineteenth century. However, already in the latter half of the century the foundations for a great revival of Torah learning were built by one of the greatest sages of all times, Rabbi Elijah, known as the Gaon of Vilna. He surpassed all other scholars by the originality of the new methods of research, which he devised, and by the magnitude of his literary accomplishments.

Rabbi Elijah ben Solomon Zalman, a descendant of Rabbi Moses Rivkes, was born in 1720 in the town of Selyets near Brest Litovsk. While he was still a small boy, his parents moved to Vilna. There he was soon recognized as a prodigy. At the age of six years, it is told, he delivered a Torah discourse which amazed the learned men of the community. He was never enrolled in any yeshivah. He studied on his own and so was not tied to any particular accepted method of study, or to any particular curriculum. Young Elijah's interest extended to many fields: Mishnah, Talmud, Kabbalah, Bible exegesis, grammar, mathematics, geography, and history. For a short time he studied under Rabbi Moses Margolioth, rabbi of Kejdany, who was a unique type among the scholars. Rabbi Moses directed the attention of his pupil to the Jerusalem Talmud. In general, little attention had been paid to the Jerusalem Talmud in Poland. The growing interest in this Talmud, which manifested itself in the Lithuanian yeshivoth during the nineteenth century was, indeed, due to the influence of the Gaon of Vilna. Rabbi Elijah was not only called "Gaon" (outstanding scholar) but "Hasid" (the pious) as well, because of his extreme asceticism. Indeed, this asceticism which he combined with complete concentration upon learning, explains the magnitude of his creative activity even in its quantity alone. He wrote about eighty works.

The Gaon's method of research was based on a direct approach to the original sources of the Halakhah. A focal point of his researches was the Mishnah. He realized that the Amoraim not only explained the Mishnah in its literal sense, but interpreted it hermeneutically as well. The Gaon therefore allowed himself sometimes to give the words of the Mishnah a somewhat different interpretation than was given by the Amoraim. He was convinced that it was imperative to know the language and life of that period thoroughly in order to understand the Halakhah. Likewise, he thought it necessary to have some knowledge of the sciences and mathematics, since certain matters having reference to them are found in the Mishnah. He therefore studied the sciences and encouraged others to study them as well. Many years were spent by the Gaon in critical examination of the text of the Talmud. His many emendations were by far more radical than those suggested two centuries earlier by Rabbi Moses Isserles and Rabbi Solomon Luria. These emendations cleared up many difficulties and made entirely superfluous many ingenious "reconciliations" that the unemended difficulties had called forth. The Gaon was a radical innovator. It was due to his prodigious scholarship and extreme piety that no one dared question his methods of study.

The Gaon was reluctant to accept the authority of the later jurists (Aharonim) and their legal writings. So, too, he was categorically opposed to the pilpul. He believed that a gradated education should be given to the pupils, which would lead them from the study of the Bible and the grammar of the Hebrew language to the more advanced subjects of Mishnah and Talmud. Rabbi Elijah rendered legal decisions only very rarely; he did not serve in the rabbinate and never taught in a yeshivah. He did not even enter into halakhic correspondence with the contemporary scholars. All his days were dedicated to Torah study. He was not interested in publishing his works, and only some of them were printed after his death by his family and a few devoted colleagues-disciples.

The literary interest of Rabbi Elijah of Vilna was very ramified. Most of his writings were, of course, devoted to the area of Halakhah. He wrote commentaries to considerable parts of the Babylonian as well as the Jerusalem Talmud. His commentary on the *Shulhan Arukh* covers all the four sections of the great code. Strange as it may look, this great rationalist was genuinely interested in the literature of Jewish mysticism. He authored a comprehensive commentary on the *Zohar, The Book of Splendor,* as well as a kabbalistic commentary on the prayer book. His interest in Biblical studies and linguistics was manifested in a commentary on the Pentateuch and a treatise on Hebrew grammar. To the area of the historical disciplines belong a geography of the Holy Land and annotations to a number of old Hebrew chronicles. And, like other true maskilim, he compiled a treatise on geometry, an extensive work on astronomy, and an essay on the four seasons and the planets.

We have seen above that the Gaon refrained from teaching in public. Only a small circle of colleagues-disciples gathered around him. All were great scholars in their own right and their spirit and outlook were akin to his. Through these men the Gaon's teachings began to spread abroad. But it was not before the beginning of the nineteenth century that a formal school was established in which the ideals of the Gaon, and his methods of study of the Halakhah found a magnificent home. Established by his most illustrious disciple Rabbi Hayim, the Yeshivah of Volozhin became the most famous school of Jewish learning in Eastern Europe. Another scholar of the Gaon's circle, Rabbi Israel of Shklov, emigrated with a group of followers to the Holy Land. They settled in Jerusalem and established there, too, an outpost of Talmudic learning in the spirit of the Gaon.

In the times of the Gaon the new movement of Hasidism began to spread in Lithuania. This movement, too, was headed by a Talmudic scholar and kabbalist of great stature, Rabbi Shneur Zalman of Lyady. He was born in the town of Lyozna in the vicinity of Vitebsk, and was younger than the Gaon by twenty-seven years. As a young noted Talmudic scholar, he became attracted to the teachings of Hasidism. He went to Mezeritch to study Torah in the court of Rabbi Dov Baer, known as the Great Magid or Preacher. After the Magid's death, Rabbi Shneur Zalman returned home and became the recognized leader of the movement in Lithuania. In 1801 he settled in the town of Lyady. During the war of 1812 he was compelled to flee. He died while en route, in a village near Kursk.

Rabbi Shneur Zalman acquired his reputation through his two works. The work *Tanya* contains his exposition of hasidic teachings known as HaBaD (*Hokhmah* — wisdom; *Binah* — understanding; *Daath* — knowledge). His other work, *Shulhan Arukh,* is the only law book produced by the hasidic movement. To compose a new Shulhan Arukh, after the work of Rabbi Joseph Karo had been accepted by Eastern Europe Jewry, was a daring act. Apparently, the Magid had encouraged him to do this. The accepted *Shulhan Arukh* had been enveloped in so many commentaries that it became rather unaccessible to the ordinary man. The people were burdened with the difficulties of everyday life, and they needed an abridged Shulhan Arukh. Consistent with his purpose, Rabbi Shneur Zalman first compiled the section *Orah Hayim,* which contains the laws of worship and the personal duties of the Jew. The work is divided into a handbook for the masses written with simplicity, and a theoretical part for the students and scholars. Similarly, the section *Yoreh Deah,* which contains the laws of ritual slaughtering, forbidden food, usury, etc., was intended for the rabbi-scholar. The work is arranged systematically, its style is lucid and readable. Rabbi Shneur Zalman also compiled a prayer book in which he changed some of the religious customs. In general, he went quite far in setting up an independent religious life for the Hasidim who followed him.

Another contemporary scholar of great stature was Rabbi Ezekiel Landau. He was the author of *Noda Biyehudah,* a collection of responsa arranged according to the four sections of the *Shulhan Arukh.* The work is one of the most important in this field of rabbinic literature. Rabbi Ezekiel was born in Opatow. In 1732 he settled together with his father-in-law in Brody, and became one of the members of the famous "Klaus," the academy of the outstanding local scholars. Later he was appointed head of the rabbinic court. From 1746 onward he served as rabbi of Jampol in Podolia. In 1755 he was appointed head of the rabbinic court of Prague. He held this position with great distinction for a period of thirty-eight years, until his death.

k

The division of Poland between Russia, Prussia, and Austria at the close of the eighteenth century made a major impact upon Eastern European Jewry in general, and upon the area of Torah learning in particular. To be sure, until the middle of the nineteenth century a semblance of uniformity was still common to the three parts of divided Polish Jewry. Thus, the post of rabbi of Vilna was offered in 1836 to Rabbi Akiba Eiger, the greatest of the scholars in the Province of Posen. Malbim, the genial preacher and commentator of the Pentateuch, held positions both in Russia and in the Province of Posen. Similarly, Rabbi Zevi Hirsh Hayes of Brody was appointed rabbi of Kalish. However, gradually such occurrences became less frequent. By the second half of the nineteenth century the Jewish inhabitants of the Province of Posen had become German Jews, and Torah study in the Eastern European way had all but vanished. In Lithuania, on the other hand, the study of Torah was flourishing and expanding. Lithuania surpassed not only the Province of Posen in this respect, but even the parts of Poland annexed by Russia. In Russian Poland the hasidic tsadiq had to some extent inherited the position of the talmid hakham or scholar. In Galicia, too. Hasidism became very powerful. Here, however, a strong counter-influence was exerted by the "Klaus" of Brody, the alma mater of many prominent scholars.

The new great era in the history of Torah learning in Lithuania was initiated by Rabbi Hayim of Volozhin (1749-1821), already mentioned as one of the closest associates of the Gaon. As a true disciple of the Gaon, he was categorically opposed to the exaggerations of the pilpul. He used to visit the Gaon every year, seeking knowledge and inspiration from the Master. In 1773, at the age of twenty-four, he accepted the position of rabbi in Volozhin, at the urging of the Gaon. He soon became renowned as one of the foremost scholars in Lithuania, and many began to address their halakhic problems to him. After the death of the Gaon he was generally acknowl-

100

edged as the greatest of all the Lithuanian rabbis. In 1802 Rabbi Hayim established a central yeshivah, which was to be conducted in the spirit of the Gaon. Its goal was to raise the standard of Torah learning in Lithuania. Rabbi Hayim issued a proclamation inviting young men interested in Torah study to enter the yeshivah, and at the same time he made efforts to interest various communal circles in supporting the new institution. Candidates for enrollment were expected to possess an exceptionally high standard of knowledge. Over one hundred candidates who met the requirements were admitted to the school. The Yeshivah of Volozhin existed until recent times, and was considered the outstanding Talmudic school of Eastern Europe. Rabbi Hayim headed the yeshivah for a period of twenty years. He consistently discouraged the use of the method of pilpul and the custom to memorize considerable parts of the text of the Talmud. His method was to train the students to penetrate deeply into the subject by means of logical analysis, and to distinguish clearly between differing opinions of the sages. He further taught them to refrain from offering artificial "reconciliations" of such differences. His son and successor Reb Itsele, as well as the third rosh-yeshivah Rabbi Naphtali Zevi Yehudah Berlin, known as Netsiv, continued to conduct the school in the ways set by its founder. The yeshivah of Volozhin attained its greatest fame in the times of Netsiv, as we shall see later. The literary heritage of Rabbi Hayim of Volozhin is not very large. A considerable part of his writings was destroyed by fire. Of his responsa only a few were published posthumously. Great popularity in the rabbinic world attained his treatise *Nefesh Hahayim*. This work is in the nature of a program of ethical conduct, composed in the spirit of the Gaon and designed for Torah students.

The founding of the Yeshivah of Volozhin set an example for the establishment of yeshivoth in other cities. Among these, was the school known as the "Yeshivah of the Forty" ("Vierziglekh") established in Vilna in 1827. One of its alumni was Rabbi Samuel Strashun whose keen annotations to the Babylonian Talmud were printed in some of its editions. It was in those years, the 1830's, that the Romm family of Vilna began to print the famous "Vilna Edition" of the Talmud. The scholarly excellence of the Vilna Talmud corresponded to the new type of learning that had risen in Lithuania. The Vilna Talmud became the most popular edition of the Babylonian Talmud and was reprinted many times. When the Second World War came to an end, the Vilna Talmud was reprinted in Germany under the auspices of the United States Army for the schools of the survivors of the death camps.

A contemporary of Rabbi Hayim of Volozhin was Rabbi Abraham Danzig, who became a great popularizer of the Jewish law. He was a native of Danzig and a pupil of Rabbi Ezekiel Landau. As a young man he came to Vilna and joined the Gaon's circle. He was first active as a merchant, but was appointed a member of the rabbinic court later in his life. Rabbi Abraham had the ability to explain complicated matters of the Jewish ritual and religious law in a way that made it easily accessible to the average man. His works *Hayei Adam* and *Hokhmath Adam* present in a popular way the laws of the *Orah Hayim* and *Yoreh Deah* sections of the *Shulhan Arukh*, and were printed many times. In many towns special societies were organized for the study of the book *Hayei Adam*.

————————

During that period Lissa was the leading community in the area of Torah learning in the Province of Posen. Its contribution was mainly due to the activities of its rabbi, Jacob Lorberbaum, a native of Galicia. Early in the century he came as a rabbi to Kalish, and in 1809 he was appointed to the same post in Lissa. Although he later again settled in Kalish, and ultimately returned to Galicia, he entered history under the name "Der Lissaer Rav." The yeshivah that he established in Lissa attracted many students and was considered the foremost school of higher Jewish learning in the Province of Posen.

Rabbi Jacob Lorberbaum was one of the most prolific

rabbinic authors of his time. Almost every branch of rabbinic literature has been enriched through his works. Unlike the majority of his contemporaries, he engaged extensively in Bible exegesis. Among his halakhic works, the most important is *Hawath Daath* on the *Yoreh Deah* section of the *Shulhan Arukh*. *Nethivoth Hamishpat,* on the *Hoshen Mishpat* section of the *Shulhan Arukh* is another major work written by him. Most popular, however, was his *Derekh Hahayim,* an edition of the prayer book with a collection of religious laws compiled for the use of the masses. This book was reprinted thirty times in twenty years.

In the rest of the Province of Posen Torah learning was declining. Torah study in the old style suffered both from the widespread clamor for the modernization of Jewish education and from the Germanizing efforts of the government. The pressure from both quarters was strong enough to make the Jews of Posen abandon their "Polish" habits, and conform to the character of the rest of the Jews of Prussia and the other German states. The process of change was completed in a relatively short time. By the middle of the nineteenth century the victory of the new trend became apparent. Nevertheless, the change was not effected without a sharp struggle between the supporters of the new trend and the protagonists of the old, traditional way of life. This struggle is conjoint with the personality of Rabbi Akiba Eiger who in those times re-established a great Torah center in the city of Posen.

To be sure, numerous Talmudic scholars lived at that time in the Province of Posen. They conducted yeshivoth and wrote valuable literary works. Such scholars were Rabbi Judah Loeb Kalisher of Lissa, Rabbi Israel Jonah Landau, author of *Meon Haberakhoth,* and his son Samuel, author of *Mishkan Shiloh.* Both, father and son, served as rabbis of Kempen. Due to the efforts of these scholars the Province of Posen surpassed all other areas of Germany in Torah learning all through the nineteenth century. It was Posen itself, however, the capital of the Province, that became a major center of Jewish learning in the times when Akiba Eiger was its rabbi.

Rabbi Akiba Eiger was born in Eisenstadt in Hungary. He studied first in Mattersdorf, and later in Breslau under Rabbi Hayim Jonah Teomim Frankel. He married the daughter of a prominent family of Lissa, and so he remained close to the Province of Posen all his life. In 1780 he settled in Lissa, where he headed a yeshivah for a number of years. His wealthy father-in-law presented him with a library and supported the yeshivah. At first the young scholar was not inclined to accept a position of a rabbi. He desired to study Torah for its own sake. Circumstances, however, forced him to enter the rabbinate. In 1791 he was appointed rabbi of Maerkisch-Friedland, one of the larger communities of West Prussia. He held this position for twenty-three years. From Maerkisch-Friedland Rabbi Akiba was called to the capital of the Province and he served as its rabbi for almost a quarter of a century. His unique greatness as a Talmudic scholar, and his outstanding communal leadership, won him great fame. His contemporaries, as well as later generations, evinced great interest in the story of his life. No contemporary rabbinic scholar, including the Gaon of Vilna, became the hero of so many biographies as Rabbi Akiba Eiger.

Rabbi Akiba Eiger was truly great both as a teacher and as a rabbinic author. Large numbers of scholars were trained in his yeshivoth. His works were widely used in Eastern Europe as a means of study and research. A considerable part of his literary work consists of concise and penetrating annotations and novellae on the Mishnah, the Gemara, and all four sections of the *Shulhan Arukh*. Of great value are the one thousand responsa which he authored. They reflect the great changes that Judaism was undergoing and the heroic efforts of the author for the preservation of the Jewish heritage. Some of the responsa were composed in the German language, to make them accessible to wider circles.

When Rabbi Akiba Eiger died in 1837, Rabbi Meir Leibush, popularly known as Malbim, was offered the position of rabbi of Posen. Malbim was a native of Volochisk in Podolia. As a child he attained such an unusual degree of knowledge, that many considered him a prodigy. When he grew up he became widely known as a preacher-orator with a superb skill of interpreting passages from the Scriptures and the Talmud to his audiences. After a stay in Warsaw, the capital of Russian Poland, where he made a great impression as an orator, he went westward to the Province of Posen. He occupied the position of a rabbi in Wreschen, where the Jewish population persuaded him to remain when he was offered the major post of rabbi of Posen. From the Province of Posen Malbim later went on to Western Europe where he held various rabbinic positions. Towards the end of his life he returned to Russia, and died in Kiev in 1879. The memory of Malbim as a great preacher has survived to this day. Among his literary works the most popular was his commentary to the Pentateuch which was studied very eagerly.

———————

Galicia too, was in this period a major center of Torah learning. The rising Haskalah movement and the spread of Hasidism seem not to have had any negative impact on the study of Torah. True, Torah learning in Galicia did not develop along "Lithuanian" lines. There was no large network of yeshivoth comparable to that of Lithuania. But Galicia had a great galaxy of illustrious scholars who had mostly acquired their knowledge through private study under the guidance of great scholars of the former generation. In general, Galicia's achievements in the area of Torah learning surpassed those of Russian Poland.

Many of the leading rabbis of Galicia at the turn of the century were part of the community of scholars whose center was the "Klaus" of Brody. This famous assembly of scholars was established about 1765 by Jacob Babad, a learned and wealthy merchant. Foremost among the scholars of the "Klaus" was Rabbi Ephraim Zalman Margalioth. He was a contemporary of Galicia and the Ukraine, including the popular hasidic both in Jewish law and in the area of mysticism. The scholars

105

of Galicia and the Ukraine, including the popular Hasidic leader Rabbi Levi Yitshaq of Berdichev, were among his learned correspondents. He was a prolific rabbinic writer, and manifested a great interest for the publication of old manuscripts.

About the time when Rabbi Ephraim Zalman Margalioth died, Rabbi Solomon Klueger settled in Brody. He was born in Komarov in Russian Poland in 1783, and spent his early years in Zamoshch. At that time lived in Zamoshch Rabbi Jacob Kranz, popularly known as "Magid of Dubno," who was a disciple of the Gaon of Vilna. Young Solomon thus had the opportunity to acquaint himself with the Gaon's ways and methods of Torah study. Rabbi Solomon served as rabbi in several Polish and Galician communities, and mainly in Brody, where he headed the rabbinic court during a period of half a century. He conducted a yeshivah and was famous for his brilliance in rendering legal decisions. Many of his decisions dealt with Jewish marriage law. His opinion that bills of divorce (gitin) are valid if sent by mail was universally accepted by the rabbis. In all his writings Rabbi Solomon Klueger manifested a tendency towards a strict interpretation of the religious law. This tendency was perhaps a reaction to the attacks which the local maskilim directed against him and his yeshivah, until it was closed by the authorities.

Rabbi Solomon Klueger was one of the most prolific rabbinic authors of all times. The bibliography of his writings lists hundreds of works in all areas of Jewish lore. Besides commentaries, novellae, and annotations on various parts of the Talmud and the *Shulhan Arukh,* he authored commentaries to several books of the Bible. He introduced a new type of rabbinic literature by writing essays in which he eulogized some of his great contemporaries. His most impressive achievement, however, were the more than ten thousand responsa which he wrote during his lifetime. They served as a practical guide at the time they were written, and became a source for Jewish legal decisions in later times. Not all of Rabbi Solomon's writings were printed. Hundreds of them, especially responsa, are still awaiting their publisher.

Younger than Rabbi Solomon Klueger was Zevi Hirsh Hayes, a native of Brody and a disciple of Rabbi Ephraim Zalman Margalioth. Besides being a great Talmudic scholar, he possessed an impressive amount of general knowledge. At an examination administered to him by the Faculty of the University of Lemberg he received a master's degree in philosophy. Unlike Rabbi Solomon Klueger he was close to the moderate wing of the Brody maskilim. The historian-philosopher Nahman Krochmal and the versatile scholar-rabbi Solomon Loeb Rappaport were his friends. In his work *Torath Neviim* he defended the traditional views on the validity of the oral law against the attacks of the radical maskilim. With equal fervor he disputed the ideas of the extremists in the Jewish Reform movement in Germany. In general, he endeavored to defend traditional Judaism with modern literary means.

Rabbi Zevi Hirsh Hayes' contribution to rabbinic literature was by and large in the field of method. Most important of all his works is his *Mevo Hatalmud, Introduction to the Talmud,* its name adequately describing its content. The work was translated into German and recently also into English *(The Student's Guide Through the Talmud).* Obviously, the usefulness of the work has not diminished since it was first published one hundred and twenty years ago. In his treatise *Darkhei Mosheh* Rabbi Tsevi Hirsh Hayes analyzed the method employed by Moses Maimonides in his Code of Laws. In another treatise, named *Darkhei Horaah,* he discussed the origin and development of the Halakhah. Rabbi Zevi Hirsh Hayes served as rabbi in Zolkiev and in Kalish. He died in Lemberg in 1855.

A contemporary of Rabbi Zevi Hirsh Hayes was Rabbi Hayim Halberstamm, a great Hasidic leader in the western part of Galicia. He was an outstanding Talmudic scholar and author. All his works bear the common title *Divrei Hayim.* Among them are commentaries on various tractates of the Talmud, responsa, and a commentary on the Pentateuch. They all count among the finest works of nineteenth century rabbinic literature. Rabbi Hayim held the position of rabbi of Sandetz

107

for almost half a century. The yeshivah that he founded and headed was a major center of Torah learning in West Galicia. Sandetz also was for many years the center of the hasidic dynasty established by him.

1

Lithuania's hegemony in the field of Torah learning lasted all through the nineteenth century. Galicia also maintained generally its former position. Among its scholars were such outstanding men as Rabbi Joseph Saul Nathanson, author of *Shoel Umeishiv,* and Rabbi Isaac Schmelkes, author of *Beth Yitshaq.* The number of the yeshivoth, however, continued to be limited. Greater changes were noticeable during the second part of the nineteenth century in the Province of Posen and in Russian Poland. In the Province of Posen the number of Talmudic scholars steadily declined. The yeshivoth have all but disappeared, and graduates of the modern theological seminaries began to occupy the rabbinic posts in the Province. The situation was quite different in Russian Poland, where several of the more important hasidic leaders started a new, great movement for the study of Torah.

In Lithuania the second part of the nineteenth century was a period when many new yeshivoth were founded. The Yeshivah of Volozhin was still recognized as the major school of Talmudic learning in the country. In fact, it was during this period that the school reached its zenith in size and importance under the dynamic leadership of its third rosh-yeshivah, the Netsiv. Studies and research were given a new impetus by the methods introduced by the associate rosh-yeshivah Rabbi Hayim Soloveichik, later famous as the rabbi of Brest Litovsk ("Rabbi Hayim Brisker"). Contemporaneously many other yeshivoth were established, such as those of Slonim, Mir, Ayshishki, Slobodka, and Telshe. It was also in this period that the Musar movement emerged and started a concentrated effort to introduce radical changes in many areas of life in the yeshivah.

A closer look at the Yeshivah of Volozhin enables us to get

acquainted with the inner life of a higher Talmudic school in Lithuania. Some of the alumni of Volozhin, outstanding as rabbinic or secular authors, have described with nostalgia life and study in their glorious alma mater. In the times when the school was headed by Netsiv the student body was composed of as many as four hundred young men from all provinces of the Russian empire. There was also always a sprinkling of students from abroad. Similarly, the budget of the school was supported by contributions from all strata of Russian Jewry. Study in the yeshivah was conducted uninterruptedly day and night. The students would gather in the halls of the large building and study in small groups their assignments in the Talmud and the Codes. The Talmudic subject on which the rosh-yeshivah was expected to lecture, was studied with special care. The daily lecture ("shiur") was given early in the afternoon and was the focal point of the program of the day. While the theme for the shiur was chosen by and large from a passage in the Talmud that lent itself to discussion, no comments were made or questions asked during the lecture. An animated debate, however, would begin as soon as the lecture was concluded. On Fridays a special lecture would be given on a portion of *Rosh*, Rabenu Asher's major commentary on the Talmud. Formal examinations were never administered in the Yeshivah of Volozhin. The leaders of the school would form over the years a definite opinion of the abilities and accomplishments of each individual student.

Volozhin's rosh-yeshivah, Netsiv, excelled also as a rabbinic author. He composed a significant commentary on the Pentateuch, *Haameq Davar,* and an equally important work on Rav Ahai Gaon's *Sheeltoth,* named *Haameq Sheelah.* Both works were consistent with his way of focusing attention on the writings of the Rishonim, that is to say the early medieval Talmudic jurists, and the halakhic midrashim. Netsiv detested useless pilpulistic thinking, though he did not discourage the keen minded from engaging in genuine dialectic discussions. Nor did he appreciate exaggerated indiscriminate memorization of portions of rabbinic literature. He insisted on depth, on the complete comprehension of the subject matter in its correct and unperverted sense.

The associate rosh-yeshivah Rabbi Hayim Soloveitchick presented his shiur along different lines. He would analyze every legal concept into its primary principles, and clarify each constituent element as a separate concept in itself. In his lectures he was not at all dependent upon the works of the later authorities. His researches were directed mainly toward the laws in the Code of Maimonides against which Rabbi Abraham ben David had leveled his strictures. The students, following in his footsteps, also concentrated mainly upon the works of the outstanding Rishonim. They would bring in the works of later authorities within the scope of their researches solely when the thinking of the latter was distinguished by a sharpness held in check by logical analysis. It is not improbable that precisely this was the original goal aimed at by the Bavarian scholars of the fifteenth century when they devised the method called hiluq or pilpul.

The student body at Volozhin was a colorful crowd of young, bright, and alert scholars. They formed a sort of an "aristocracy" in the world of yeshivah students. While in most schools of a similar nature the students were given meals in the homes of the local Jewish families ("eating days"), this was not the case in Volozhin. A considerable number of the students came from middle-class families and were supported by their parents. The less fortunate were usually cared for by the school. Quite unusual for a yeshivah was the endowment fund established in Volozhin by the wealthy Israel Brodski of Kiev. This fund provided generous maintenance scholarships for a number of gifted students. They were called by their colleagues, not without envy, the "Brodskians."

Since Netsiv became head of the yeshivah in 1853, he had to struggle against repeated efforts on the part of the Czarist authorities to close the school. Several times the yeshivah was actually closed under various pretexts, and mostly because secular studies did not have their proper place in the curriculum. When the yeshivah was closed again in 1892, it seemed as if this was the end of the ninety years old illustrious school. The entire Jewish world reacted with expressions of regret at the loss of the great institution of learning. Isaac Friedman, a student at the Yeshivah of Telshe, described the event in a play entitled *The Drama of the Closing of the Yeshivah of Volozhin.* As it turned out, however, the despair was unwarranted, and the yeshivah reopened in 1895 to exist for almost half a century longer. It ultimately went down from the historical scene in the years of the Nazi holocaust.

Second in importance to the Yeshivah of Volozhin was the school founded in Telshe in 1880 by Rabbi Eliezer Gordon. A native of a small town in the vicinity of Vilna, he came early in his life to Kovno where he studied under Rabbi Israel Salanter (see further). Prior to the establishment of the school in Telshe he held the position of rabbi of Kelm. Under his leadership the Yeshivah of Telshe gained great fame. When Rabbi Eliezer Gordon died in 1910 in London while on a mission in behalf of the school, his son-in-law Rabbi Joseph Loeb Bloch became his successor. The impact of the personality of the new rosh-yeshivah was remarkable, and the school of Telshe gained additional importance. In fact, between the two World Wars, when the Yeshivah of Volozhin was in a state of decline, the school of Telshe reached the highest point in its development. It was very popular among the yeshivah youth of Poland, Germany, and America, and many of them flocked to Telshe. Like the Yeshivah of Volozhin, the school of Telshe, too, existed to the days of the destruction of Eastern European Jewry by the Nazis. A part of the faculty and of the student body succeeded to escape during the war to the United States. They re-established the Yeshivah of Telshe in the city of Cleveland, and opened branches of the school in other localities with a large Jewish population.

The methods of study followed in the two leading yeshivoth differed considerably. In Telshe a definite attempt was made to set up a regulated order of study. In this respect the Telshe yeshivah was almost a modern school. True, Netsiv in Volozhin had also striven for order, but he refrained from exercising a too close supervision over the student body. He wanted to achieve order through the free, co-operative efforts of the students. That explains why no examinations were held in Volozhin; nor was attendance at the shiur compulsory. In Telshe, instead, some form of "classes" was introduced. Attendance at the shiur was made obligatory, and examinations were held frequently. Also the form of the shiur was different from that in Volozhin. In Telshe the rosh-yeshivah would not actually lecture. He would rather endeavor to evoke a discussion between the students and himself. In this way the students were trained for independent participation in a Talmudical dialogue. Following an old custom practiced in the yeshivoth of Eastern Europe, the same tractate of the Talmud was studied in all the grades of the Telshe school. Each class, of course, studied the text in accordance with its level of knowledge. The tractates mostly studied in Telshe were those of the orders Nashim and Neziqin, the Jewish marriage law and the Jewish civil law.

We have seen how the yeshivoth of Volozhin and Telshe differed in matters of arrangement and order. More basic changes in the nature of the yeshivoth were introduced by the Musar movement created by Rabbi Israel Salanter. His doctrines, as well as the movement he initiated, profoundly affected many areas of Jewish life. His main efforts, however, were directed towards the yeshivoth. The changes he sought to introduce into them did not concern the manner or method of study, but rather the curriculum. To the subjects usually studied in a yeshivah, the Musar movement sought to add the writings of the Jewish moralists. It wanted the yeshivoth not only to increase the students' knowledge and to train their capacities of comprehension, but also to open their hearts to the ethical values of Judaism, so that they may become better human beings.

The Story of Torah Learning in Eastern Europe

The founder of the movement, Rabbi Israel Lipkin, was born in 1810 in Zhagory, where his father was a melamed. As a youth he came to Salanty and thus became known as Rabbi Israel Salanter. In this town he found an inspiring mentor in Rabbi Joseph Zundel, a learned layman of great piety. Rabbi Joseph Zundel directed his young friend's attention to the writings of the Jewish moralists. The impact that these writings made upon young Israel was so great, that he began to neglect the study of Talmud. He soon realized his error and set up for himself a program of study which included both legal and moralistic Jewish literature. In the 1840's, after having served for a short time as instructor in one of the yeshivoth in Vilna, he opened a yeshivah of his own, to introduce the combined curriculum which he developed while still in Salanty. He put special emphasis on the study of the classical works of the Musar literature, *Hovoth Halevavoth (Duties of the Heart)* of Rabbi Bahye ibn Paqudah, and *Mesilath Yesharim (The Path of the Upright)* of Rabbi Moses Hayim Luzzatto. He was also instrumental in having reprinted forgotten medieval ethical works. In addition, he preached constantly about the improvement of the morals in everyday life. He was also in favor of physical labor. From Vilna Rabbi Israel went to Kovno, where he established another yeshivah with a "Musar-Shtuebel" next to it. Rabbi Israel spent his last years in various cities in Western Europe. Wherever he went he found support for his ideas. His great desire now was to bring the world of the Talmud to the attention of Western Jewry. In line with this he made serious, though unsuccessful, efforts to have the Talmud translated both into German and French. He now felt so much at home among the German Neo-Orthodoxy that he even became a citizen of Prussia. In Memel, a Lithuanian Jewish community on German territory, he published a weekly journal "Tevunah" for the propagation of the Musar ideals. These activities of the founder of the Musar movement in Western Europe established a close and firm contact between Germany's modern Orthodox Jewry and the world of Torah learning in Lithuania, that lasted many decades.

113

Rabbi Israel was quite a prolific author. His literary work, like the new curriculum he introduced into the yeshivah, consisted of writings in the area of Jewish law and in the field of ethics. All his works attained high regard in the Jewish world. Even "secular" circles showed interest in his works and studied them. By far most popular among his books is *Igereth Hamusar, Epistle of Musar,* recently translated into the English language. This work offers a description of the ideals of the Musar movement, and was written to be a guide to a better way of Jewish living. Rabbi Israel died in Koenigsberg in East Prussia in 1883.

It has been mentioned above that the Musar movement first directed its attention to the laymen. This tradition was followed by one of Rabbi Israel's disciples, Rabbi Mosheh Yitshaq, the famous magid (preacher) of Kelm. He travelled from city to city and from town to town preaching to the masses to follow the path of righteousness and to keep away from sin. When, however, Rabbi Isaac Blazer, Rabbi Simhah Zisel Braude, and Rabbi Nota Hirsh Finkel, three of the closest disciples of Rabbi Israel Salanter established their own Musar yeshivoth (in Kovno-Slobodka and in Kelm), a great controversy arose in the yeshivah world. Many feared that an excessive preoccupation with Musar literature would lead to a neglect of the study of Talmud. After some time the Musar movement emerged the victor, though its victory was not complete. In most of the Lithuanian yeshivoth limited time began to be allotted for study of Musar and for discourses of the rosh-yeshivah in matters of ethical conduct. For the first time the position of a spiritual adviser *(mashgiah ruhani)* of the students was created. The mashgiah, with functions somewhat similar to those of a dean of men of the modern university, became in the Musar yeshivoth a leader of great influence. In Telshe it became the practice to study a Musar work for half an hour each day. The extreme wing of the Musar movement was not satisfied with a partial victory. It wanted Musar to be the most important subject in the yeshivah curriculum. The first yeshivah of this type was established in Novogrodok by Rabbi Joseph Yozel Hurwitz. These yeshivoth were called "kibbutzim," and the students were named after the location of the prototype, "Navardoker."

————

A rise in the general level of Torah knowledge could be noticed in Congress-Poland in the second half of the nineteenth century. There the various houses of worship, the "house of study" (beth midrash) of the general Jewish community, and the "shtuebel" of the Hasidim performed an educational function similar to that of the yeshivoth in Lithuania. Once a boy would become of age and attain sufficient knowledge to graduate the most advanced heder of the town, he would transfer to the beth-midrash, if he intended to continue to study full time. There he would meet other young people who studied on their own, without supervision and almost entirely without guidance. These young men generally strove to become erudite, that is to study the entire Talmud over and over again. In addition, the practice of memorizing Gemara was very popular in the beth midrash. The laymen enthusiastically encouraged this way of Torah study, and awarded prizes to students who were able to recite an impressive number of folios of the Talmud by heart. This way of learning was described by its critics as *Gemara davenen,* to "pray" Gemara. They protested the mere learning by rote without understanding the subject matter sufficiently. Much better was the situation in those cities and towns, where scholars-rabbis had the desire to teach the young. Such men would attract groups of young and eager scholars and give them informal instruction in the Talmud and the later rabbinic literature. In this way small "private" yeshivoth were founded in many cities and towns. From these schools emerged a large proportion of the scholars who served as rabbis at the end of the nineteenth and the beginning of the twentieth century.

Rabbinic literature in Russian Poland in this period was more significant than could be expected. The works of men like

Rabbi Jacob Joshua Trunk and Rabbi Hayim Eleazar Wax count among the finest products of rabbinic literature of the nineteenth century. Some of the great hasidic leaders, too, made significant contributions in this area. The founder of the tsadiqim dynasty of Gora Kalwarja ("Gur") Rabbi Yitshaq Meir Alter, and his grandson Rabbi Judah Loeb, were both great rabbinic authors, and are commonly known by the names of their books

A scholar who courageously blazed a new trail in rabbinic literature was Rabbi Gershon Henoch Leiner, one of the most remarkable personalities among the hasidic leaders. At an early age he conceived the idea of collecting from the entire Talmud and the midrashim all the discussions and statements relevant to the laws of those parts of the Mishnah for which there is no Talmud (Gemara). He arranged all this material to form some semblance of a tractate of the Babylonian Talmud. In addition, he composed twin commentaries to this quasi Talmud tractate in a manner resembling the commentaries of Rashi and the Tosafists to the Babylonian Talmud. The work evoked admiration in some quarters, antagonism in others. A real storm arose in the rabbinic world, when Rabbi Gershon Henoch announced that he had rediscovered the *hilazon,* the creature from which the blue dye *(tekheleth)* had to be extracted for the *tsitsith* (Numbers 15:38). Both Rabbi Gershon Henoch and his opponents defended their respective views in numerous treatises devoted to this specific question. And, although his views were accepted only by his devoted followers (the Hasidim of Radzyn), Rabbi Gershon Henoch remains in the literary history of the nineteenth century rabbinic world a most remarkable and exciting figure.

It was due to all these events that in spite of the lack of a network of formal yeshivoth, Torah learning in Russian Poland was on the rise all through the second part of the nineteenth century.

m

With the advent of the twentieth century new processes

developed in the life of Eastern European Jewry, that had a decisive impact upon the Jewish educational scene. The Zionist movement was spreading rapidly, and it began to stress the importance of a curriculum centered around the study of the Hebrew language and the Bible. This, of course, could be achieved only by a curtailment of the time allotted in the school to the study of Talmud. Other factors that greatly influenced Jewish education were the Bolshevist Revolution in Russia and the reunification of Poland at the end of the First World War. True, the emergence of the new Poland resulted in the unification of the large Jewish communities of Russian Poland, Galicia, and parts of Lithuania. At the same time, however, the equally important Jewish communities of White Russia and the Ukraine were cut off from the bulk of Eastern European Jewry and from the world of Torah learning.

All these political, communal, and cultural developments had manifold results. The avowed hostility of the Communist regime toward religion made it all but impossible for Torah learning to continue to exist in Soviet Russia. Here and there devoted individuals were conducting hadarim and yeshivoth in a "Torah underground." After some time, however, all Torah learning had disappeared from among the millions of Jews in Soviet Russia. A yeshivah in Moscow with a handful of students, opened in recent years, is all that remained in Russia of its great Torah world after less than half a century of Soviet domination.

Not too favorable an impact on Torah learning had the establishment of a public school system in the new Poland. Tens of thousands of Jewish school children had left the traditional heder to be absorbed by the public schools in which practically no Jewish education was given to them. Devoid of religious education were also most of the Yiddish schools founded by circles whose avowed purpose was to create a secularistic school program for the Jewish children.

A positive attitude to the study of Torah was prevailing in the Zionist schools where Hebrew was the language of

117

instruction. In practice, however, most of the time allotted to the specifically Jewish subjects was given to the study of the Bible and Jewish history. The study of Talmud occupied a rather limited place in the curriculum of the Zionist school. Similar was the situation in the modern, Zionist inspired, Jewish school in the newly created republics of Lithuania and Latvia.

Under the impact of these developments, Orthodox Jewry, which was committed to the ideal of centering Jewish education around the Talmud as the main subject of study, was compelled to make a number of important adjustments. Far reaching were the changes introduced into the school by the religious Zionist movements, such as the Mizrahi. While still insisting on ample time to be given to the study of Talmud, the Mizrahi school, too, allotted considerable time to the study of the Hebrew language, Bible, and Jewish history.

Closest to the type of the old heder were the "Yesodei Hatorah" schools established by the Agudas Yisroel movement. In these schools the study of Talmud was still conducted for many hours daily. Hebrew as a language was rarely taught, but certain books of the Bible did become a part of the curriculum. Secular subjects, mainly the Polish language and arithmetic, were taught an hour or so daily in the evening.

Torah learning on the yeshivah level was also undergoing a process of change. True, the old Lithuanian yeshivoth, such as those of Volozhin, Telshe, Slobodka, and Novogrodok, remained largely unaffected by the radical changes introduced into the Jewish elementary and secondary school. There was always an impressive number of young men who were willing to devote all their time to the study of Talmud. In fact, some of these yeshivoth reached the highest point in their development after the First World War. We have seen that the Yeshivah of Telshe had then become very popular even among the Jews of Germany.

In religious Zionist circles, however, tendencies began to emerge already at the beginning of the century to experiment with the foundation of "modern" yeshivoth. In 1904, Rabbi Jacob Isaac Reines, founder of the Mizrahi, established such a yeshivah in the Lithuanian town of Lida where he served as rabbi. The curriculum of the yeshivah was designed to give the students an opportunity to acquire an extensive knowledge of the Talmud and rabbinic literature, and of certain secular subjects. In this manner Rabbi Reines endeavored to furnish the layman as well as the rabbi with the knowledge necessary for the Jew facing a changing world. The modern character of the yeshivah with regard to its curriculum was paralleled by a more modern organizational structure. The school was divided into formal classes and examinations were held regularly. The Yeshivah of Lida existed for ten years and was closed during the First World War.

Shortly after the establishment of the Yeshivah of Lida, a group of Zionist maskilim in Odessa conceived the idea of reorganizing the local yeshivah that was founded in the 1860's. Rabbi Chaim Tchernowitz, a noted scholar with a modern, critical approach to the Talmud, became the head of the school. He, as well as the board of overseers, attempted to develop the yeshivah along the lines of a modern rabbinical seminary in Western Europe. Besides the study of the Talmud and the Codes, the curriculum included such subjects as Hebrew grammar, Jewish history, and philosophy. The secular part of the curriculum included the Russian and the German languages, history, geography, mathematics, and the natural sciences. The faculty included such illustrious men as Hayim Nahman Bialik and Joseph Klausner. The school existed till 1919, when it was closed by the Soviet authorities.

————————————

The First World War inflicted many hardships upon the yeshivoth of Lithuania. Many were compelled to leave their locations and to settle temporarily in the Ukraine and in the interior of Russia. When the hostilities came to an end, most of the yeshivoth were able to return to Lithuania and Poland. Most prominent among the yeshivoth of Lithuania were now those of Telshe and Slobodka. Several members of the faculty of the Slobodka school together with a part of the student body migrated to the Holy Land and established a yeshivah in Hebron. After the Arab riots of 1929 the school moved to Jerusalem, but retained the name "Yeshivah of Hebron."

Among the many yeshivoth of Polish Lithuania the school of Mir was the leading institution of learning. Its student body equalled in numbers that of Volozhin in its prime. Like the school of Telshe, the Yeshivah of Mir attracted many students from abroad, primarily from Germany and the United States. At the time of the Nazi invasion of Poland, about three hundred students fled together with part of the faculty across Soviet Asia to Japan. During the years of the war the yeshivah continued its activities in the Far East. When the war came to an end the entire school was able to reach the shores of the United States. The school is now located in Brooklyn and is considered one of the leading yeshivoth in America.

In general, the level of Torah knowledge was very high in Polish Lithuania. The number of learned laymen was large, and the rabbis of the communities were almost all trained in the Lithuanian yeshivoth. Many of them were distinguished rabbinic authors, as were also many of the rabbis in former Russian Poland. Rabbinic literature reached a hitherto unknown degree of productivity. Suffice it to say that in the two decades between the World Wars more books in the field of rabbinic literature were published in the Republic of Poland than during the entire seventeenth and eighteenth centuries.

Most distinguished among the Talmudic scholars in Polish Lithuania were Rabbi Israel Meir Pupko, known by the name of his work *Hafets Hayim,* and Rabbi Hayim Ozer Grodzenski of Vilna. Between the two World Wars Rabbi Israel Meir Pupko was probably the oldest man in the Polish-Lithuanian rabbinate. He was one of the finest products of the Musar movement. His popularity was unequalled, and to many he was a legendary personality. He lived most of his life in the small Lithuanian town of Radun, where he founded and headed a yeshivah with about three hundred students. He was a distinguished scholar in the area of the Jewish law, as is manifested by his work *Mishnah Berurah,* a commentary on the *Orah Hayim* section of the *Shulhan Arukh.* But unlike most of the great Lithuanian rabbis, it was not the civil law to which he devoted his writings. His great concern was the piety and the ethical conduct of the individual Jew. The theme of his main work, *Hafets Hayim,* is thus a discussion of the laws designed to keep the Jew away from slander and evil and idle talk. His other books similarly give guidance and instruction to the individual Jew how to live a life of piety and righteousness. In general, Rabbi Israel Meir was considered a symbol of Eastern European Jewry's highest religious and ethical ideals, and many saw in him a true saint. It is worth noting that Hafets Hayim firmly believed in the imminent coming of the Messiah and in the rebuilding of the Temple in Jerusalem and the renewal of the sacrificial service. It was for this reason that he included in the curriculum of the Radun yeshivah the study of the generally neglected tractates of the Talmud that describe the rules of the sacrificial service. Rabbi Israel Meir died in 1933 at the age of ninety-five years.

A different type of Talmudic scholar was Rabbi Hayim Ozer Grodzenski. Although a graduate of the Yeshivah of Volozhin, he did not follow the new method of research in the Talmud developed by the associate rosh-yeshivah Rabbi Hayim Brisker. On the contrary, he was very much interested in the historical aspects of halakhic research. He had acquired a thorough erudition in the legal works of the later authorities. Thus, following the old Vilna tradition of learning, he preferred broad clarification to fine analysis. His approach was very popular among the scholars of Vilna and they accepted him as their leader. His method of study found brilliant literary expression in his work *Ahiezer,* a collection of responsa arranged to follow the order of the *Shulhan Arukh.*

Rabbi Hayim Ozer served as head of the rabbinic court of Vilna for many years. He did not establish a new yeshivah, nor was he teaching at any of Vilna's schools of Talmudic learning.

Instead, he devoted all his efforts to the task of securing for the yeshivoth a certain degree of financial stability. The Jews of the Republic of Poland, and to a great degree also those of Lithuania, were undergoing an uninterrupted process of pauperization. Consequently, organized financial aid for the yeshivoth became imperative. Rabbi Hayim Ozer Grodzenski, with the co-operation of Hafets Hayim, therefore organized the "Vaad Hayeshivoth" — Committee for the Yeshivoth — as a central agency for the support of the schools of Talmudic learning. The Vaad Hayeshivoth achieved a great degree of success, and shortly before the outbreak of the Second World War it aided seventy-eight yeshivoth in Poland and Polish Lithuania with a total of about 6,000 students. The Vaad Hayeshivoth obtained a considerable part of its funds from abroad, and mainly from the United States. The yeshivoth of the Republic of Lithuania were generously supported both by American and German Jewry. In 1930 the yeshivoth of Eastern Europe received a single bequest of hitherto unknown magnitude. Professor Waldemar Mordecai Haffkine, a renowned bacteriologist whose fight against contagious diseases in India had gained international fame, conceived the idea of establishing a "Foundation for the Benefit of Yeshivoth." For this purpose he deposited in a bank in Lausanne, Switzerland, the amount of one and a half million Swiss francs with the provision that the proceeds should be distributed among the yeshivoth of Eastern Europe. According to his will, the "Hilfsverein der Deutschen Juden" was to administer the Fund. The Haffkine Foundation thus became a major source for support of the yeshivoth in the last years before the outbreak of the Second World War.

n

The rise in the general level of Torah knowledge in Russian Poland continued during the last generation as well. More and more young men were studying in the hasidic houses of worship (shtueblekh). The number of junior yeshivoth multiplied till there were hundreds of them. Torah study on the adult level was equally popular. In the large cities the interest in study was remarkably rising, especially in the circles of the working youth, the craftsmen, and the storekeepers. Sabbath study groups were organized in Warsaw, in Lodz, and in many other localities. Especially numerous were the Mishnah study groups, *hevroth mishnayoth*, where the Mishnah was studied together with the commentary of Rabbi Obadiah of Bertinoro and that of Rabbi Israel Luepschuetz, *Tifereth Israel*.

It was in this time that Poland's two Orthodox movements, Agudas Yisroel and Mizrahi, established in the capital city of Warsaw central schools for the avowed purpose of training young rabbis. The two schools, *Methivta* and *Tachkemoni*, differed basically with regard to their curricula, which expressed the different ideological attitudes of the two movements.

The Methivta, mainly supported by the circles of the Rebbe of Gur, existed until the outbreak of the Second World War, and it produced many rabbis for the communities. Unlike the Lithuanian yeshivoth, the emphasis here was placed upon a comprehensive knowledge of the *Shulhan Arukh* and its ancillary works. In this way the students received adequate preparation to answer questions on the ritual usually directed to a rabbi in a Jewish community. The course of study at the Methivta was spread over several years. The Talmud and the Codes were studied for the largest part of the day, and an hour or two were allotted to the study of secular subjects. Candidates for graduation were examined by a board of rabbis composed for the most part of members of Warsaw's Communal Rabbinate. After passing the tests, the students received a certificate of ordination, *Hatarath Horaah*. The Yesodei Hatorah network of *hadarim* served as preparatory schools for the Methivta.

The Mizrahi movement in postwar Poland, reminiscent of the experiment conducted by Rabbi Jacob Isaac Reines early in the century, established another modern rabbinical school named *Tachkemoni*. The school was to produce rabbis who would possess a broad knowledge of Talmud and rabbinic literature, as well as secular knowledge equal to that offered in a public high school. The Tachkemoni Seminary existed for almost twenty years. Beginning with the year 1927 a number of students were each year ordained as rabbis. Great scholars and noted Hebrew writers taught the rabbinic and Judaic subjects. The school was headed by famous scholars, such as Rabbi Hayim Heller, Rabbi Moses Soloveitchik, and the historian Majer Balaban. Nevertheless, the school did not achieve its avowed purpose. The secular subjects and the study of Jewish history and Hebrew literature absorbed too much time to allow the students to obtain a profound knowledge of the Talmud and the widely ramified rabbinic literature. Only a few of the Tachkemoni graduates held rabbinic positions. They were usually students who had acquired broader knowledge of the Talmud prior to their admission to the Tachkemoni Seminary. And yet, there was much need in Poland for a rabbinical school of this type. Large segments of Polish Jewry were undergoing a process of "westernization." Social and cultural conditions gradually became similar to those that existed in Western Europe in the second part of the nineteenth century, when even Orthodox Jewry realized that there was a need for rabbis versed both in Jewish and secular knowledge. If not for the destruction of Poland's entire Jewish community during the Second World War, the Tachkemoni Seminary would certainly have had a greater role to play in the future. It is worth noting that a number of the graduates continued their studies in various universities in Western Europe. Some of them presently occupy important teaching positions at various schools of higher Jewish learning.

————————

In the period between the two World Wars Torah learning in Galicia was also undergoing significant changes. While during most of the nineteenth century East Galician scholars made a major contribution to the rabbinic literature, it was now West Galicia that became a great center of Torah learning. Rabbi Meir Arik, the rabbi of Tarnow, was a Talmudic scholar as famous as the leading Lithuanian rabbis. Equally important as a scholar was Rabbi Joseph Engel, the head of the rabbinic court of Cracow. He was one of the most prolific rabbinic authors of all times. He composed over one hundred works on Halakhah, Agadah, and Kabbalah. In addition he compiled a kind of Talmudic encyclopedia in thirty-two volumes. Many of his works were published under the name *Otseroth Yosef*.

An organized network of yeshivoth also developed in this period in West Galicia. The origin of the network goes back to the year 1880, when Rabbi Solomon Halberstamm established a school of higher Talmudic studies. He was a descendant of Rabbi Hayim of Sandets, author of the works named *Divrei Hayim* (see above). The tradition of study established by him was kept alive in later generations when his decendants, the tsadiqim of Bobow became the most influencial hasidic leaders in West Galicia. It was this tradition of learning that prepared the ground for Rabbi Solomon's yeshivah. The yeshivah existed for more than thirty years and was closed in the turmoil of the First World War. In 1921 the yeshivah was reopened in Cracow by Rabbi Ben Zion Halberstamm, at that time head of the Bobow dynasty. The yeshivah, named *Ets Hayim* achieved great success. After some time Rabbi Ben Zion began to establish branches of the school in the various cities and towns of West Galicia, and even in some localities in Central Galicia. The network kept on growing, and at the outbreak of the Second World War about sixty yeshivoth were affiliated with it. The Ets Hayim network of the Bobow yeshivoth thus became a great factor in the Torah world of Galicia.

The yeshivoth established between the two World Wars in the former Russian Poland and in Galicia created in these two regions conditions for the study of Torah partly similar to the conditions prevailing in Lithuania. At the time Eastern European Jewry was destroyed by Hitler's hords, all the land from the Baltic Sea to the Carpathian mountains was thus one great area where tens of thousands of Jewish young men were engaged in the age old noble calling of the Jewish people — the study of Torah.

———————

The enthusiasm for the study of Torah that had encompassed Poland's Orthodox Jewry reached its climax with the establishment of *Yeshivath Hakhmei Lublin*. As the name indicates, the school was located in Lublin, the cradle of Torah learning in Eastern Europe. We have seen how Rabbi Shakhna, Poland's first native scholar, had founded there the school of higher Jewish learning in which Moses Isserles was trained, and at which Maharshal, Maharam, and other great men taught. All through the centuries Lublin has remained a major center of Eastern European Jewish life and learning. Majer Balaban, Polish Jewry's great historian, has depicted with rare beauty the Jewish Lublin in his book *Die Judenstadt von Lublin*.

In the early 1920's Rabbi Meir Shapiro, a man of great vision, conceived the idea of returning to Lublin its glory as East European Jewry's outstanding place of learning. A native of Bukovina, he was at the time a rising star in the Torah world of the Republic of Poland. Like Rabbi Shakhna of Lublin, he too, was the son of a wealthy merchant. He never studied under the hard conditions that prevailed in the yeshivoth of Eastern Europe. Only when he became rabbi of Sanok in Galicia he became aware of the plight of the contemporary young Torah student. It was then that he conceived the idea of establishing in Lublin a school where young and gifted Torah scholars would be able to study in comfort, without the need to obtain their sustenance in the hitherto practiced undignified manner ("eating days"). His plan was to gain for his gigantic project the support of the Agudas Yisroel movement, which he had joined. When he announced the plan at the Congress of Agudas Yisroel held in Vienna in 1923, he was given enthusiastic encouragement. At the same Congress he also presented a major plan for adult studies in the Talmud. The proposal called for all nonprofessional Torah students to study daily one and the same folio of the Talmud. He prepared a detailed scheme according to which the entire Talmud would be studied during a certain period of time by hundreds of thousands of Jewish men. Few Jewish educational projects in recent generations met with a success equal to that of the *daf yomi* ("daily folio"). Even now, after the destruction of East European Jewry, tens of thousands of Jews all over the world study the *daf yomi* cycle after cycle. It has become customary for Jewish daily newspapers and calendars to print the order of the daily folio. Several recent editions of the Babylonian Talmud also included the calendar of the *daf yomi* in all the tractates.

In 1924 Rabbi Meir Shapiro began to work for the implementation of the yeshivah plan. During the next six years he devoted his boundless energy to the effort of obtaining the financial means necessary for building the campus. His duties as rabbi of Sanok, and later of Piotrkow, as well as his work as a Jewish representative in the Polish parliament (Sejm), seemed to be secondary to the task of building the school. Although he was able to collect for the project considerable amounts of money in Poland, he had to go on a ten months journey to the United States to secure additional funds.

On Lag B'omer 1924 work on the building was begun. The blueprints called for the erection of lecture-halls, a large library, dormitories for hundreds of students, and dining halls. In the spring of 1930 the school was opened in the presence of a large number of rabbis and hasidic leaders. At the same time the Council of the Jewish Community of Lublin elected Rabbi Meir Shapiro to the post of the communal rabbi. It was only logical that the man who built the magnificent school for Torah learning, and was its head, should hold — like Rabbi Shakhna four hundred years earlier — also the position of the rabbi.

The main purpose of the new school was not to prepare rabbis as religious functionaries, but to train the very gifted young men to study Torah for its own sake. In accordance with this purpose, Rabbi Meir Shapiro chose for the curriculum the tractates of the Talmud of the order *Qodashim,* which had until

127

then remained to a large extent untouched by research. We have seen that also Hafets Hayim emphasized in his yeshivah in Radun the study of the tractates that discuss the rules of the sacrificial service.

The fame of the Yeshivath Hakhmei Lublin increased steadily. Books for its library poured in from everywhere. Travelers passing through Poland would stop at Lublin just to visit the yeshivah. Here a new type of yeshivah life began to emerge. However, the school was founded at a very late date. Moreover, its founder Rabbi Meir Shapiro died suddenly in 1934 at the age of 46 years. At the time of the destruction of East European Jewry therefore the expected results had not yet materialized. Nevertheless, the Yeshivath Hakhmei Lublin was a most significant achievement, the last great effort of Polish Jewry in the field of Torah learning.

———————

Our generation has witnessed the destruction of Eastern Europe's great Jewish community. The greatest center of Torah learning that had ever existed in Europe became a thing of the past. And when we conclude the story of this great Torah center, we recall the words that Nathan Hanover wrote three centuries earlier: "Matters that are well known need no proof, for throughout the dispersions of Israel there was nowhere so much learning as in the Kingdom of Poland . . . "

V

THE JEWISH POPULATION IN RENAISSANCE ITALY

Originally published in Jewish Social Studies, vol. 13 (1951), pp. 3-24

Statistics on the Jewish population in any period usually present a difficult problem for historians. The data available for calculating the size of a population in a distant period are particularly complicated when they refer to a persecuted minority, which is not the master of its own fate. For the most part, the particular figure in a contemporary source is incorrect, and occurs not incidentally but in relation to a specific need. This renders the source suspect and the historian does not always have the means to check that source or to distinguish between its tendentious aspect and the grain of truth imbedded in it.

As far as the investigation of statistics on the Jews of Italy is concerned, there are in fact further difficulties to be overcome. Until the last quarter of the nineteenth century Italy comprised a multiplicity of states, large and small. The treatment of the Jews varied widely; while those in one area enjoyed a measure of freedom their contemporaries in another suffered oppression. It is, therefore, necessary to examine the data bearing on the individual republics, duchies and towns. In the end one may hope to ascertain the approximate extent of the Jewish population in the peninsula as a whole, during the period in question.

a

This study will deal with the number, distribution and

communal divisions of the Jewish inhabitants of Renaissance Italy (1300-1600). It was during these centuries that separate groupings developed within the Jewish population. On the threshold of this age began the mass immigration from Germany,[1] and two hundred years later came the refugees from Spain and Portugal. Groups from the same countries continued to arrive during the sixteenth century, the end of which saw the immigration of the Levantine Jews, particularly to the important center at Leghorn. The age of the Renaissance consequently transformed the composition of the Jewish population; the original homogeneous *italiani* now lived together with Ashkenazim, Sephardim, and Levantines.

A study of the distribution of this population must reckon with the fundamental fact that it consisted of migratory groups. It is a general rule that after their arrival immigrants tend to change their residence within the new country. In the case of the Jews who migrated to Renaissance Italy, this tendency was intensified by two circumstances: the widespread expansion of loan banks,[2] and the political disunity of the peninsula. The settlements of the Ashkenazim arose in towns to which a Jew was invited for the purpose of opening a pawnbroking establishment. He received the privilege of residence for himself, his family and others attached to the household. The agreement was limited to a specified number of years and upon its expiration either party frequently declined to renew it. This marked the end of the residence of the Jewish group in the given town and its transfer to another.

A rather instructive example is offered by the duchy of Parma-Piacenza. Between 1562 and 1578 the 16 localities, which harbored Jewish money-lenders, declined to eight. Characteristically, thereafter the Jews remained in these eight towns until

---

1 The author has dealt at length with this immigration in his article, "Ashkenazic Jewry in Italy," published in this volume.

2 *Cf.* Colorni, Vittore, *Il prestito ebraico e communità ebraiche nell' Italia centrale e settentrionale* (Bologna 1935) and the author's Hebrew article on the problem of the establishment of Jewish communities in Italy in *Sinai*, vol. x.

the nineteenth century, the only places with any recorded Jewish population in the duchy.[3]

It was the Jews of Rome and vicinity who started the trend of new loan establishments, which sprang up to the north, south and east of that city. Thus, these established Jewish residents of Italy, no less than the newcomers, contributed to the spread of the Jewish population.

The second circumstance reflected in the population shifts which was mentioned above was the division of Italy into numerous political units. When one state expelled the Jews they simply moved to a town in an adjacent state under another ruler. Small-scale expulsions of this type were particularly frequent throughout the fifteenth and sixteenth centuries. There were, indeed, towns which invited the Jews to return after their expulsion and repeated the procedure again and again.[4]

In brief, the characteristic feature of the Jewish scene in Renaissance Italy was migration within the country's borders. This makes it all but impossible to depict the distribution of the Jewish population without, however, having much bearing on the question of the total number of Jews in Italy. This feature of Italian-Jewish history evidently had little relation to the numerical growth or decline.

b

How many Jews were living in Italy at the beginning of our period, at the end of the thirteenth century? There is as yet no way of answering this question, but the geographic distribution of the population can be established. There were few, if any, Jews north of the Rome district, in which their number was fairly large. The movement of moneylenders from Rome to numerous small towns[5] marks the beginning of the spread of the Jewish population and implies a rather large group in

[3] Cf. Bachi, Roberto in the Dante Lattes jubilee volume, p. 272, n. 2. See also Cassuto, U., *Gli ebrei a Firenze nell' età del Rinascimento* (Florence 1918) p. 230.

[4] For a list of these expulsions see Bachi, *op. cit.*, p. 269.

[5] Cf. Colorni, *op. cit.*

their original place of residence. This trend apparently did not cause any sharp decline in the size of the Jewry of Rome, whose natural increase was presumably sufficient to make good the loss.

To the south, in the Kingdom of Naples,[6] there was an equally dense Jewish population until the beginning of our period. It was just at this point that the first Angevin kings carried out their systematic policy of forced conversion.[7] The story of the Jews' resettlement in southern Italy during the age of the Renaissance will be presented in a later portion of this study. At this point we need only mention that, apart from the groups who adhered to Judaism in secret, there were very few Jews in the Kingdom of Naples in 1300.

There was, on the other hand, a large Jewish population in Sicily. As early as the twelfth century Benjamin of Tudela provides figures greater than those referring to the Italian mainland.[8] Whatever our judgment of this traveller's reliability in regard to statistics there is no doubt that in visiting this area he received the impression that the Jews of Sicily outnumbered those of the peninsula. To this must be added the fact of the considerable number of communities in the Sicilian towns.[9] There is no reason to suppose that these consisted for the most part of tiny groups, such as spread later in other parts of Italy, on the basis of contracts for moneylending activities.

In what way did this scene change during the ensuing three centuries? The question of whether an upward or downward trend occurred is a complicated one. The period was, on the one hand, one of relative tranquility and freedom for the Jews. Despite the recurrent anti-Jewish actions, it was essentially a

6 *Cf.* Ferorelli, N., *Gli ebrei nell' Italia meridionale,* (*Turin* 1915) p. 42 ff.

7 See the articles by U. Cassuto in the Hermann Cohen *Festschrift* (Berlin 1912) p. 389 ff. and in the memorial volume for Asher Gulak and Samuel Klein, p. 139 ff. See also Starr, Joshua, "The Mass Conversion of Jews in Southern Italy (1290-1293)," in *Speculum,* vol. xxi (1946) 203-11.

8 Benjamin of Tudela, *Masaot,* ed. Grünhut (Frankfort 1904) p. 12 ff. and p. 100 ff.

9 According to Giovanni di Giovanni's *L'ebraismo della Sicilia* (Pelermo 1748) p. 19 ff, there were 55 Jewish communities in Sicily.

favorable era, one in which we would find a substantial increase, particularly in view of the influx from the north and from the Iberian peninsula. The increase was stemmed, however, by trends toward conversion produced by passing phases of political pressure, as will be shown below, and secondly, by the fact that Sicily was included in the decree of Ferdinand and Isabella. It may be doubted whether the refugees from Sicily, who crossed the Strait of Messina *en masse*, settled there.[10] Throughout the sixteenth century we find Sicilian Jews only in a few southern towns and in Rome, but none farther north.[11] This contrasts with the fact that Sicilian congregations spread throughout the Near East.[12] We can only conclude that the Italian mainland was merely the first stop in the migration of the Jews from Sicily in 1492 to the Levant (the Balkans in particular).[13]

The main factor in the growth of the Jewish population was the waves of immigration, the first of which brought Jews from Germany.[14] Even before 1300 we find Ashkenazic communities in the region under the Republic of Venice, and as the fourteenth century advances the references become increasingly frequent. These immigrants attained a numerical strength reflected in their flourishing communities in northern Italy, which had no Jewish population at the time the Ashkenazic influx began. According to the account of Elijah Capsali, the principal source for this area, the Ashkenazic population was extremely large, but one must discount the exaggeration in view of this scholar's penchant for painting the local scene in the brightest of colors. At all events, the Ashkenazim clearly formed the

[10] *Cf.* Ferorelli, *op. cit.,* p. 79. A small number of Jews from Sardinia also came there (*l. c.,* p. 81).

[11] In M. Stern's *Urkundliche Beitraege über die Stellung der Paepste zu den Juden* (Kiel 1893) vol. i, p. 91, there are references to refugees from "Sicily" in several cities of Le Marche. Careful reading of the Latin text reveals, however, that these references are to the Kingdom of Sicily and not to the island of Sicily.

[12] *Cf.* Rosanes, S. A., *Dibre yeme yisrael betogarma,* vol. i, p. 150 ff. and *Sefer masaot* of Rabbi Moshe Bassola, ed. by Yitshak Ben-Tsvi (Jerusalem 1938) p. 36, 39, 67.

[13] See Milano, A., *Richerche sulle condizioni economiche degli Ebrei di Roma durante la clausura nel ghetto* (1931) p. 7.

[14] See n. 1.

largest group among the Jewish immigrants who came to Italy during the Renaissance.

The second wave brought Jews expelled from France in 1394, who crossed the border into Savoy, a mixed French and Italian region. As the chronicler Joseph Hakohen relates:[15] "After their departure from France, Jews lived happily in Savoy, *where they waxed greatly in strength.* And it came to pass thereafter that they were expelled in the year 5221, which is 1461, and they went to live in the land of Lombardy and Romagna, and remained there unto this day." Thus, the number who settled in the Lombardy-Romagna was greater than the number who immigrated from France sixty-seven years earlier. The Piedmont area, on the northwestern frontier of Italy, likewise received an influx of refugees from France (1410),[16] an event which accounts in part for the numerical rise of the Jews in Lombardy during the latter part of the century.[17]

The third move, which brought the Spanish Jews, was apparently smaller in extent than the influx from Germany, yet much greater than the number who came from France. Jews from Spain were a familiar sight in Italy, beginning with the persecution of 1391,[18] and the connection between the two countries became very close with the conquest of the Kingdom of Naples by Aragon. After the expulsion of 1492 the tide of immigration swelled,[19] and of the estimated 9,000 persons who came to Italy in that year,[20] many remained after the others departed eastward.

Although each of the three waves is associated with a particular period they respectively occupied a span of years. The

15 *Emek habakha* of Rabbi Joseph Hakohen, 2d ed. (Cracow 1895) p. 88, 94.

16 *Ibid.*

17 Invernizzi, C., *Gli Ebrei a Pavia* (Pavia 1905) p. 4.

18 *Cf.* Stern, *op. cit.,* p. 21, 36; Colorni, V., *Legge ebraica e leggi locali* (Rome 1945) p. 367; Ciscato, A., *Gli Ebrei di Padova* (Padua 1901) p. 12 f.

19 *Cf.* Marx, Alexander, *Studies in Jewish History and Booklore* (New York 1944) p. 85 ff. and the author's *The Jews in Spain from the Year* 5151 *to the Expulsion,* in Hebrew (Jerusalem 1947) p. 41 ff.

20 Cassuto, U., in *Encyclopaedia Judaica,* vol. viii, p. 694.

influx from Germany reached its peak toward 1400,[21] but immigrants continued to arrive in larger or lesser numbers throughout the ensuing two centuries. A similar curve may be perceived in the case of the Spanish Jews who in 1492 went to Portugal, which presently decreed their forcible conversion.[22] Throughout the entire sixteenth century there was a steady stream of marrano families, arriving singly or in groups from the Iberian peninsula, who threw off the cloak of Christianity in Italy. In 1513 there came from Sicily alone 400 marranos, part of the population which had not left in 1492.[23] Similarly, Jews from France continued to migrate to Italy for years after the main group of immigrants appeared. The partial expulsion from Provence in 1491 brought immigrants as far south as Palermo (Sicily).[24] A case of a Provencal Jew, settled in Mantua, occurs as late as 1566.[25] In the sources for our period, individuals hailing from all parts of the Mediterranean world (Corfu, Tunis, Ragusa, Tripoli, Balearic Isles) are mentioned, indicating a small but steady immigration in addition to the important waves discussed above.

In the middle of the sixteenth century, the Levantine sector of the Jewish population, consisting of immigrants from Palestine and other parts of the Near East, began to achieve prominence, and in the following century this new element assumed considerable importance. In Venice, the Levantines attained their prominence as early as the first half of the sixteenth century.[26] In later years their progress kept pace with the strengthening of the connection between Italy and Palestine,[27] culminating in the leading role of the Levantines in the development of Leghorn, the youngest of the leading Jewish

---

[21] Cf. Elijah Capsali in *Revue des études juives*, vol lxxix, p. 28.
[22] *Emek habakha*, p. 108.
[23] Cf. Roth, Cecil, *The History of the Jews of Italy* (Philadelphia 1946) p. 284.
[24] Giovanni di Giovanni, *op. cit.*, p. 96.
[25] Cf. *Hatsaa al odot haget* (Venice 1566) 30 b.
[26] Roth, C., *Venice* (Philadelphia 1930) p. 61.
[27] See the author's Hebrew work, *Rome and Jerusalem, the History of the Relations between the Jews of Italy and Palestine* (Jerusalem 1944) p. 72.

centers.[28]

Some increase in population also resulted from the ransoming of Jewish captives brought to Italy. This activity forms one of the brightest chapters in the social life of Italian Jewry, and it would require an extensive collection of material to show its full scope. Here we can only take into account the fact that over the centuries the liberated captives totalled more than a negligible addition to the population. A few examples may be cited. In 1509 all of the Jews captured by the Spaniards in Tripoli were transported to Naples.[29] No doubt many of them succumbed to harsh treatment, but the survivors remained in Italy. When Charles V attacked Tunis in 1535, Jewish captives were brought to Genoa and Naples, where 150 were ransomed.[30] When Andrea Doria took the Greek towns of Modon, Coron and Patras in 1533, part of his many captives were also ransomed in Italy.[31]

The factors which favored the upward population trend were entirely counterbalanced by various contrary factors. To begin with, the exodus from the Kingdom of Naples, which continued for some decades,[32] must have reduced the number of Jews,[33] even though some of the refugees gradually found a haven elsewhere in Italy. Apart from such cases, Jews often emigrated from specific localities, when the situation made it necessary. Thus, in 1509, when the war of the League of Cambrai struck the large Ashkenazic center, many of the Jews indeed went to Mantua and Ferrara, "but many went to Germany to look for a peaceful place."[34] Again, under the impact of the hostile policy of Pope Paul IV, another reduction occurred and "the poor folk sailed away in ships for Turkey."[35] Added

28 Roth, *The Jews of Italy*, p. 347.
29 *Emek habakha*, p. 110.
30 *Ibid.*, p. 118.
31 *Shalshelet hakabala* (Lemberg 1862) p. 173.
32 Ferorelli, *op. cit.*, p. 218 ff.
33 *Emek habakha*, p. 118; *Dibre hayamim lemalkhe zarfat umalkhe bet-Ottoman* (Amsterdam 1733) vol. ii, p. 28a.
34 *Revue des études juives*, vol. lxxix, p. 56.
35 *Cf.* "The History of the Pope Paul IV," in *Tarbiz*, vol. ii, p. 347.

to this was the migration to Palestine, which rose to a high level under the stress of the persecution in the Papal States.[36]

In considering the effect of conversions to Christianity, we must naturally distinguish individual cases and large groups. The low rate of individuals forsaking Judaism is attested by the large community of Ferrara, where conversion claimed no more than 94 persons in a seventy year period (1531-1600).[37] Much more significant for their effects on the numerical strength of Italian Jewry were the recurrent cases of mass conversion, usually a result of official persecution. First in this series was the Kingdom of Naples, where the Jews had re-established themselves following the mass conversion effected under the first Angevin kings. After almost two centuries, however, they fell prey to the fanaticism of a conqueror, King Charles VIII, and only secret Jews remained in southern Italy. In a letter of 1504, written by Fernando Gonzales de Cordoba, the Spanish viceroy, extant in the library of the Jewish Theological Seminary in New York, we read that the number of converts far exceeded the loyal Jews.[38] Despite the fact that the former continued to practice Judaism in secret, the conversion unquestionably diminished the size of the Jewish population. In the end the marranos either left the Kingdom of Naples and migrated to other lands or became indistinguishable from their neighbors.

The second instance of this type occurred as a result of the policy of Pope Paul IV. Benjamin Nehemiah, the most important chronicler for this period, reports that in a certain small town "seventeen persons were converted together, while elsewhere in the Papal States a few here and there were converted, so that there was no city without an apostate."[39] A document of 1582 attests the conversion of many of the wealthier Jews of Rome.[40] We have also a letter from Cori, which states that

[36] Shulvass, *Rome and Jerusalem*, p. 69 f. and p. 74 f.
[37] Livi, L., *Gli Ebrei alla luce della statistica* (Florence n. d.) p. 290.
[38] An English translation of this letter was published in the *Register* of the Jewish Theological Seminary for 1940, p. 65 ff.
[39] *Tarbiz*, p. 346.
[40] Milano, *op. cit.*, p. 47.

"every day there come families of the great and the small, the wise and the intelligent, the poor and the rich, who change their religion . . . "[41] The disillusionment, which followed the exposure of Asher Laemlein, the false messiah, likewise took the form of numerous conversions.[42]

The rate of natural increase among the Jews of Renaissance Italy, it should be noted, was quite low. As Rabbi Judah Mintz explicitly indicated, "it is not customary for the *Romaneschi* (Jews of Rome or families which came from Rome) to marry girls of minor age."[43] Where data are available, we find families averaging no more than two or three children each.[44] The theory of a student of Sicilian Jewish history that polygamy prevailed in that group[45] cannot be proven. The refugee families from Spain, moreover, were fairly small.[46]

These various popuplation changes extended down to the very end of the Renaissance. About a century later, Rabbi Simone Luzzatto estimated the number of Jews as 25,000.[47] This important figure refers to the year 1638, by which time the migrations into and out of Italy were a thing of the past, so that the numerical strength of the country's Jewry was governed until the mid-nineteenth century almost entirely by the rate of natural increase. In view of Luzzatto's profound grasp of economic and political affairs we may assume that his estimate was well-founded.

The figure of 25,000 must be considered in the light of

41 Published in the Hebrew edition of Graetz, ed. by S. P. Rabinowitz, vol. vii, p. 420.
42 *Shalshelet hakabala*, p. 64.
43 *Responsa* of Judah Minz, no. 2.
44 Of the eight Jewish families living in Asolo in 1547, five had 2 children each, one had 5 children, one had 3 children, and one had 1 child. *Cf.* Osimo, M., *Narrazione della strage compita nel 1547 contro gli Ebrei di Asolo* (Casale Monferrato 1875) p. 27. Rome had 1,772 Jews and 373 families in 1520 (Bachi, *op. cit.*, p. 271, n. 1), making an average of 3 children to each family. Only one instance is found of a family of 9 children (*cf.* Azariah de Rossi, *Meor Enayim*, ed. Benjacob, pt. i, Kol elohim, p. 11).
45 Giovanni di Giovanni, p. 21.
46 In a group of 11 families that came from Spain to southern Italy in 1492, there was a total of 28 children, averaging less than 3 children per family (*cf.* Ferorelli, p. 84, n. 1).
47 *Discorso circa il stato degli Ebrei* (Venice 1638) p. 91.

the losses suffered during the severe epidemic of 1630-1631, and as a consequence of the entry of the Imperial army into Mantua.[48] It would, accordingly, follow that in 1630 the Jewish population numbered about 30,000. This estimate, however, appears somewhat conservative; our estimated figures, covering most of the political divisions of Italy, yield a total of about 35,000 (see section d, below) .

If either of these estimates be accepted, we must conclude that the number of Jews on the mainland *and* Siciliy in 1300 dropped considerably during the Renaissance period. On the other hand, on the Italian mainland there was a greater number at the end of the period than at its beginning. This increase means that the losses resulting from the persecution in the Papal States were outweighed by immigration. This numerical rise is one of the factors in the unique development of social and cultural activities which marks the life of the Jews of Renaissance Italy.

c

The influx of Jews from other countries changed the composition of the population, which had been culturally homogeneous in the preceding period. Small as the population was, various groups now lived side by side, Italian, German, Spanish, French and Levantine, together with a sprinkling from the Greek islands and North Africa. The three groups which set the tone of communal life were the Italian, the German and Spanish Jews. The Levantines began to play a prominent role only at the close of the Renaissance, while the French group lost its identity and left only some families with a vague memory of their origin.[49] The French prayer ritual persisted only in the three northwestern communities, Asti, Fossano, Moncalvo (the *Afam mahazor*).

[48] *Cf.* the chronicles *Olam hafukh* of Abraham Catalano, Kobets al Yad, n. s. bk. iv; *Hagaluth Vehapeduth* of Abraham Massaran, Hayekev (St. Petersburg 1894) .
[49] An example of this was the family of Leon Modena. See his autobiography, *Haye yehuda,* ed. by A. Kahana (Kiev 1912) p. 10.

While the three principal groups *(tre nazioni)* represented distinctive cultural-religious currents, each had its regional focus in a particular Italian region. This geographic distribution was a result both of the diverse directions from which the immigrant groups arrived and of the internal migrations; that is to say, the result of the resettlement of Italy as a whole by Jews during the Renaissance period. The earliest movement was that of the Jews of Rome and vicinity who sent forth settlers to new localities.[50] While starting their loan-banks they founded communities in Le Marche and later in Romagna and Umbria. There they spread northward as far as Padua, while others at the same time moved in the opposite direction and began to penetrate into the Kingdom of Naples.[51] The influx from Germany brought immigrants to Friuli and later to Istria; expanding eastward, this group re-established a Jewish population in Dalmatia, then a Venetian colony.

Concurrently there arose communities on Venetian territory, closer to the capital, and as far west as Brescia and Cremona. The German Jews came into contact with the established Jewish groups to the southwest of Venice, in the Po Valley. It was not long before the newcomers increased to the point of putting an Ashkenazic stamp on the Jewish scene at Padua, a change facilitated by the temporary suspension of the loan-banks and the departure of the Italian-Jewish residents.[52] The growth of the German element in the cities of the Republic prior to 1509 is clearly portrayed in the chronicle of Elijah Capsali. In the Duchy of Milan (Lombardy), which saw a considerable increase in the Jewish population between 1400 and the time of Francis Sforza, the Ashkenazim likewise predominated.[53] The names of the first Jews to reappear in Pavia are Ashkenazic, and a document of 1459 designates one as *hebreus de Alemania,* an

50 *Cf.* Colorni's study mentioned in n. 2.

51 Ferorelli, *op. cit.,* p. 72 f.

52 Morpurgo, E., *L'Università degli Ebrei in Padova nel XVI secolo* (1909) p. 19.

53 Invernizzi, *op. cit.,* p. 4, and Emek habakha, p. 92.

immigrant from Germany.[54] In the principalities of Monferrato and Piedmont, where French and Spanish refugees were the first Jewish settlers (see section d, below), the residue of the Jewish population was again Ashkenazic. This is shown by the retention of their prayer ritual to our own day. The once flourishing Ashkenazic congregations of Venice and Padua, on the other hand, ultimately adopted the Spanish and Italian ritual, respectively.[55]

The Spanish Jews were concentrated in the Kingdom of Naples, which received the main body of the refugees in 1492,[56] and even after the great majority became nominal Christians the remainder consisted primarily of Sephardim. The well-known document in which David Ibn Yahya lodged his complaint against the Naples community[57] makes it clear that the leaders and most of the population were Sephardim.

In sum, the Jews in the north were chiefly of German origin, in central Italy Italian, and in the south Spanish. Within the three geographic divisions there were other groups as well, largely as a result of the expulsions. As noted above, in 1461 French Jews had to move from Savoy to Romagna, where the Italian element predominated. Following the final expulsion from Naples, many Spanish Jews found a haven in Le Marche: Ancona, Fano, Ascoli and Camerino.[58] The war of the League of Cambrai drove many Ashkenazic Jews from Venetian territory southward, particularly to Mantua and Ferrara.[59]

The mixed character of the Jewish population in the big cities was primarily a result of the fact that these centers attracted Jews of diverse background. This was especially true of Rome, Venice and Ferrara. At the beginning of the sixteenth century the non-Italian elements in the Rome community became strong

[54] *Ibid.,* p. 13, n. 2.
[55] *Lunario israelitico* (1928) ed. by F. Servi.
[56] Ferorelli, *op. cit.,* p. 78 f.
[57] Published by Alexander Marx in *Hebrew Union College Annual,* vol. i., p. 616 ff.
[58] Stern, M., *op. cit.,* p. 91.
[59] Capsali, in *Revue des études juives,* vol. lxxix, p. 56.

enough to vie for communal power. When the struggle ended, as a result of the mediation of Daniel da Pisa, the power was shared between the Italian and the more recent elements, although the former retained some minor privileges.[60] At this junction non-Italians evidently formed about half of the Jewish population of Rome, but during the course of the century the Italian Jews regained their predominance. Following the closing of the Ashkenazic synagogue, as a result of the machinations of the Inquisition,[61] the local Ashkenazim scarcely figure in the community life during the rest of our period. By an order of the state, in 1571, the council of the community *(congrega)* was to consist of 60 members, of whom 35 should be Italians, thus reflecting the relative decline of the non-Italian groups within the Jewry of Rome.

The community of Venice was divided into three major "nations," of which the German was the dominant sector. Yet the Spanish and Levantine groups, reinforced to a degree by the Italian, rose in importance and ultimately the Spanish Jews wrested the control of the community from the Ashkenazim. The influx of non-Ashkenazic Jews into Venice, attracted by the city's economic opportunities and the liberal regime, coincides with the flight of such Jews from nearby Padua, which was mentioned above. The majority status of the German Jews declined until the Spanish and Levantine Jews together gained a majority in the communal executive committee, a trend which continued in the same direction thereafter.[62]

The development of the Spanish Jews' preponderance in Ferrara is especially noteworthy. Around 1500 this was one of the most important cities in Italy, with a total population of close to 100,000 (as compared with 30,000 at present) , and the capital of a duchy, which played a prominent role in the politics of that day. So great was the influx of Jews from Spain that the

---

60 Milano, A., in *Rassegna mensile di Israel*, vol. x, p. 324, 330.

61 Berliner, A., *Censur und Konfiscation hebräischer Bücher im Kirchenstaate* (Berlin 1891) p. 5.

62 Roth, Cecil, *Venice*, p. 129.

city's limits had to be enlarged in order to accommodate them.[63] The number grew following the flight of marranos from Portugal, where the Inquisition was established in 1531. Joseph Hakoheń relates that "most of them returned to the Lord, God of our fathers, who had mercy on them, and they worshipped the Lord, God of Israel, and Ercole, Duke of Ferrara, permitted them to dwell in his land . . . "[64] Again, a decade later, many Spanish Jews, including the Abrabanel family, when compelled to leave the Kingdom of Naples, came to Ferrara. This important city likewise attracted Ashkenazim, who founded a synagogue in 1532.[65]

There were other places as well in which the Jewish population included "cultural islands" in addition to the predominant group. But the tripartite concentration of the major categories, which was indicated above, remained until the last decades of the Renaissance period, when the Spanish Jews lost their stronghold in the south. Thereafter this group formed compact units elsewhere in Italy; in time, as the Leghorn community became a flourishing center, the Jewry of Tuscany as a whole took on a Sephardic complexion.

d

We have thus far described the Jewish population in general terms, for one cannot reconstruct the demographic picture in every one of the divisions of the Italian peninsula. The effort must, nevertheless, be made to obtain at least a partial picture. The materials in the writer's possession provide a basis for certain conclusions, which, despite their incompleteness, may contribute toward the understanding of the historical course of the Jews of Italy.

The Republic of Venice

On Venetian territory, where the settlement of Jews pro-

[63] Pesaro, A., *Memorie storiche sulla communità israelitica ferrarese* (Ferrara 1878) p. 16.
[64] *Emek habakha*, p. 108.
[65] Pesaro, *op. cit.*, p. 19.

ceeded in accordance with agreements between the moneylenders and the town councils, the Jews appear in the smaller towns first and in the larger places afterward. Until 1516 the Jewry of Venice proper — from which Jews were excluded — resided not in the capital but at Mestre, a small town on the adjacent mainland. In the case of Verona, the important document published by Salo W. Baron indicates that while the Jews settled in the nearby villages, they did not take up residence in the city until it was annexed by the Republic of Venice (1408).[66] The Jewish population in the small towns persisted long after the Renaissance, as late as the second half of the eighteenth century. The list of places inhabited by Jews is sufficiently broad to warrant the generalization that they were scattered throughout Venetian territory.

The size of this Jewish population cannot be estimated with any certainty. At all events, in the writer's opinion, the number in the three principal centers (Venice, Padua and Verona) exceeded the combined number in all other parts of the Venetian state. Typical of the tiny communities was Asolo, with seven Jewish families (37 persons) about 1550.[67] One must bear in mind that in the small towns, in which the basis of the residence of Jews was a *condotta,* we must assume that they numbered only one or two families. The account of the attempt of Jews to settle in the fortress-town of Palmanova, which was built at the end of the sixteenth century, indeed refers to a single family from an adjacent small town.[68] It would accordingly not be far from the truth to estimate the combined Jewish population of each 25 small local groups under the Republic of Venice as about 1,000 persons.

Our information regarding the three principal cities is clearer. The Jewish population of Venice rose from less than a thousand in the middle of the sixteenth century to 1,694 in

66 Baron, S. W., in Samuel Krauss *Festschrift.*
67 Osimo, *op. cit.*
68 Published in *Italia,* vol. i, p. 26 ff.

1586.[68a] The reason for this rapid increase is obscure, but the fact that the number grew from 923 to 1,424 between 1556 and 1563, suggests a connection with the flight of Jews from Rome (under Paul IV and thereafter). This persecution, which culminated in the expulsion of 1569, probably accounts for the continued upward trend in Venice during the years 1563-1586. The influx of Jews into Venice was in fact greater than that reflected by the net population figures, for one must take into account those who left in 1571, fearing that the order of expulsion issued that year would be enforced.[69] The figure for 1586 also reflects the mortality due to the plague of 1575.[70] The sudden decline of the population from 1,694 to 1,043 in a seven-year period (1586-1593) has yet to be explained. At the close of the Renaissance there were about a thousand Jews in Venice.

In Padua the Jews numbered about 600-700. This estimate is based on the fact that the plague of 1576 killed 220 Jews, while the population numbered 439 in 1603 and 721 in 1631.[71] In Verona there were more than 400 Jews at the end of the sixteenth century.[72] Their number probably rose in 1597, when refugees from Lombardy arrived.[73]

Lombardy

The Jews were expelled from the duchy of Milan in 1225.[74] Then in the latter part of the following century (1387), Jews received authorization to establish loan-banks in the duchy.[75] In Pavia, one of the chief cities, there were at this date more than 50 Jews.[76] The population increased in the fifteenth century with the arrival of the French Jews, who were driven out of

[68a] Roth, Cecil, *Venice*, p. 106, n. 12.
[69] *Emek habakha*, p. 153, and *Hamagiah*, printed with the *Emek habakha*, p. 167.
[70] *Hamagiah*, p. 171.
[71] Isaac Cantarini, *Pahad yitzhak* (Amsterdam 1685) 10 b.
[72] Baron, *op. cit.*
[73] *Hamagiah*, p. 184.
[74] Invernizzi, p. 4.
[75] *Ibid.*, and Colorni, *op. cit.*, p. 41.
[76] Ivernizzi, p. 10.

their temporary haven in Savoy[77] and were welcomed by the famous Duke Francis Sforza.[78] In 1489, however, a century after the restoration of the Jews to this state, Lodovico Moro, the son of Sforza, decreed the expulsion of the Jews.[79] A second restoration ensued on the basis of the *condotta* of 1522, which authorized 80 families to settle, indicating a total population of at least 400, all dependent on moneylending. In addition, we may assume that Jews engaged in other pursuits joined the bankers. A number of those expelled from Bologna and its district by Pope Pius V settled in the Milan region.[80] Cremona with a Jewish population of more than 450 had an important community at this time.[81] There were small groups inhabiting other places as well; the historians of the Jews of Pavia and Brescia mention a considerable number of localities in which individual Jews or small groups are recorded.[82] Cecil Roth estimates the Jewish population as a whole in 1550 as about 900.[83] At the time of the expulsion of 1597, the Jewish bankers were concentrated in Cremona, Pavia, Allesandria, and Lodi. The capital, Milan, was closed to Jews as a place of residence.[84]

Piedmont and Monferrato

The settlement of Jews in Piedmont and Monferrato begins much later than that in the eastern portion of north Italy. The first to appear in Piedmont were the French Jews in the fifteenth century,[85] and the refugees from Savoy (1461) [86] were evidently

---

77 *Emek habakha,* p. 94.
78 *Ibid,* p. 92.
79 *Ibid,* p. 98.
80 *Hamagiah,* p. 159; *Invernizzi,* p. 62, n. 1, 63.
81 The volume published by the Union of Jewish communities of Italy in 1914 (p. 25) gives a figure of 456 Jews in Cremona in 1588. This is probably based on an article on the Jews of Cremona that escaped my investigations.
82 Invernizzi, p. 25; Glissenti, F., *Gli Ebrai nel Bresciano* (Brescia 1890) .
83 *History of the Jews of Italy,* p. 322.
84 Invernizzi, p. 76, 85.
85 *Emek habakha,* p. 88.
86 *Cf.* Foà, Salvatore, *Gli Ebrei nel Monferrato* (Alessandria 1914) p. 7, 9, 66, 73, 74, 75, 124 (n. 58) .

Spanish Jews came to Monferrato in 1492 and by 1509 the population was sufficiently large to warrant the appointment of a state official *(conservatore)* to deal with the community. Some years later (1522), when the sum of 25,000 scudi was appropriated for the army, the Jewry was taxed 500 scudi. In view of the disproportionate share of the taxes regularly levied on this group, I am inclined to consider that it constituted one percent of the total population, and paid double that ratio of the the first to settle in Monferrato. There are signs that some military levy. Later in the same century the importance of the bankers in the Jewish population became pronounced, a change attributable not only to the arrival of French Jews from the Savoy and of Jews from Spain but to the migration of German Jews. This hypothesis is supported by the remarkable persistence of the Ashkenazic prayer ritual, which was pointed out above. The documents name numerous towns, to which the *condotta* applied, but the list was repeatedly revised and it is doubtful whether Jewish bankers settled in all of these places. The existence of local Jewish groups is, however, certain in those places where we know both of a *condotta* with the regime of Monferratto and the papal authorization. The papal authorization was undoubtedly obtained for the specific purpose of taking advantage of the *condotta* by Jews about to settle in the localities in question. We have a list of 13 towns, for which papal approval of Jewish residence was obtained in 1589-1594, which attests the distribution of the Jewish population in the smaller centers. These were tiny groups, and only in those in which a synagogue is known to have existed (such as Capriata or Monastero) may we assume that the population comprised ten male adult Jews. The bulk of the Jewish population was naturally concentrated in Casale, the capital, an important community in post-Renaissance times, and four other towns (Acqui, Asti, Moncalvo, Nizza Monferrato). In the second half of the sixteenth century the Jewry of Piedmont likewise increased. Duke Emanuel Philibert issued in 1572 a sort of official invitation to the Jews,[87]

---

[87] The text is published in *Revue des études juives*, vol. v, p. 231.

of all varieties — Italian, German, Spanish Portugese, Levantine, North African, and Syrian — which undoubtedly brought a number of newcomers.

In regard to Monferrato, we have an important item in a memorial addressed by the Jews to the state (1601), to the effect that the Jewry comprised 100 families, many of which were large. This justifies an estimate of 600-700 persons.

Mantua

The capital of a small but strong duchy, Mantua was from the fifteenth century one of the most celebrated Jewish communities in Italy. This Jewry was noted for its unusually rich communal activity, which implies a degree of numerical strength. Like Venice, this Jewry was composed of groups of diverse origin. Founded in the familiar manner by moneylenders, the original Italian-Jewish settlers from the Rome area were joined by immigrants from Germany (Speier, Erfurt, Nuremberg, Heidelberg) and the region around Venice. In the second half of the sixteenth century came the French Jews from Piedmont. Within this mixed population the Italians formed about two-thirds of the total.[88] As the influx into Mantua continued, this group grew with the arrival of exiles from Romagna under Pius V,[89] who had been preceded fifty years earlier by Ashkenazim fleeing from Padua.[90] At the close of our period came a number of exiles from Lombardy, likewise chiefly Ashkenazim. The names figuring in the sources for this century also attest the presence of Jews of other origins (Tunis, Provence, Corfu). Although as early as 1431 there appeared a Spanish Jew at Mantua,[91] surprisingly few came from that country toward the end of the century; considering the large influx of exiles into Ferrara, this situation is enigmatic and calls for investigation.

[88] *Cf.* Colorni, in *Rassegna mensile di Israel,* vol. ix, p. 219.
[89] *Hamagiah,* p. 159.
[90] Capsali, *op. cit.,* p. 56.
[91] Colorni, *Legge ebraica . . . ,* p. 367.

At the end of the Renaissance period there were close to 2,000 Jews in Mantua,[92] (twice as many as in Venice) constituting, according to some authorities, 20 percent of the city's total population.[93] The relative position of the Jewish group in Mantua in respect to its sister communities in Italy was paramount, and the local Jewry's social and cultural activities were correspondingly noteworthy.

Ferrara, Modena, Reggio, Parma

Ferrara was a typical Renaissance development. The dukes of Este succeeded in building a small but strong state, the principal cities of which, besides the capital, were Modena and Reggio, and which comprised a great number of small towns and villages. The house of Este had a very liberal Jewish policy and the duchy had a relatively dense Jewish population. During the fifteenth century a number of Ashkenazim settled in Ferrara beside the established Italian community but were too few as yet to have need of a separate synagogue.[94] The population rose quickly in 1492, as was seen above. The number in Modena and Reggio likewise increased, but these were apparently Ashkenazi centers.[95] In the early part of the succeeding century we also find Jews scattered in the villages around Reggio.[96]

Throughout this century Ferrara received Jewish exiles from other parts of Italy, belonging to the various groups. In 1510 came those who fled Padua (chiefly Ashkenazim) during the war of the League of Cambrai.[97] In 1531 there arrived many marranos from Portugal,[98] and a decade later the exiles from the Kingdom of Naples, including the Abrabanel family. The

[92] *Ibid.*, p. 338; also in *Rassegna mensile di Israel,* vol. ix, p. 230.
[93] *Cf.* Kahana, Abraham, in *Hagoren* (5682) 178. I was not able to consult the works of Carnevali and Rezasco.
[94] Pesaro, *op. cit.,* p. 16 f.
[95] *Cf.* Balletti, A., *Gli Ebrei e gli Estensi* (Modena 1913).
[96] This is evident from a responsum by Rabbi Azriel Dayena, published in *Kiryat sefer,* vol. xiv.
[97] *Sefer hapesakim* (Venice 1519) p. 34a.
[98] *Emek habakha,* p. 108.

two latest additions to the population came from the Papal States: a large part of the wealthy class from Rome in 1556[99] and the exiles from Bologna and Romagna in 1565.[100] The constant stream of immigration during this period in which Ferrara reached the zenith of its power resulted in a Jewish population estimated as about 2,000 by a reliable local historian.[101]

In 1597 Duke Alphonso II died without issue, whereupon the pope annexed Ferrara, leaving the new duke to rule Modena and Reggio. As a contemporary chronicler succinctly describes the exodus from Ferrara: "There went out Don Cesare (the duke) and the Jews."[102] According to the modern historian cited previously, however, the number leaving was one-fourth of the Jews, so that 1,500 remained.[103]

No doubt a large part of those who left Ferrara came to nearby Modena and Reggio, as did some of the exiles from Lombardy,[104] who preferred not to settle in Ferrara under papal rule. Thereafter the importance of that city's Jewry declined considerably, while Modena and Reggio assumed greater importance during the seventeenth and eighteenth centuries.

In the duchy of Parma, the western neighbor of Ferrara, the residence of Jews was likewise based originally on the *condotta*.[105] In 1562 we learn of 16 towns to which Jewish moneylenders were admitted, but in 1578 there were only 8. The Jewish population persisted in these eight localities down to the nineteenth century.

Tuscany

The Jewry of Florence, the principal city of Tuscany, had

99 *Tarbiz*, vol. ii, p. 346.
100 *Hamagiah*, p. 159.
101 Pesaro, op. cit., p. 33.
102 *Hamagiah*, p. 187.
103 Pesaro, p. 34.
104 *Hamagiah*, p. 184.
105 Loevinson, E., "Gli Ebrei di Parma, Piacenza e Gaustalla," in *Rassegna mensile di Israel* (1932).

its beginnings at the opening of the Renaissance, and the names of the earliest residents point to Rome.[106] The community remained predominantly Italian almost throughout this period. Rabbi Joseph Colon mentions the arrival of newcomers[107] but without indicating where they hailed from. Few of the Spanish exiles came here or elsewhere in Tuscany and this region is not mentioned in our principal source regarding the distribution of that population in Italy.[108] Here and there, nevertheless, we meet with individual families, such as the Y a h y a in Pisa (1495).[109] The number of Jews in Tuscany increased as a result of the persecution in the Papal States and the expulsion from Romagna, [110] which brought chiefly Italian Jews.

The distribution of the population outside of Florence in 21 towns of the district is attested by the fact that in 1571 the Jews thereof were concentrated in the newly established ghetto at Florence. Somewhat later a similar concentration took place in the ghetto of Sienna, and the circumstances imply that the population outside of the two cities was quite limited. In Florence, according to one scholar, the ghetto period opened with some 500 residents.[111] The researches of Umberto Cassuto tend, however, to make this appear somewhat too high.

Papal States

During the Renaissance the Papal States rose in extent to second rank among the states of the peninsula. This domain comprised nearly all of central Italy from coast to coast and in the north took in Romagna with its capital Bologna. As the period ended the pope also added Ferrara.

As far as the pattern of the Jewish population was concerned, the essential feature of this state was the concentration of the

---

106 *Cf.* Cassuto, U., *Gli Ebrei a Firenze,* ch. i.
107 No. 172.
108 Marx, *op. cit.*, p. 86.
109 *Shalshelet hakabala,* p. 91.
110 *Hamagiah,* p. 159.
111 Livi, *op. cit.*, p. 24.

Italiani within its borders. While it is impossible to make any reliable estimate, the number must have formed a high ratio of the total Jewish population in Italy. The list of Jews taxed for the *Casa dei Catecumeni* in 1569 covers 42 towns in the Rome district, in which synagogues existed; there were in addition 34 such towns in Le Marche and 13 in Romagna. This is in accord with the fourteenth-century report, which mentions money-lending establishments in 30 towns in the latter province. [112] We may accordingly figure that the total number of local communities was about 80. This agrees with the impression given by the chronicler Benjamin Nehemiah,[112a] who as a captive traversed the route from Civitanova on the Adriatic to Rome and found Jews living in virtually every one of the places he passed through.

In 1527 there were close to 1,800 Jews in Rome,[113] and in 1556 about 1,500.[114] The downward trend undoubtedly continued beginning with the reign of Paul IV. According to a report of unknown reliability, however, more than 200 families returned under Sixtus V (1585-1590).[115] The number in Bologna is estimated as 800-900 persons,[116] and there were a few hundred or more at Ancona.

Among the smaller towns, in 1566 there were 200 Jews in Cori, after the conversion of a substantial number.[117] In view of the numerous communities scattered throughout the Papal States, and especially in the Rome area, and of the fact that they did not originate on the basis of the *condotta,* we may assume that their combined Jewish population was relatively great. I would conjecture that the smallest numbered no less than 100 and some had 200 or more.

Throughout the first half of the sixteenth century the Papal States received Jews from other areas. There were during

---

[112] Colorni, *Il Prestifo* . . . p. 32; Stern, *op. cit.,* p. 144 f.
[112a] *Tarbiz,* vol. ii, p. 480 ff.
[113] Livi, *op. cit.,* p. 23.
[114] Milano, *op. cit.,* p. 71.
[115] *Cf.* Natali, E., *Il ghetto di Roma* (Rome 1887) p. 217.
[116] Cassuto, U., in *Encyclopaedia Judaica,* vol. iv, p. 926.
[117] Graetz, Hebrew ed., vol. vii, p. 421.

1492-1511 five waves of immigration to Rome from Spain, Sicily, Portugal, Navarre, Provence, Naples, Calabria and Tripoli, as a result of which the newcomers formed a slight majority of the Jewish population.[118] The province of Le Marche, for its part, received an influx from the Kingdom of Naples; the exiles came to Ancona, Fano, Ascoli and Camerino.[119]

On the basis of the foregoing figures and the estimates for the smaller communities, the Papal States comprised half of the total Jewish population of Italy, as estimated by Luzzatto (25,000) or one third according to the writer's conclusion (see below). These figures refer to the middle of the sixteenth century, after which a decline occurred under the pressure of the policy initiated by Paul IV. The numerical loss was the result both of mass conversions and departures, as pointed out above. Regardless of the occasional return of some Jews to Rome and Bologna conditions were unfavorable for checking the numerical decline and the population was clearly smaller in 1600 than in 1500.

Duchy of Urbino

Jews appeared in Urbino, the duchy in which the Adriatic port of Pesaro is situated, at the beginning of the fourteenth century.[120] Under the Montefeltre and the first of the Rovere dukes, the political situation was favorable for the Jews, and we may assume that their number rose during the fifteenth and sixteenth centuries. It is known that many of the wealthier Jews in the papal provinces of Le Marche and Umbria moved to Urbino, immediately after the famous bull of Paul IV against the Jews.[121] A number of the exiles from Romagna came to Urbino and Pesaro.[122] The expulsion of the marranos from Pesaro in

---

118 *Cf.* Milano, A., in *Rassegna mensile di Israel,* vol. x, p. 325 f.
119 Stern, *op. cit.,* p. 87, 91.
120 Luzzatto, G., *I banchieri ebrei in Urbino* (Padua 1902) p. 21.
121 *Tarbiz,* vol. ii, p. 346.
122 *Hamagiah,* p. 159.

1558[123] presumably did not affect the size of the Jewry, since the former were recent refugees from the Papal States and their sojourn was temporary, while awaiting an opportunity to proceed to Turkey. At the end of our period the number of Jews in the duchy was about 1,500,[124] divided into Italian, Spanish and Levantine groups;[125] German Jews do not figure in the sources.

Kingdom of Naples

The Jewish situation in the Kingdom of Naples, which was the largest of the Italian states, was subject to recurrent changes. The history of this Jewry, which goes back to antiquity, was terminated at the end of the thirteenth century, as has already been mentioned. Shortly afterward the Jews reappeared and in 1311 they received the privilege of re-establishing synagogues in various towns, a sure sign of the rise of new communities. In 1393 the Jews of the Balearic isles received a special invitation to immigrate. The distribution of this population extended to the provinces on the northern frontier and Jewish communities were found in various towns in the Abruzzi hills.[126] We have already had occasion to see how the influx of Italian and German Jews increased the population.

The immigration of Spanish exiles was quite considerable, and was supplemented by others from Portugal, Sicily and Sardinia. Although the absolute total is not known, these immigrants outnumbered the resident Jews (regnicoli) two to one.[127]

[123] Emek habakha, p. 136; Revue des études juives, vol. xx, p. 70; Jewish Quarterly Review, vol. iv, p. 510.

[124] Luzzatto, op. cit., p. 43.

[125] A takkanah of one of the rabbis of Pesaro, in the year 1584, (published in Louis Finkelstein's Jewish Self-Government in the Middle Ages — New York 1924 — p. 315) contains a passage implying that there were at least three groups in the community.

[126] Ferorelli, op. cit., p. 63 f.

[127] Of a tax of 6,000 ducats imposed on all the Jews of the kingdom, 2,000 ducats were paid by the regnicoli and 4,000 by the immigrants (Ferorelli, N., Immigrazione degli Ebrei spagnoli nel Napoletano durante e dopo il 1492—1906—p. 7). We can assume that the immigrants were not burdened with a disproportionate share of the taxes, thus indicating that they made up two-thirds of the Jewish community.

But no sooner did the new arrivals settle than a new conqueror, Charles VIII of France, decreed a persecution. The Spanish conquest was followed by the restoration of the Jews, including small groups of immigrants or captives of war who had been ransomed. At this stage, however, the plans for the final expulsion (1540) were ripening. The population during these closing decades was prosperous but small in number.

The greatest expansion was undoubtedly that which occurred in the latter part of the fifteenth century. The Jewish population at this time was distributed in at least 153 localities.[128] There is, however, no means of estimating the extent of this population and Ferorelli's calculation of 150,000, based on certain taxation data,[129] is plainly a gross exaggeration. That figure is entirely out of keeping with the restricted scope of the cultural and social activities of the Jewry of southern Italy and is not reflected in any way in the Jewish sources. It is, nevertheless, amazing that there were small towns in which according to Ferorelli, hundreds of Jews are known to have lived.

As for the composition of the Jewish population, the first to return to this kingdom were moneylenders from the Rome area. Later came the German and Provencal Jews.[130] After 1492, however, the population was predominantly Spanish.

Sicily, Malta, Sardinia

It will be recalled that Sicilian Jewry was relatively populous on the threshold of the Renaissance era, and it retained its density until the expulsion of 1492. There were some 50 communities, the largest of which greatly outnumbered the population of the principal mainland communities. Visiting the island in 1488, Obadiah of Bertinoro reported 850 Jewish families in Palermo,[131] or about 5,000 persons, a figure corroborated by non-

---

128 A list of these is given in Ferorelli, N., *Gli Ebrei nell' Italia meridionale*, p. 98, n. 1.
129 *Ibid.*, p. 97 f.
130 *Ibid.*, p. 71 f.
131 *Igeret Obadiah mibertinoro*, p. 8.

Jewish sources.[132] Elsewhere this traveler found 400 families in Messina, 5,000 persons in Syracuse, and lesser groups in Trapani, Catania and Agrigento. While Giovanni di Giovanni's claim that the Jews formed 10 percent of the island's total may be fairly correct, his estimate of 100,000 Jews is definitely too high. This is made clear by statements of the Jews submitted to the regime on various occasions in reference to taxation.[133]

The rulers of Sicily usually held Malta and Gozzo, where the Jewish situation was similar. About 1250 there were 25 Jewish families on Malta and 8 on Gozzo. By the time of the expulsion a century and a half later, the number had risen to 500 and 350 persons, respectively, judging from the tax records.[134] Of the Jews of Sardinia we know only that in 1492 the exiles landed at Gaeta and Naples.[135] This was apparently a very small population, which has left no traces in Jewish literature.

e

Summarizing the population figures and estimates presented above, we arrive at the following:

Region	Jewish Population
Venice (city)	1,000
Padua	700
Verona	400
Other localities *(ca. 50)* under Venice	2,000
Lombardy	900
Monferrato	700
Mantua (city)	2,000
Ferrara (city)	2,000
Florence	400
Papal States	12,500
Urbino (duchy)	1,500
Total	24,100

[132] Güdemann, M., *Hatora vehahayim*, vol. ii, p. 264.
[133] Giovanni di Giovanni, *op. cit.*, p. 21 and *passim*.
[134] Roth, C., *The Jews of Malta* (London 1931) p. 191, 195.
[135] Ferorelli, *op. cit.*, p. 83, 95, n. 1.

The foregoing list does not include several places, for which no estimates are available, namely, Piedmont, Mantua (outside of the capital), Reggio and vicinity, Modena and vicinity (both in Ferrara), the duchy of Parma, and Tuscany. With the exception of Parma, all of these had a fairly important population in the seventeenth and eighteenth centuries. The Piedmontese communities, those in the vicinity of Mantua and the two large centers of Modena and Reggio[136] with the smaller groups in the vicinity, all played an important role in Italian-Jewish communal and cultural life down to the last years of the eighteenth century. We may accordingly estimate that there were some 10,000 Jews in the places named. If so, the total Jewish population of Italy at the close of the Renaissance was about 35,000.

[136] In the second half of the 17th century, for example, there were about 900 Jews in Reggio.

VI

ASHKENAZIC JEWRY IN ITALY

Originally published in Yivo Annual of Jewish Social Science,
vol. VII (1952), pp. 110-131.

a

Beginning in the second half of the 13th century and continuing for about three hundred years, Italian Jewry experienced
the most important phase of its history: the transformation from
a culturally homogeneous Jewish group *(Italiani)* to a composite
group of Italian, Ashkenazic, Sephardic and Levantine Jews.
This process has had a large share in shaping the destiny of
Italian Jewry to this day.

This process began at a time when Italian Jewry had
decreased greatly both numerically and geographically. Up to
about the 12th century Jews could be found all over Italy.[1] Then
the situation changed. North Italian Jewry disappeared for
reasons and under circumstances that have as yet not been
sufficiently elucidated. South Italian Jewry was virtually destroyed in the battle of extermination waged against it by the
first kings of the Anjou dynasty.[2] Only two groups of Jews
remained in Italy: one in central Italy, mainly in Rome and its
environs, and the other in Sicily. Sicilian Jewry followed its

---

[1] An attempt to give a panoramic picture of Italian Jewry at that time is
found in Milano, A., *Gli Ebrei in Italia nei secoli xi-xii* (Citta di Castello
1938). The report of Rabbi Benjamin of Tudela, who travelled in Italy about
1160, is taken as a point of departure.

[2] *Cf.* Feroreli, N., *Gli Ebrei nell' Italia meridionale* (Turin 1915) p. 53;
Cassuto, M. D. A., in *Cohen-Festschrift* (Berlin 1912) p. 389 ff. and in the
Sefer hazikaron in memory of Asher Gulak and Samuel Klein, p. 139 ff.; also
the study by Joshua Starr in *Speculum,* vol. xxi (1946) p. 203 ff.

own course and never really constituted a part of Italian Jewry.[3]
Hence there remained only the group in the vicinity of Rome,
fairly numerous, firmly established and possessing a demograph-
ically high expansion potential.[4]

In the second half of the thirteenth century the Jews of
Rome and vicinity (hereafter we shall refer to them as Italiani)
began to spread to the south and to the north. The motive for
this expansion was entirely economic. It was not the pressure
of economic distress but rather the urge to economic expansion
— in this case the idea of establishing banks that lent money
on pledges — that gave rise to this movement. It therefore, was
an "emigration" of individuals or families and not a mass
exodus. The Italiani thus took the first step toward the recolonization of Italy by Jews.[5] The real recolonization, however, was
the result of a large immigration of foreign, non-Italian Jews,
who came from three directions, Ashkenazim from the north,
Provencal and Spanish Jews from the west and Levantine Jews
from the orient. The first to arrive were the Ashkenazim from
Germany.[6] Although we do not know the exact number that
came it is quite certain that they constituted the largest group
among the new arrivals. They possibly even exceeded in numbers the Italiani. One thing is certain: the immigration of
Ashkenazim to Italy brought back Jews to northern Italy, from
Dalmatia and Istria to the French border. The Sephardim, who
came during the entire course of the 16th century, merely enlarged the already existing communities, but, with the exception
of Leghorn, established practically no new communities.

[3] See the author's paper read at the First World Congress of Jewish Studies in Jerusalem, published in *Sinai*, vol. xi, 44.
[4] The Jewish population in Rome is to this day the human reservoir of
the Jewish community in Italy and practically the only place where the birth
rate exceeds the death rate. *Cf.* Bachi, R., *La demografia degli Ebrei Italiani
negli ultimi cento anni* (Rome 1931) p. 69.
[5] On the process of this bank colonization, *cf.* Colorni, V. *Il prestito
ebraico e communita ebraiche nell' Italia centrale e settentrionale* (1935).
[6] The Levantine Jewish merchants who came possibly very early to Venice
(*cf.* Cecil Roth's *Venice*, Philadelphia, 1930, p. 10 ff.) were individuals who
stayed there temporarily. The real immigration of Levantine Jews took place
in the 16th and 17th centuries, simultaneously with the Sephardic immigration.

The effects of the Ashkenazic immigration into Italy and the destiny of the Ashkenazic Jews in Italy are among the most important problems in Italian Jewish historiography. The author of this article hopes sincerely that he will be able to undertake a thorough study of Ashkenazic Jewry in Italy. The present article is a by-product of work done by the author in collecting material for his book, *Jewish Life in Renaissance Italy*. The data presented here allows for several general conclusions. At the same time the author will endeavor to point out the main problems that emerge in connection with this topic.

b

The first reports of groups of Ashkenazic Jews in Italy date from the last years of the 13th century. It may be assumed that Ashkenazic Jews had begun to come to Italy some time earlier, but the first explicit information about them is from the years 1294 and 1296. In 1294 Ashkenazic Jews were recorded in Treviso and in 1296 in Cividale del Friuli.[7] In the area between these two cities, which occupied a large part of the territory of the Venetian republic, were many small towns which, from later reports, had Ashkenazic communities. Since economic and political conditions in all these places were the same as in Cividale del Friuli and Treviso we may assume with certainty that at the end of the 13th century there were many more Ashkenazic communities there than those we know about.

This fact would also indicate that at the end of the 13th century Ashkenazic immigration reached only as far as the central areas of the republic of Venice. To be sure, individual Ashkenazic Jews were found also farther south. In the entourage of Immanuel of Rome, who, is as well known, spent his years in south and central Italy, was the poet Jacob "the Ashkenazi."[8] These were isolated instances, however.

In the fourteenth century the immigration of Ashkenazic Jews to Italy began to increase. Reports about them now became

[7] Colorni, *op. cit.*, p. 33.
[8] *Mahberot Imanuel haromi*, ed. Wilheimer (Lwow 1870) p. 161.

more frequent in Jewish as well as non-Jewish sources. Among the Ashkenazim in Italy the tradition persisted that they had arrived there in the 14th century, mainly in the second half. Rabbi Elijah Capsali of Crete, who studied in the Ashkenazic yeshiva of Rabbi Judah Mentz in Padua and whose books are full of much useful information about the Ashkenazim in Italy, stated that the Ashkenazim had come to Italy "one hundred and thirty years ago or longer."[9] This would mean some time between 1360 and 1380.

The colonization of the Ashkenazim in Italy proceeded quite naturally from north to south. In the vicinity of Verona, for instance, Ashkenazic Jews were scattered throughout the smaller towns already in 1408, when Venice annexed the city.[10] Further south the Ashkenazim appeared a little later: in Mantua in the 15th century, in Ferrara toward the end of the 15th century and in Rome only in the beginning of the 16th century.[11] The case of Padua is of particular significance. It was the northernmost point of the movement of the Italiani from the neighborhood of Rome and there Ashkenazim and Italiani met. A document of 1432 lists the Jewish bankers in the city (seven in number) with their households and employees.[12] The majority of these were Italiani, and their surnames indicate that they were natives of various places in central Italy. The surnames of the Ashkenazim indicate that they were no recent arrivals from Germany but second generation Jews who adopted the names of the Italian cities in which they had previously lived, or at any rate men

[9] *Revue des études juives,* vol lxxix, 33.

[10] *Cf.* the important document published by Salo Baron in his study "Sikhsukh kehilot beverona," in *Sefer hayovel* for Samuel Kraus (Jerusalem 1937) p. 9.

[11] For Mantua see the study of Vittore Colorni in *Rivista Mensile di Israel,* vol. ix, p. 219; for Ferrara see Pesaro, A., *Memorie storiche sulla comunità israelitica ferrarese* (Ferrara 1878) p. 17. In 1511 we find in Rome Rabbi Israel (Isserlin) Ashkenazi, a disciple of Rabbi Judah Mentz, *cf.* Mortara, Marco, *Mazkeret hakhme italia* (Padua 1886) p. 5. Rabbi Israel Isserlin is mentioned in *Sefer hapesakim* (Venice 1519), in the Library of the Jewish Theological Seminary in New York, p. 23. *Cf.* also Rabbi Judah Mentz, *Sheelot uteshuvot,* par. 14. Elijah Levita came to Rome shortly afterward.

[12] Published by A. Ciscato, *Gli Ebrei in Padova (1300-1800)* (Padua 1901) p. 242 ff.

who after their arrival from Germany had lived in northern cities in Italy and thence moved to Padua.

The same conditions obtained in the western parts of northern Italy: Lombardy, Piedmont and Monferrato. Jews lived in groups in the cities and in very many small townships and villages, although not quite to the same extent as in the eastern areas.[13] There is much evidence that the predominant majority of these Jews were Ashkenazim.[14] There, too, an expansion southward was manifest. A classical example is the fact that when the Jews (Ashkenazim) were expelled from Lombardy they migrated to Modena, Reggio, Mantua and Piedmont.[15] A similar occurrence had taken place earlier, in 1510, when the main center of Ashkenazic Jews in Italy, mainly the one in Padua, had been dealt a severe blow in the war of the League of Cambray against Venice. At that time many Jews left Padua and its vicinity for Ferrara and Mantua. Some also returned to Germany.[16]

Considering all the aforementioned events, three phases can be distinguished in the Ashkenazic colonization of Italy. First, German Jews came and established a large number of small and larger communities. In the second phase a number of Ashkenazim left their new homes and migrated further south. The third phase consisted of a later and constant immigration from Germany, which no longer established new communities but strengthened the Ashkenazic element in the country and particularly in the cities with a mixed Jewish population. A typical example was Padua. First Italiani settled there. Later Ashkenazim arrived. In 1430 the Italiani were still the dominant group. Later on the Ashkenazim became the majority and toward the

[13] Cf. Glissenti, F., Gli Ebrei nel Bresciano (Brescia 1890) passim and Invernizzi, C., Gli Ebrei a Pavia (Pavia 1900). The materials on the Jews in Lombardy are not sufficiently known.

[14] Suffice it to mention the fact that precisely in the western parts the Ashkenazic ritual has persisted more stubbornly than in the eastern parts.

[15] See the report of the unknown chronicler who described himself as the magiha (corrector), printed at the end of the Emek habakha by Rabbi Joseph Hakohen (2d ed. Cracow 1892) p. 184 ff.

[16] Report of Elijah Capsali in Revue des études juives, vol. lxxix, 56.

end of the 15th century Padua became a thoroughly Ashkenazic community, even the outstanding Ashkenazic community in Italy (in Venice there was as yet no Jewish community). This development was undoubtedly the result of a continued immigration of new Ashkenazic elements.

The wave of Ashkenazic immigration proceeded southward and in the Po Valley it encountered the Italiani who had come from central Italy. This encounter undoubtedly weakened further Ashkenazic expansion to the south, for the further south we proceed the fewer Ashkenazim we meet. There were some in the more important cities like Ancona and Pesaro and some even reached as far as Naples and Brindisi.[17] But these were only individuals or small groups. In Ancona, for instance, the number of Ashkenazim was so small that they could not organize their own synagogue according to the Ashkenazic rite and worshipped in the synagogue of the Italiani.[18] In Rome the Ashkenazim did have their own synagogue up to 1557. At that time the Inquisition confiscated various Hebrew books there, and this incident sufficed to have the synagogue closed and never reopened again.[19]

These facts lead to a very important conclusion, which clearly illuminates the character of the Ashkenazic immigration to Italy. It was a colonizing immigration. Wherever it encountered cities and areas that had no Jews it established new communities. When it came to areas settled by Italiani it generally stopped. Only individuals and small groups proceeded farther south.

The question why German Jews migrated to Italy is a difficult one. The generally accepted opinion is that it was brought

[17] Rabbi Jacob Landau, author of *Haagur,* one of the most typical of Ashkenazic rabbis in Italy, lived in Naples where there were many Ashkenazic printers. On Naples see the introduction to the *Agur* and Bloch, J., *Hebrew printing in Naples* (New York 1942); on Brindisi, Vernale, E., *Gli Ebrei nel Salento* (Lecce 1933) p. 7.
[18] Compare the study of Rabbi Chaim Rosenberg in *Rivista Mensile di Israel,* vol x, 312.
[19] Berliner, A., *Censur und Confiskation herbäischer Bücher im Kirchenstaate* (Berlin 1890) p. 5.

on by the persecutions in Germany and that Italy was chosen because of its proximity.[20] This would be plausible if only Jews from southern Germany had come to Italy. But this was not the case. Rabbi Judah Mentz tells of Ashkenazic Jews in Rome who had relatives in Weissenburg, which is presumably in Alsace.[21] The Ashkenazim in Mantua came from Speyer, Erfurt, Nürnberg and Heidelberg.[22] Jews thus came to Italy from a large area of Germany (from Thuringia to Alsace) and from regions that were distant from the Italian border. The opinion that it was the proximity of Italy that attracted the Jewish immigration from Germany is not sufficient to explain the phenomenon.

It should also be borne in mind that Jewish immigration to Italy began precisely at the time when communication between Germany and Italy was drastically severed because of the final defeat of the Hohenstaufens. Nevertheless the immigration gained in intensity and Jews immigrated even from regions in Germany that were far from the Italian border. The conclusion is inescapable that we have here a combination of political, economic and social causes (neither should the possibility of social equality for the individual that the Renaissance proclaimed be overlooked) that must be thoroughly studied in order to furnish a satisfactory explanation for the phenomenon of the expansion of Ashkenazic Jewry southward. Mention should also be made here of the contemporary Ashkenazic immigration to Byzantium and the Balkan countries which has not yet been investigated at all.

It should, of course, not be forgotten that during the third phase of Ashkenazic immigration to Italy Polish Jewry was also in fairly close contact with Italian Jewry. Gumprecht of Szczebrzeszyn wrote his poems in Venice; Rabbi Mordecai Jaffe, author of the *Lebush,* was in Italy; Rabbi Jacob Soresina of

---

[20] A confirmation of this opinion can be found in the document about Verona published by Salo Baron, p. 9.

[21] *Sheelot uteshuvot,* par. 14.

[22] *Cf.* the above mentioned article by Vittore Colorni on the Jews of Mantua, p. 219.

Cracow settled in Castelazzo and later in Venice;[23] and members of the Katzenellenbogen family came from Venice to Poland.

No less complex is the problem of the number of Ashkenazic Jews who came to Italy and their proportion to the Italiani. We still know very little regarding this question. Rabbi Elijah Capsali's account[24] gives the impression that vast numbers of Ashkenazic Jews lived in northern Italy. This, however, is undoubtedly exaggerated, as is everything that he wrote concerning the Jewish center in northern Italy. He saw the destruction of this Jewish center at the time of the war of the League of Cambray, and everything that had existed before that appeared to him beautiful and significant. That the number of Ashkenazic Jews in Italy had not attained tens of thousands can also be seen from the report of Rabbi Simone Luzzatto in his famous work, *Discorso circa il stato degli Ebrei*. In his time (1637) there were in all of Italy about 30,000 Jews, and this was after the arrival of many Sephardim following the expulsion from Spain, after many marranos had reverted to Judaism in the 16th century and after the establishment of the Jewish community in Leghorn. While we cannot arrive at exact statistics of the number of Jews in Italy on the basis of the data on Jews in the various communities now available, it is clear that Rabbi Simone Luzzatto's estimate was not far afield.

How many Ashkenazim were there? Were they always few in number or was their number drastically reduced by the reemigration to Germany in 1510 described by Capsali? The only way to arrive at a partly satisfactory answer to this question is by painstakingly gathering all possible details and attempting to establish a total on that basis.

c

Upon their arrival in Italy the Ashkenazim came into contact with other Jewish "tribes." In the first place there were, as

[23] See the introduction to his *Seder hanikur* (Venice 1595). Soresina is a locality in Lombardy. We may assume that Jacob lived there after his arrival from Cracow and so acquired his surname.

[24] *Revue des études juives*, vol. lxxix.

stated above, the Italiani, the old established settlers, perhaps the first Jews in Europe. Then there was a large number of Provençal Jews, who were not in such close relations with the Ashkenazic Jews as were the Jews of northern France. Toward the end of the 15th century large groups of Spanish and Portuguese Jews began coming. (Individuals had come earlier, mainly to southern Italy.) Levantine Jews, too, were no rarity in Italy.

The Ashkenazim assumed a very prominent place, both numerically and in their influence upon the shaping of Jewish culture and public life. The question therefore arises: What were the relations between the Ashkenazic and the other Jews? It should be stated at the outset that the following principle seemed to obtain: Where the Ashkenazim were the predominant majority a degree of tension developed between them and the Italiani. Wherever there were three groups — Ashkenazim, Sephardim and Italiani — the Ashkenazim sided with the Italiani and formed with them a united front against the Sephardim.

Wherever the Ashkenazim were in the minority and not in a position to build their own synagogue they joined the synagogues of the Italiani and never those of the Sephardim. The same tendency existed among small groups of Italiani who lived in communities in which there was rivalry between large groups of Ashkenazim and Sephardim. The Italiani always aligned themselves with the Ashkenazim.

There were conflicts between Ashkenazim and Italiani and occasionally the Ashkenazim broke away from the Italiani and established their own synagogues. But the prevailing rule remained: the Ashkenazim and Italiani felt a closer mutual kinship with each other than with the Sephardim. A cogent illustration is found in Ferrara.[25] In 1492 the Italiani were in the majority in Ferrara and the Ashkenazim in the minority. Suddenly such a large group of Sephardim, exiles from Spain, arrived that the duke was compelled to enlarge the city to almost twice

---

[25] *Cf.* for the following the previously mentioned book of Abraham Pesaro, p. 16, 17, 19 and 31. For Ancona see the aforementioned study of Rosenberg.

its size. The Sephardim naturally established their own synagogue, but the Ashkenazim worshipped in the synagogue of the Italiani until 1532 when they built their own synagogue. In 1571 an earthquake destroyed Ferrara.[26] The Ashkenazim united again with the Italiani but the Sephardim retained their isolation.

Two years before the Ashkenazim completed their synagogue in Ferrara an Ashkenazic synagogue was established in Mantua (1530).[27] In those years, apparently, the Ashkenazic element in the Po Valley had gained in strength and had begun to think of independence. It was also natural that where the Italiani and Ashkenazim were about even in strength conflicts should arise concerning the synagogue ritual.[28] Occasionally the Italiani would utter a few unfriendly words at the expense of the Ashkenazim, as in the case of one of the Italiani who attempted to dissuade his friend from going to Ashkenazic Venice to study. He wrote: "I heard it said that the community in Venice is degenerate, with many people of unclean lips in the midst thereof, impudent and hating the Italiani . . . "[29] This, however, is mild in comparison with the explicit animosity that the great Sephardic chonicler, Joseph Hacohen, author of *Emek habakha,* displayed toward the Ashkenazim in Italy. In his opinion they had bad manners and were responsible for a series of disasters and expulsions that occurred in Italy at that time. He never failed to add to the name of a culprit that he was an Ashkenazi.[30] Great tension between Italiani and Ashkenazim was also manifest in cases of business or marital conflict in which one party was Ashkenazic and the other Italiani. In such instances the

[26] This is the earthquake so beautifully described by Azariah de' Rossi in the first chapter of his *Meor enayim.*

[27] Stern, M., *Urkundliche Beiträge über die Stellung der Päpste zu den Juden* (Kiel 1894) p. 74.

[28] A similar instance was told by Rabbi Azriel Dajjena in a reply from which S. Asaf has published an extract in his work *Sheelot uteshuvot rabi azriel dajjena* (1938) p. 26.

[29] Published by Alexander Marx in his study "Rabi Yosef ish Arli betor more verosh yeshiva besiena," in *Sefer hayovel likhvod Levi Ginsberg limlot lo shivim shana* (New York 1946) p. 299.

[30] Cf. *Revue des études juives,* vol xvi, 35; *Emek habakha,* p. 122, 141, 143 and 148.

Ashkenazic party sought the protection of Ashkenazic rabbis and the other party demanded the intercession of Italianic rabbis. Charges of partiality were often made. Rabbi Isaac ben Immanuel de Lattes, an Italianized rabbi of Provençal origin, twice accused the Ashkenazic rabbis of faithless dealing. He wrote: "For it is their custom (that is of the Ashkenazic rabbis in Italy) . . . to side with the Ashkenazim . . . whether they be right or wrong and to decide against the Italiani . . . "[31] But all these minor incidents cannot obscure the fact that in the meeting of the various Jewish groups in Italy the Ashkenazim and Italiani were close to each other and that the kinship of their spiritual interests was pronounced.

This fact led to partial assimilation of Ashkenazim into the Italiani community, although we believe that the number of Ashkenazim was not smaller than that of the Italiani. A contributing factor to the "victory" of the Italiani was the fact that they spoke Italian or a Judeo-Italian dialect, and the Ashkenazim, although they continued speaking Yiddish for a long time (see the following section), nevertheless had to learn Italian. Although Ashkenazic cursive script survived to the 18th century the Ashkenazim came increasingly to use Italian cursive script. The author of this study has published a historical manuscript, written in the republic of Venice by an Ashkenazic Jew in the last third of the 17th century. The text is in wonderful Ashkenazic cursive script but the introduction to the work was written in Italian cursive script.[32] This indicates the tendencies toward assimilation among the Ashkenazic Jews in Italy. The same development also took place among the Provençal Jews in Italy. But no such tendency was manifest among the Sephardim in Italy. Quite the contrary, in some cities, like Leghorn, they have even retained their Spanish idiom almost to this day. When the Sephardic Jew Gedaliah ibn Yahiya, author of *Shal-*

---

31 *Sheelot uteshuvot rabi Yitshak ben Imanuel Milates* (Vienna 1860) p. 149 ff. See also in the book *Ele hadevarim* (Mantua 1566) , the response about the divorse of Samuel of Perugia and Tamar Tamari of Venice.

32 *Hebrew Union College Annual,* vol. xxii.

shelet hakabala, transcribed a work of his father (second half of the 16th century) into Italian cursive script, he apologized and emphasized the fact that he did it to make the manuscript accessible also to non-Sephardic Jews in Italy.[33] This story would also indicate that all Jews in Italy used, or at least knew how to read, Italian cursive script.

Considering the problem of the relations between Ashkenazim and Sephardim in Italy, we come to the following conclusions: The Sephardim concentrated in places where the main element was Italiani (southern Italy, Tuscany, the middle-Adriatic ports and Ferrara), or where the Ashkenazim were in the minority (for example, Ancona and Ferrara), or represented by a few individuals only (various communities in Tuscany). If a struggle broke out there it was fought almost without the intervention of the Ashkenazim. In Verona, one of the outstanding Ashkenazic communities, a true conflict flared up between the Ashkenazim and the Sephardim. In Venice the administration of the Jewish community was in the hands of seven people, three Ashkenazim, three Sephardim and one Levantine.[34] Hence, the Ashkenazim were in the minority on the administrative board, although they constituted a large majority of the Jewish community. The reason for this disparity in representation derived from the system of election, which granted the franchise only to those members paying a minimum tax to the community. Since the Sephardim had a wealthier membership than the Ashkenazim their influence on the administration of the community was correspondingly larger.

It is therefore quite understandable that when Sephardim began to settle in the completely Ashkenazic Verona the leaders of the community took measures to prevent the Sephardim from gaining control over the community. Even when the community was forced to agree to a separate *minyan* (conventicle) for some of the Sephardic Jews it enumerated the names of those permitted to worship there, while the other Sephardim had to

---

[33] *Kiryat sefer,* vol. iii, 237.
[34] Roth, Cecil, *Venice* (Phila. 1930) p. 129.

continue to worship in the (Ashkenazic) main synagogue. When the Sephardim came to constitute 25 percent of the taxpayers in the community and began a fight for equality they gained their end only with the aid of the Venetian government, where the Sephardim of the capital had considerable influence.[35]

d

What was the character of the inner life of the Ashkenazic Jews in Italy? To what extent did they retain their Ashkenazic way of life and to what extent was this way of life modified in the new environment? The first problem that arises is that of language. To what extent and how long did the Ashkenazic Jews in Italy continue to speak Yiddish? There is no doubt that at the time of the flowering of the Ashkenazic immigration, up to the time of the war of the League of Cambray and shortly thereafter, Yiddish was the main language of the Ashkenazic Jews in Italy. Furthermore, Yiddish even influenced the Hebrew in northern Italy, just as it had influenced the Hebrew of medieval Germany and Poland. When Rabbi Elijah Capsali, a guest from Crete, wishes to indicate that the Talmudic discourses in the yeshiva of Padua were delivered by heart, he uses the Hebrew term *"mibahuz"* (from without), a mechanical translation of the Yiddish *"fun oysnveynik,"* instead of the regular Hebrew term *"baal pe."*[36]

Instructive is also the following fact. The literature in the Italo-Judean dialect consisted almost exclusively of liturgical or Biblical works: prayer books and individual prayers.[37] The literature in Yiddish included religious works of a non-liturgical character as well as *belles-lettres.* The conclusion is clear. The Italiani, who spoke Italian or one of the Judeo-Italian dialects, satisfied their desire for general reading in Italian. They had to translate the Hebrew prayers into Judeo-Italian for the women or for those men who did not understand Hebrew. The situation

[35] See the documents published by Isaiah Sonne in "Avne binyan letoledot hayehudim beverona," in *Zion,* vol. iii (1929) 143 ff.
[36] *Revue des études juives,* vol. lxxix, p. 34.
[37] A list of this literature is to be found in *Revue des études juives,* vol. lxxx, 63 ff.

was quite different among the Ashkenazim. Some of them did not know enough Italian to read it. Such persons needed a non-liturgical religious as well as secular literature in Yiddish. We may, therefore, infer that Ashkenazic Jews spoke Yiddish and also understood Italian. It may also be assumed that in a place where various Jewish groups came together Hebrew occupied a definite place as a medium of communication. The aforementioned Rabbi Elijah Capsali tells that when the French scholar, Rabbi Hayim Carmi, arrived in Padua and discoursed on Talmudic problems with Rabbi Judah Mentz the language they used was Hebrew.[38] It should also be noted that the Ashkenazim adjusted their pronunciation of Hebrew to that of the Italiani — an additional proof of their tendency to assimilation with the latter. The Sephardim were far more independent in this respect. In Tuscany the Sephardim still pronounce the Hebrew letter *zadi* (ts) as "s."

Yiddish was spoken in Italy well into the 17th century. In 1595, a Polish immigrant from Cracow, Rabbi Jacob Soresina, published in Venice a manual for *menakrim*,[39] in which the appropriate terminology is given in Yiddish, Italian and Judeo-Spanish. He wanted, he said, that his handbook should be used by all Jews in Italy, "each city and community according to its language."[40] This would indicate that Yiddish was still spoken in Italy. That Yiddish was understood in Italy thirty years later can be seen from the fact that Rabbi Jacob Halpern used many Yiddish words in his book, *Nahalat yaakov* (Padua 1623).[41] Most important: Rabbi Judah Leon Modena stated expressly in his *Historia dei riti ebraici,* which contains a description of Jewish life in Italy, that the Ashkenazic Jews in Italy spoke "German" (Yiddish).[42]

[38] *Op. cit.,* p. 35.
[39] Porgers, who make the meat ritually fit for consumption by excision of the veins and fat.
[40] See the introduction to Rabbi Jacob Soresina's *Seder hanikur* (Venice (1595).
[41] Paragraph 1: "Gar sheanu korim belashon ashkenaz takh"; The roof, which in Yiddish we call *takh;* par. 42: "helzlekh."
[42] First edition Venice 1638. *Cf.* Part II, ch. i, par. 1.

171

During the latter half of the 17th century nothing more is heard of Yiddish in the literature of the period. A few years after Judah Leon Modena made the above statement, the Yiddish language in Italy began to decline rapidly. Even the wave of Polish immigrants that arrived as a result of the massacres of 1648 could not bring about its revival. There is no doubt that although Yiddish was still understood and spoken it was progressively falling into oblivion. This process it seems, began in the middle of the 16th century. A letter from that period which discusses the problem of engaging a teacher, suggests that "you stipulate with your honorable teacher, may his Rock and Redeemer guard him, to teach the written law in the language of Ashkenaz (Yiddish) and the oral law in Italian . . . "[43] From this we may conclude that children at home still spoke Yiddish and that they were taught the Pentateuch in Yiddish. When they grew older and began the study of the Talmud, the language of instruction was Italian. A hint at the decline of Yiddish may possibly also be found in the epilogue of Abraham Bassevi to the Yiddish romance, *Paris un Viene,* stating that some people may find the book difficult to read, but that with a little practice, they will understand it.[44] Mention should also be made of the fact that the Ashkenazim in Italy introduced into the Yiddish language Italian words that became so thoroughly a part of the Yiddish language that only linguists are able to recognize their origin.[45]

We have already indicated that because of the presence of Ashkenazic Jews Hebrew was used in Italy as the medium of communication between Jews of various origin. We should add that this apparently was also the reason why there were no official proclamations in Yiddish in such distinctly Ashkenazic communities as Venice (in its early period) and Verona, as was

[43] *Revue des études juives,* vol. cv, 56.
[44] The quotation is found in Max Erik's *Geshikhte fun der yidisher literatur fun di eltste tsaytn biz der haskole-thufe* (Warsaw 1928) p. 437 ff.
[45] *Cf.* Weinreich, Max *Bilder fun der yidisher literatur-geshikhte* (Vilna 1928) p. 143 in the paragraph about "A maase midantsik" and *Shtaplen* (Berlin 1923) p. 80.

the case in the communities of Poland and Germany. Technical terms, however, were expressed in Yiddish, as for example in the *pragmatica* of Venice of 1543[46] or in the aforementioned *Seder hanikur* of Rabbi Jacob Soresina, which confirms the fact that the porging terminology that was used in Venice was Yiddish. Another example is the term *yortsayt,* which was taken over from Yiddish speaking Jews, and is used throughout Italy to this day.

The Ashkenazim clung tenaciously to the Ashkenazic form of their names. Names like Mendlin and Yoslin (similarly women's names) abound in the responsa of Rabbi Joseph Colon, written in the second half of the 15th century, and in the responsa of Rabbi Judah Mentz. Similarly in the literature that came into being as a result of the controversy over the ritual bathhouse in Rovigo (at the end of the 16th century) there are many purely Ashkenazic forms of names.[47] In the chronicle *Sipur hatsarot sheavru beitaliya,* written in the last third of the 17th century, occurs the name "Aaron called Zelikman." This indicates that even then the Yiddish every-day name usurped the place of the "real" name. A more impressive example is found in the name "Mordecai called Gumprecht of Bassan" (born about 1540).[48] Although at that time every Mordecai in Italy was called Angelo, and no Hebrew name was so consistently changed to an Italian name as Mordecai to Angelo, an Ashkenazic Jew nevertheless retained the well-known combination Mordecai-Gumprecht.

All this refers merely to given names. The surnames of the Ashkenazic Jews rapidly became Italianized. Most Jews in Germany had no surnames and were called by their place of domicile. The Ashkenazic Jews followed the same procedure in

---

[46] See Sonne, Isaiah, *Avne binyan letoledot hayehudim beverona,* part 2, *Kovets al yad* (new series), vol. iii, p. 159 (the word *kimpetorins* lying-in women). Pragmaticas in Italy were sumptuary laws of the communities regulating extravagance in all its forms.

[47] See the appropriate chapter in the second part of L. Blau's *Leo Modena's Briefe und Schriftstücke* (Budapest 1906).

[48] *Mashbit milhamot* (Venice 1606) 896 b.

Italy, hence their surnames showed so few traces of Ashkenazic origin. It may safely be taken for granted, however, that every Italian Jew whose surname derives from a north Italian city is of Ashkenazic descent.[49] Of Ashkenazic origin too are names like Tedeschi, which means Ashkenazi, and the popular Ashkenazic surnames Morpurgo and Ottolenghi. These families came originally from Marburg and Ettlingen.[50]

Apart from language and names, the inner life of the Ashkenazim became rapidly adjusted to their new surroundings. This was due to their close relations to Renaissance life which they encountered in Italy. This important problem, however, shall be discussed separately later on.

It is as yet difficult to determine to what extent the main institutions of Jewish social life, the *kehila* and the rabbinate, retained their Ashkenazic form in Italy. As yet little is known regarding the general organization of the Jewish communities in Italy. It is certain, however, that at the time the immigration of the Ashkenazim began the *kehila* in Italy was not a powerful institution. The individualist inclinations of Renaissance man did not permit the establishment of a *kehila* that would restrict him too much. A second element in the weakening of the *kehila* was the fact that Italian Jewry was no longer homogeneous and the various groups displayed particularistic tendencies. Later on, when the Jews were forced into ghettos, the *kehila* came naturally to assume greater importance. One of the reasons why the *kehila* in Venice was so strong was the fact that the ghetto had been introduced there in 1516, fifty years prior to the movement to establish ghettos in the other provinces of Italy.

What was the role of the Ashkenazim in the weakening of the *kehila*? To what degree did they "take advantage" of the situation in order to retain their own *kehila* traditions in those places where they lived by themselves? How did they affect the

---

[49] Surnames of Jews in present day Italy were compiled by Samuel Scherf in *I cognomini degli Ebrei d'Italia* (Florence 1925).

[50] A monograph on the Morpurgo family was written by Edgardo Morpurgo, *La famiglia Morpurgo di Gradisca* (Padua 1909). In this monograph we find people named Marpurg who resided in Germany.

organizational structure of the *kehila* in places with a mixed Jewish population? Answers to all these questions cannot be given before source materials are gathered. Practically none of the minute-books of the Italian communities or communal associations have as yet been published. The only thing that can be said at present is this: Ashkenazic Jewry in Italy never created the kind of *kehila* that it created in Poland. The *kehila* in Poland, although dominated by aristocratic groups, was nevertheless based on the Jewish masses. It was originally established for the benefit of the religious and social interests of the masses. The Italian *kehila* in the newly colonized places was very frequently an institution established by one family for its religious needs. It required the establishment of the ghetto to give the forces that fought for the democratization of the community a chance for victory.[51]

Although it is as yet impossible to come to definite conclusions on the general character of the rabbinate in Italy, and particularly on the Ashkenazic rabbinate, it can be said with certainty that the rabbinical organization, *"hayeshiva hakelalit,"* which was characteristic of large areas in Italy, was largely the result of Ashkenazic influence. The Ashkenazim had many more rabbinic scholars than the Italiani and they sought to express their opinions on matters of practical religious life. The solution was the creation of the *yeshiva kelalit,* in which were represented all scholars who had attained a certain degree of rabbinical authorization (that is they had received the title *morenu* [teacher], *haver derav* [associate teacher], and the like), and where the functioning rabbi or rabbis were "first among their peers." The form of the *yeshiva kelalit* as a rabbinical institution was ideal for a country with a heterogeneous Jewish population. Here Italiani could sit next to Sephardim and Levantines, and since the oldest member was always the chairman of the group his selection did not lead to friction between majority and minority groups. Notwithstanding the existence of a collective

[51] *Cf.* my study "Letoledot kehilat rovigo (levaayat hithavut hakehilot beitaliya) ," in *Sinai,* vol. x.

rabbinate things were not always smooth-running. In Mantua there was a separate Ashkenazic rabbinate. In a book of rabbinic decisions we read: "We members of the Ashkenazic yeshiva in Mantua . . . " The question involved referred to a decision on a practical matter and was not just an academic discussion. This means that the "Ashkenazic yeshiva" was in Ashkenazic rabbinical court in a city of mixed Jewish population.

Of special interest were the conditions in the *yeshiva kelalit* in Venice. There were tendencies to give the decisive voice to the Ashkenazic members. One of the Italiani scholars, Rabbi Judah Saltaro, remonstrating against this practice,[52] wrote: "Far be it from you to say, as it seems to you, that leadership is appropriate to the . . . Ashkenazim, and that the Lord has kept back from honor the Italiani, the Levantines and the Westerners . . . "[53] Several years later, however, we find the signature of a Levantine scholar in first place on a rabbinical decree.[54]

We cannot conclude our comments on the organization of the rabbinate without mentioning the prominent role occupied by the district rabbi in the regional organization of the Jewish communities in the various provinces. There were many factors that gave rise to the district rabbinate. As far as the Ashkenazic areas in Italy were concerned it must be stressed that the institution was not intended to provide a structure for a centralized organization. The institution of district rabbi arose from the first needs of religious life, when the community was not yet sufficiently organized and the few Jews who had just arrived from across the Alps and had settled in small towns had to bring their religious problems to the rabbi in the neighboring town. That rabbi automatically became the district rabbi.[55]

---

52 *Mikve yisrael* (Venice 1607) p. 9a.
53 The Sephardim were called *"ponentini,"* who came to Italy from the west, from the Italian *ponente*, which means west.
54 Solomon de Rossi, *Hashirim asher lishlomo* (new edition) (Frankfurt a.M. 1925) p. 6a.
55 This would explain the fact that not only rabbis sent questions to Rabbi Joseph Colon but also Jewish laymen and entire communities. A similar condition, although on a smaller scale, is found in the responsa of Rabbi Judah Mentz.

The arrival of the Ashkenazim in Italy led to a new flowering of Jewish scholarship. Northern Italy was covered with a large network of *yeshivoth* during the years up to the war of the League of Cambray.[56] In this respect the impact of the Ashkenazim upon the Italiani was very great. Even before this time Italian Jewish scholarship had been strongly under the influence of the classical Ashkenazic *halakha* (the Tosafists, Rabbi Meir of Rothenburg and others). Now the Italiani took advantage of the opportunity and studied assiduously in the schools of the Ashkenazim. A prominent representative of the Italiani like Rabbi Judah son of Yehiel, known as Messer Leon, himself head of a famous yeshiva, sent his son to study in the Ashkenazic yeshiva in Padua.[57] Padua was a sort of Italian Volozhin. Its yeshiva existed for over a hundred years and it was headed by a series of scholars who represented the specifically Ashkenazic tradition of Jewish learning. Owing to the influence of the Padua yeshiva the study of the *Tosafoth,* and the *pilpul* spread extensively in Italy. To be sure, the Italiani too had yeshivoth but they devoted considerable time to secular studies and to the art of Hebrew espistolography. Jewish studies, therefore were limited. In Padua the only subject was *Torah,* just as in the German and the Polish yeshivoth.

The 16th century brought a change in the whole situation. The Ashkenazic center of learning in Italy was partly destroyed in the war of the League of Cambray and never recovered its former glory. On the other hand, the urge to Jewish studies became intensified among the Italiani, particularly in the second half of the century, when there was a marked rise in religious feeling among the Italian Jews. The picture changed even more during the 17th century, when the Sephardim established a number of important yeshivoth and the Levantine Jews strengthened the desire for the study of the Torah and the Kabala. The Ashkenazim no longer enjoyed their previous monopoly on the

[56] See the description by Elijah Capsali, p. 33.
[57] This and the following topic are discussed in detail in the author's book *Jewish Life in Renaissance Italy.*

study of Torah, although Padua and other Ashkenazic communities continued to be important centers of study.

Several of the most important Ashkenazic works on Halakha were written in Italy. These were *Leket yosher, Agur,* the *Responsa* of Rabbi Judah Mentz and of Rabbi Meir of Padua. In this field as in the field of the Yiddish language the Ashkenazic Jews in Italy made a substantial contribution to Ashkenazic culture.

e

It was no mere accident that the Ashkenazic immigration to Italy coincided so plainly with the Italian Renaissance. We have briefly indicated above that one of the factors that attracted German Jews to Italy was the prospect of social equality opened for them in Renaissance Italy.

The Renaissance was, as is well known, a movement of the upper social classes. But it also possessed an immanent democratic sense and admitted without hesitation people that fitted into its framework even though they were without aristocratic tradition. To this latter category belonged the Jews. Jews who were either wealthy or talented found many doors open to them in Renaissance Italy and they were allowed to participate in the cultural life of the country.

From this standpoint the Ashkenazic Jews were a very suitable element for Renaissance society. Their immigration was associated with the establishment of banks, and huge wealth was therefore concentrated in their hands. Rabbi Elijah Capsali, the most important source on the Ashkenazim in northern Italy up to 1510, constantly emphasized their enormous wealth.[58] Asher Meshulam (Anselmo del Banco), the famous leader of the Ashkenazim and courageous opponent of the establishment of a ghetto in Venice, was considered by his contemporaries the richest Jew in Italy.[59] The path to the culture of the Renaissance

[58] *Op. cit.*, p. 28. See also p. 36 for details on the family of Anselmo del Banco. Details on the wealth of this family are also found in the work of the famous diarist Marino Sanuto, *Diarii* (Venice 1879-1903) vol. lv, p. 30.
[59] *Sefer hapesakim* (Venice 1519) p. 12b.

was therefore open to many of them.

The Ashkenazic Jews utilized this opportunity on a very large scale and began avidly to enjoy those higher forms of life which had been barred to them in their previous home. The approach to the culture of the Renaissance among the Ashkenazim, however, was different from that of the Italiani.[60] The Italiani were firmly established in Italy, the seat of classical Roman culture. For them the culture of the Renaissance, with its rediscovery of classical antiquity, was a natural continuation of a culture that was present before their eyes. The dominant tendency among them was a longing for the culture of classical antiquity — the Graeco-Roman and Jewish cultures. They carried on intensive scientific studies and from their ranks came most of the Jewish humanists. They likewise exhibited the general Renaissance aspiration to achieve perfection.

The attitude of the Ashkenazic Jews was different. They came from an entirely different culture and from a milieu in which Jews were barred not only from participation in the general culture but also from all contact with the non-Jewish population. They never produced any great Latin scholars, eminent physicians, copyists of old manuscripts, poets or humanists. The Ashkenazim seized upon the external aspects of Renaissance culture — the richer forms of life, the striving for external splendor. They, more than the other Jews, produced the type of "Renaissance man," the strong individual, the fighter that goes on indefatigably to his goal and is full of stormy passions.

A few facts may serve to illustrate this difference. One of the very wealthy Ashkenazic Jews, Joseph Castelfranco of Brescia, had a copy of the Talmud made for him on parchment and in such exquisite fashion that the work cost him a fortune. Naphtali Hirz Wertheim of Padua started to build a private synagogue in his house with walls covered with gold. He was denounced and the authorities ordered the construction stopped. They did not want the synagogue to be too stately. He succeeded by other

[60] See the report of my paper read at the first Judaistic Congress in Jerusalem, in the summer of 1947, published in *Siani*, vol. xi (1948) 45.

means, however, in making his synagogue ornate. The account of the funeral of Rabbi Judah Mentz in Padua abounds in descriptions of external splendor. Nowhere in the Jewish world prior to 1800 was there such a funeral for a rabbi or a head of a yeshiva. The description is more reminiscent of the funerals of princes.[61]

We find the most striking examples of Renaissance men among the Ashkenazim. We have a detailed description of the banker Jonathan Finzi of Reggio which reveals him in all sorts of situations: how he conducted his business, how he lived, fought and carried on intrigue against his opponents.[62] The total picture is one like that of the famous "passionate" men of the Renaissance. Another militant figure was Rabbi Abraham Mentz, successor to his father, Rabbi Judah Mentz, as rabbi in Padua.[63] Of similar mettle was the aforementioned Naphtali Hirz Wertheim, who waged a fight against Rabbi Judah Mentz because he was refused permission to hang a curtain with his coat of arms in the Synagogue. Rabbi Meir of Padua tells that Naphtali Hirz Wertheim, "because of his great wealth and power" disregarded the rabbi "and forcibly put it (the curtain) up in the synagogue. Whereupon the old man (Rabbi Judah Mentz) left the synagogue angrily, and very many quarrels ensued on account of this . . . "[64] A similar type was Asher Meshullam. He had more personality and his passions found expression in a political struggle against the establishment of the ghetto in Venice. To his last day, sixteen years after the establishment of the ghetto, he did not relent in his fight for the right of unrestricted settlement of the Jews in the entire city.[65]

We shall not dwell at length upon the relationship between

[61] Cf. the stories of Elijah Capsali, op cit.

[62] Balletti, A., Gli Ebrei e gli Estensi (Modena 1913) p. 20 ff.

[63] See the Sefer hapesakim (Venice 1519) and the study by Alexander Marx, "A Jewish Cause Celebre," in Abhandlungen zur Erinnerung an Zebi Perez Chajes (Vienna 1932) p. 149 ff. and reprinted in Studies in Jewish History and Booklore (New York 1944) p. 107 ff.

[64] Cf. Sheelot uteshuvot avkat rokhel, par. 65.

[65] Roth, Venice, p. 45.

the Jewish and non-Jewish world, which is one of the most important points in characterizing Jewish Renaissance society in Italy. In this as in many other respects the Jewish capital was neither Rome nor Florence but Ashkenazic Venice. It was primarily against Venice that the Jewish leaders spoke in their anxiety lest the people become too deeply immersed in the alien culture. We have many reports on this point. Here we wish merely to cite the outspoken opinion of Rabbi Azriel Dajjena, one of the great rabbis of the period and himself a man of the Renaissance. He wrote:

> I have heard of no city that was as dedicated to the laws of the nations and the courts of the nations as Venice, a city famed for wealth, whose leaders are the princes of the holy people, which were of old, men of renown, whose merchants are the honorable of the earth. How can these men tolerate such sins . . . [66]

We have stated already that there were fewer humanists among the Ashkenazim than among the Italiani. But the Ashkenazim too had their humanists. Suffice it to mention the name of Elijah Levita. He was a humanist through and through, and there was not a trait in his entire mode of life or work that did not fit the concept of a humanist. That he was not an isolated case can be seen from the lampoons he wrote against his enemies.[67]

The name of Elijah Levita is also linked with the Yiddish literature of northern Italy. This is not the place for a description of this literature. One point, however, must be emphasized, namely, the close connection between this literature and the Renaissance. The *Bovo bukh* and *Paris un Viene* are versions of Italian romances. Elijah Levita not only borrowed the materials for his romances from the Italian epic of chivalry but also treated it in the manner of Ariosto and introduced into Yiddish literature the literary form of the romance in stanzas. He thereby

[66] I have this quotation in my notes but unfortunately I do not have any indication as to its source.

[67] For instance the poem "Hamavdil," published by N. Shtif in *Tsaytshrift*, vol. i (1926) 150.

established contact between the Yiddish readers in the Ashkenazic sphere and the culture of the Renaissance, a fact that is of
great general moment in the history of Jewish culture.

f

What became of Ashkenazic Jewry in Italy? The answer
is quite clear. In the course of the centuries all elements of the
specific Ashkenazic culture disappeared completely. Only the
Ashkenazic order of prayer remained, which is still used in
several communities. Even this ritual, however, did not succeed
in maintaining itself everywhere. Venice, for instance, which
was the capital of Ashkenazic Jewry in Italy, today uses the
Sephardic ritual.

How and when did all this happen, is a much more difficult
question. Surveying Jewish life and the changes it underwent in
Italy in the past two hundred and fifty years, the impression is
gained that there was a constant attenuation of the Ashkenazic
elements in the life of the Ashkenazim in Italy. We have pointed
to the assimilationist tendencies and their causes. The main
cause was undoubtedly the severance of direct contact between
the Ashkenazic Jews in Italy and their brethren in Germany.
The break, of course, was not sudden. Güdemann was of the
opinion that the expulsion of the Jews from Carinthia and Styria
in 1496 was the cause of the break.[68] It is possible that this
expulsion did have some effect but it is by far not enough to
account for it entirely. It seems to me that an important factor
in the break with Germany was the war between the League of
Cambray and the republic of Venice. In the first place, as indicated above, many Jews returned to Germany because of the
catastrophe. This had a discouraging effect upon subsequent
immigration to Italy. Moreover, Ashkenazic Jews, because of
their association with Germany, were accused of aiding the
German assailants. This alone was sufficient cause for the Jews
in Italy to review critically their relations with the Jews in

---

[68] *Hatora vehahayim,* vol. iii, p. 200.

Germany. To this negative cause was added a positive motive. As a result of the invasion of the armies of the League of Cambray the Jewish community of Venice was established. With the establishment of this large community there came the characteristic loyalty and love of the Jews for the republic of Venice, so frequently expressed in the writings of Leon Modena, Rabbi Simone Luzzatto, David de'Pomi and others. It is therefore understandable that Jews ceased to be German Jews and began to become Venetian Jews. When, in the course of time, the great wave of immigration also declined, the link between Ashkenazic Italy and Germany was severed.

Among the results of the break with the original Ashkenazic Jewry were the transition to the use of Italian (certainly not at once, but gradually), the abandonment of the Ashkenazic pronunciation of Hebrew and, certainly, the obsolescence of a number of customs and forms of social life. All these phenomena still require more thorough study.

At present there are only about a score of Jewish communities in Italy that use the Ashkenazic ritual.[69] But the impact of Ashkenazic immigration to Italy was historically of the greatest significance. The Ashkenazic element fulfilled its historic mission, saving Italian Jewry from the danger of extinction several hundred years ago and imparting to it the character of an ethnically composite Jewish community. In this ethnic heterogeneity possibly lies the secret of the great cultural and social accomplishments of historic Italian Jewry.

[69] According to the calendar, *Lunario israelitico,* published by Servi in 1928, eighteen communities use the Ashkenazic ritual, sixteen of which are in northern Italy, mainly small places in Piedmont and Monferrato. This calendar is not a reliable source. Nevertheless a general impression may be gained from its data. The largest community that has retained the Ashkenazic ritual is Verona. Venice uses now the Sephardic ritual and Padua the Italiani.

VII

THE KNOWLEDGE OF ANTIQUITY AMONG THE ITALIAN JEWS OF THE RENAISSANCE

Based on a lecture delivered at the Annual Meeting of the American Academy for Jewish Research in 1948, and published in its Proceedings, vol. 18, pp. 291-299.

a

Jacob Burckhardt, the greatest historian of the Italian Renaissance, maintained that the rediscovery of the world and man together with the reproduction of the classical world, form the principal contents of the culture of the Renaissance. I had the occasion elsewhere[1] to speak of the Jews' inclination towards the culture of the Renaissance in general. This inclination becomes obvious as soon as one examines the attitude of the Jews to the various spheres of this culture.

One can also find in the sources proof of the interest of the Jews in the ancient Greek and Roman world. This interest manifested itself in a positive attitude to the cultural tradition of the ancient world and in an effort to acquire the knowledge of this world. While the Italian Jews maintained quite a definitely critical attitude towards the religious tradition of Christianity, they displayed a pronounced interest in the mythological tradition of the pre-Christian world. They strove to acquire the knowledge of both classical languages, Latin and

[1] In my lecture at the First World Congress of Jewish Studies which was held in Jerusalem. The context of the lecture was published in *"Sinai"* vol. 2 p. 44 f.

Greek, and to master the Greek and Latin literatures, the history of Antiquity, its religion, mythology, and way of life.

The interest in the ancient world and its culture is evident in the Hebrew literature of the period. The famous work of Abraham Portaleone, *Shiltei Hagiborim*, furnishes us with detailed descriptions that yield a truly clear picture of the ancient world and its way of life. Besides, one must not forget that this work — as the author assures us[2] — was an act of penance and it aimed to replace his secular studies. Nevertheless, the writer devoted a considerable part of the book to a description of the classical world. Obviously, he thought that a Jew who is repenting does not need to refrain from pursuing classical studies.

A further confirmation of the above-mentioned phenomenon can be found in the following fact: When Leon Modena translated the Christian ethical book *Fior di virtu* into Hebrew, he replaced all passages mentioning the dogmas or saints of Christianity with passages from rabbinic literature, but retained all the legends and tales about Greece and Rome.[3] The Jews of the sixteenth century evinced a great interest in the *Dialoghi di amore* of Judah Abravanel because it offered explanations of many Greek legends.[4] It is beyond doubt that Gedaliah ibn Yahya included in the *Shalsheleth Hakabbalah*[5] the chapter which describes ancient idolatry and the detailed information about the ancient world and its history for the purpose of satisfying a deep curiosity about these subjects among the Jews.

We have seen that the interest in the ancient world brought about a strong desire to learn Greek and Latin. Azariah de' Rossi sincerely regretted that he did not know Greek sufficiently.[6] In general, the sources to the history of Jewish education in

---

[2] See the introduction to *Shiltei Hagiborim*.

[3] The Hebrew name of the booklet is *Tsemah Tsadiq*. It appeared in Venice in the year 1600.

[4] Cf. the study of I. Sonne in *"Tarbiz"* vol. 3 p. 287 f.

[5] *Shalsheleth Hakabbalah*, Lwow 1862 p. 140 f.

[6] *Meor Ainayim* (ed. Ben-Jacob) p. 2.

Italy in the sixteenth century[7] indicate that the study of Latin was a subject which one could not omit. It was thus in the spirit of the time when Rabbi Obadiah of Bertinoro stated that Greek is the most beautiful of all the European languages.[8] The immigrant Don Isaac Abravanel was also a great admirer of the classical world. In his commentary on the Pentateuch he had many words of praise for the Greeks and Romans. He admired their political wisdom, their heroism, and even their physical appearance.[9]

b

Although the Jews of the Renaissance were equally interested in both classical languages, the knowledge of Latin was far more widespread than that of Greek. Various factors were responsible for this. To begin with, Jews who spoke Italian found it much easier to learn Latin than Greek. In addition, the knowledge of the Latin language had a practical value in everyday life. The Renaissance had developed an excellent epistolography and rhetoric in Latin in addition to the Neo-Latin literature. Everyone who desired to let his son have a good education was obliged to let him acquire a thorough knowledge of that language. Thus we find among the Italian Jews men who were acquainted with Latin, from the beginning of the Renaissance until its end.[10] They acquired the knowledge

[7] Cf., for example, the collection of letters related to education, published by S. Assaf in vol. 4 of his *Meqoroth Letoldoth Hahinukh* p. 20 f. and the material published by Alexander Marx in his study on Joseph Arli in the Hebrew Jubilee Volume in honor of Louis Ginzberg. The curriculum of the Jewish University which David Provenzali intended to found, includes also, naturally, the study of the Latin language. Cf. the text of the curriculum *"Halevanon"* vol. 8 (1868).

[8] Tractate *Sheqalim* chapter 3, mishna 2. References concerning the positive attitude of the Rabbis to the languages of the *benei Japheth* may be found in various sources, as for example *Genesis Rabbah* chapter 36 (ed. Leipzig p. 64) and *Deuteronomy Rabbah,* at the beginning of chapter 1.

[9] The Commentary on the Pentateuch, ed. Hanau 1710 folio 40 p. 1.

[10] As for example Judah Romano, the friend of Giannozzo Manetti, the Florentine scholar Emanuel (see U. Cassuto, *Gli Ebrei a Firenze nell'eta' del Rinascimento,* p. 275) Elijah del Medigo, Azariah de' Rossi, Jacob Mantino, Joseph Zarfatti, Judah Moscato, Abraham Portaleone and others.

of the language either by studying with private tutors or in yeshivoth. Had we compiled a list of Italian Jews of the Renaissance who knew the Latin language, it would have to include many authors, rabbis, and scholars. The historian of the Jews in South Italy, Nicola Ferorelli, has pointed out[11] the extensive knowledge of Latin among the Jews in the Kingdom of Naples. The participation of South-Italian Jewish scholars in the major effort of translating scientific works from Arabic into Latin was equally impressive. This effort began in the late Middle Ages and continued all through the period of the Renaissance.[12] At the same time, there appeared in Italy translations from Hebrew into Latin and vice versa.[13] We also find a certain number of Jewish authors who wrote original works in Latin prose.[14]

While most of the scholars had merely a literary knowledge of Latin, some were able to make practical use of it as a spoken language. The physician David de' Pomis, author of the trilingual Hebrew-Latin-Italian dictionary *Tsemah David,* delivered a long speech in Latin in the presence of Pope Pius IV and the cardinals.[15] Avtalyon de Modena also had an opportunity to address in Latin Pope Gregory XIII. In his speech which lasted two hours Avtalyon pleaded for permission to print the Talmud.[16] It should also be noted that in the middle of the sixteenth

[11] Cf. N. Ferorelli, *Gli Ebri nell' Italia meridionale,* Turin 1915, p. 102, and especially note 8.

[12] Cf. R. Strauss, *Die Juden im Koenigreich Sizilien,* Heidelberg 1910, p. 91 about the unique position of the Jewish translators at the court of Emperor Frederic II of Sicily.

[13] Cf. M. Steinschneider, *Allgemeine Einleitung in die juedische Litteratur des Mittelalters,* p. 92. Steinschneider wrote that the translations from Hebrew to Latin appeared in Italy until the middle of the 16th century. In fact, however, we find them also later. Moses Alatini, for example, translated a number of books, from Hebrew to Latin at the turn of the 17th century. See the Jubilee Volume in honor of Abraham Berliner, p. 272. Among the other translators may be mentioned Calonymos ben Calonymos, Jacob Mantino and Azariah de' Rossi.

[14] As for example David de' Pomis and Abraham Portaleone who wrote several Latin books, or Lazzaro da Viterbo who wrote a lengthy Latin tractate, in which he wished to prove to Cardinal Sirleto that the text of the Bible in the hands of the Jews is genuine. See *JQR,* vol. 7, p. 283.

[15] See his autobiographical introduction to the *Tsemah David,* also available in Nepi Ghirondi, *Toledoth Gedolei Israel.* Cf. ibid. p. 89.

[16] Cf. the autobiography of Leon Modena, *Hayei Yehudah,* Kiew 1911, p. 12.

century the former Portuguese Marrano Didacus Pyrrus, who was living in Ancona as a Jew, was one of the most famous Neo-Latin poets.[17]

Some of the scholars who knew Latin also knew Greek,[18] but rarely reached in it the same degree of perfection as in Latin. This can be seen from the fact that the number of Jewish translators from Greek into Hebrew was far smaller than that of those who rendered from Latin into Hebrew. We have also seen how Azariah de' Rossi deplored his poor knowledge of Greek.[19]

Of course, there were exceptions. For example, Abraham Yagel Gallico, who lived at the end of the period, was able to translate a chapter of IV Ezra from Greek into Hebrew.[20] But Abraham Portaleone surpassed everyone in his knowledge of Greek and in his efforts to encourage its study. He knew that there are five dialects in the Greek language, and he was even able to classify the ancient Greek poets according to the dialects in which they wrote. He printed in his work the Greek alphabet, and he stated clearly that he was doing it to make it possible for the Jews to learn the language. He went as far as to advise them to buy Christian prayerbooks and to use the Greek parts for the study of the language. In addition, he printed a regular course of Latin in his work.[21]

c

The knowledge of the classical languages was accompanied by a wide dissemination of the knowledge of Graeco-Roman literature and the cultural tradition of the ancient world. The many Italian translations of works of the classical literature made it possible for everyone to become familiar with the

[17] Cf. C. Roth, *The History of the Jews of Italy*, Philadelphia, 1946, p. 300. It is probable that also David, the son of Messer Leon, was a Neo-Latin poet. Cf. *HB* vol. 12, p. 33.
[18] As for example Elijah del Medigo, Joseph Zarfatti, Judah Moscato.
[19] *Meor Ainayim* p. 2.
[20] "*Qovets Al Yad*," 1888, p. 38.
[21] Cf. *Shiltei Hagiborim*, the introduction called *Leshonoth Hagoyim* folio 4, p. 1; 8, p. 1 and 2; 9, p. 1 and 2.

culture of the Antiquity, even without an adequate knowledge of its languages. For instance, we find a common man quoting the Iliad in a letter to a relative.[22] Obviously, some knowledge of the ancient culture also penetrated into uneducated circles.

A profound knowledge of classical literature was, of course, found only among the scholars. Here again Abraham Portaleone and Azariah de' Rossi surpassed all others. The starting point of Portaleone's description of the various fields of knowledge was the science of the Antiquity. When he described the architecture of the Temple in Jerusalem, he referred continuously to the works of Vitruvius, the greatest architect of the Antiquity. His knowledge of the classical literature was broad enough to include the comedies of Terence and Plautus. An almost equally thorough knowledge of the Roman and Greek writers had Azariah de' Rossi, who quoted in his work more than one hundred Roman and Greek authors.[23] Judah Moscato, the great writer and preacher, quoted besides Plato and Aristotle, also Seneca, Ovid, Cicero, Quintilian, and others.[24] In his sermons he liked to use material from the Roman and Greek legends as illustration of his thoughts.[25]

Quotations from the classical literature are frequently found in the writings of other Jewish authors as well. In a poem dedicated to the history of music, Samuel Archevolti wrote about Pythagoras as the "rediscoverer" of music. Judah Moscato likewise knew of him as the restorer of the art of music.[26] Abraham Faresol, the greatest geographer among the Jews of the Renaissance continuously referred in his Igereth Orehoth Olam to the geographical writings of Ptolemy. Messer Leon and Judah Moscato, who wrote about rhetoric from the theoretical point of view, derived their knowledge from the writings of Aristotle,

22 See Rivista Mensile di Israel vol. 1, p. 37 f.
23 Cf. the biography of Azariah written by Zunz in Ben-Jacob's edition of Meor Ainayim, and the list of authors in Cassel's edition, part Matsref Lakesef, p. 161.
24 Cf. Nefutsoth Yehudah, the introduction and folio 2, 26 and 128, p. 1.
25 Cf. the study of Israel Bettan, HUCA, vol. 6, p. 305.
26 Cf. Arugath Habosem folio 118 p. 1 and Nefutsoth Yehudah sermon 1, called "Higayon bekhinor."

Cicero, and Quintilian.[27] In his own sermons, Judah Moscato strictly adhered to Cicero's plan, and his oration consisted of four parts: the exordium, preposition, analysis, and conclusion. Azariah Pigo, another great preacher of the Italian-Jewish Renaissance, composed his sermons in the same manner.[28]

The Hebrew epistolography of the Renaissance imitated both the contemporary Neo-Latin writers and Cicero.[29] Now and then we also find works which made use of material from the Greek-Roman religion and mythology. The playwright Leone de' Sommi introduced many figures from the classical mythology into his Italian plays,[30] and likewise did Judah Moscato in his sermons. Needless to say, almost all authors made use of the writings of Philo[31] and Josephus. Many also quoted Plato extensively. The knowledge of Antiquity was further fostered by a deep interest in its archeological remnants. For example, David Finzi of Mantua was the owner of a collection of ancient coins which Azariah de' Rossi used to study.[32] The physician Enoch of Ascoli was sent by Pope Nicholas V, a great admirer of the ancient world, to acquire old manuscripts for him in Greece, the Balkan Countries, France, and Germany.[33] Abraham Portaleone tells that the Jews had a passion for collecting "gold medals . . . old bronze figures and other objects, such as vessels . . . "; to this report Portaleone added a warning to his Jewish contemporaries not to spend too much money for such acquisitions.[34] Obviously, the passion of the Jews to collect

[27] Cf. *Nofeth Tsufim* in several places and *Nefutsoth Yehudah* folio 78, p. 1.

[28] See the study by Israel Bettan, *HUCA*, vol. 7, p. 467.

[29] Cf. the study by Alexander Marx on Joseph Arli, *"Tarbiz,"* vol. 8, p. 172.

[30] Cf. Isaac (Ignacy) Schipper, *Geshikhte fun yiddisher teater kunst un drame*, vol. 1, Warsaw 1927, p. 48.

[31] See the study of R. Marcus, *HUCA*, vol. 21, p. 29 f. that Azariah de' Rossi was one of the first who critically examined Philo's works in a thoroughly comprehensive manner. He is also the translator of the Greek name Philo into Yedidyah Haaleksandroni. And generally Philo was very popular among the Italian Jews in this period.

[32] *Meor Ainayim*, part *Yemei Olam*, p. 188.

[33] Cf. E. Natali, *Il Ghetto di Roma*, Rome 1887, p. 186.

[34] *Shiltei Hagiborim*, folio 60, p. 2.

190

archeological objects surpassed normal limits and assumed dimensions characteristic of the epoch of the Renaissance.

———————

These facts confirm the impression we get whenever we study the sources of this epoch: the interest in the Renaissance and in the various branches of its culture was more than incidental. It was accompanied by genuine efforts to acquire this culture. But the Jews did not become totally absorbed in the pursuits of the Renaissance, as did certain parts of the Christian population. The Jews remained firmly attached to Judaism, and only adopted the culture of the Renaissance in a "moderate" form.[35] Abraham Portaleone tried to further the knowledge of the ancient civilization among the scholars through his writings, while Gedaliah ibn Yahya did the same for the common man in his *Shalshelet Hakabbalah*. The scholar and the common man responded to this challenge in a positive way, and their knowledge of Antiquity contributed to the influence which the Renaissance had on the life of the Italian Jews.

[35] In my lecture at the First World Congress of Jewish Studies mentioned in note 1.

VIII

ROME — EUROPE'S OLDEST JEWISH COMMUNITY

To the memory
of Eli Rogozik
(1910 - 1939)

a

Rome is called the Eternal City. It can also be called the Eternal Jewish Community. It is perhaps the only Jewish community from which the Jews were never expelled. Uninterruptedly a Jewish kehillah has existed in Rome for the past two thousand years.

The first Jewish inhabitants of Rome were probably the captives whom Pompey brought from Palestine after he had captured Jerusalem in the year 63 B.C.E. Thereafter the relationship between the Roman state and Palestine became ever closer, and the Jewish settlement in the city of Rome kept on growing. Aristocrats from Judea were attracted by the high culture and beauty of the metropolis. Other newcomers were restless revolutionaries who were brought over after every unsuccessful attempt of the Judeans to free their land from Roman yoke. Sooner or later the captives-slaves were redeemed by their brethren of the young Roman Jewish community, and some of them came to rank among its respected members. In the sixteenth century seven or eight families were still trying to "prove" that they alone belonged to the four families who, according to tradition, were brought by Titus from Jerusalem after the Temple was destroyed.

The constant rise of Rome's Jewish community evoked well-known reactions on the part of the adversaries of the Jews. In addition, the pagan writers were unable to distinguish between Jews and Christians. Anti-Christian feelings thus contributed to the development of so-called "ancient anti-Semitism." In general, however, the Jews lived quite peacefully in pagan Rome. Julius Caesar was their great friend. When he prohibited the existence of all private organizations *(collegia)*, he explicitly permitted the Jewish community to continue its activities as an organized social body. This was an act of great historical significance as we shall see later.

With few exceptions the Roman emperors continued the friendly policy towards the Jews of the Eternal City. They were opposed to an independent Jewish state in Judea, but were tolerant to the Jewish inhabitants of their capital. When the Emperor Caracalla granted in 212 C.E. Roman citizenship to all the inhabitants of the state, the Jews also became citizens of the Empire.

When Christians began to ascend the throne of Rome, the situation of the Jews became less advantageous. Constantine the Great (323-337) was the first to deprive the Jews of some of their rights. Many of his successors did the same, and when Christianity was raised to the position of the state religion, the Jews lost the rest of their civil rights. In addition, early Christianity waged a bitter literary feud against its mother religion and issued a flood of propaganda to exclude the Jews from society and to degrade them. Such was the position of Rome's Jewry at the time of the fall of the Empire (476 C.E.) and so it remained all through the Middle Ages.

In spite of their abased civil and social position, and the fact that Rome was a perpetual target of the medieval wars, the Jews clung to the city. Like their Christian neighbors they were great and sincere Roman patriots. They participated in the uprising of the popular hero Cola Rienzi in 1347, when for a moment it seemed that the old glory of imperial Rome was returning. A few decades later a Roman Jew, who lived in another city, remembered Rome in his last will and gave a certain amount for "the fortification of the walls of Rome, my native city." Like the ancient Roman, who proudly declared at every occasion *civis Romanus sum* (I am a Roman citizen), the Jew of medieval Rome liked to mention that he was *Ish Romi* — a man of Rome.

The end of the Middle Ages brought better times for the Jews of Rome. During the period of the Renaissance religious differences seemed to have lost much of their bitterness. The important thing now was to fill life with cultural experience, poetry, music, and study. The new esteem given to the languages and cultures of Antiquity shed its grace upon the Jews, who were the keepers of the ancient Hebrew language and Hebraic culture. The popes collected antiques and old manuscripts, and Jewish scholars worked for them enthusiastically. The Hebrew grammarian Elijah Levita *(Elijah Bahur),* an immigrant from Germany, had among his pupils some of the highest dignitaries of the Church. For many years he lived in the palace of Cardinal Egidio da Viterbo, who was one of his students. The mysterious David Reubeni, who came to Rome in 1524 as the "ambassador" of an imaginary Jewish kingdom, was received by Pope Clement VII with great honors. Jewish poets, musicians, and scholars felt at home in the spiritual realm of the Roman Renaissance.

The happy times of the Renaissance did not last too long. In 1527 the city was ransacked by the Emperor's soldiery *(Sacco di Roma).* The Jews suffered along with the other citizens; but the blow was not as hard as that which came about thirty years later. In the year 1555 an old monk, Cardinal Caraffa, ascended the papal throne as Paul IV. In the four years of his reign he succeeded in destroying most of the cultural achievements of the Renaissance. One of the things he disliked most was the rapprochement between Jews and Christians, which was a major result of the Renaissance. The Jews were forced into the notorious Roman Ghetto, whose walls did not fall until 1870. Social relations between Jews and Christians were forbidden. The entire Jewish community was compelled to earn its livelihood by trading in old clothes. For more than three hundred years the Jewish community fought with dignity against the inhuman conditions imposed on it. Although a relentless missionary activity was conducted among the Jews, an average of no more than ten of them annually converted to the dominant religion. A well organized system of social welfare, which included more than sixty charitable societies, cared for the needy. A class of skilled garment workers emerged among the traders in old clothing. Other traders in secondhand merchandise became noted antique dealers. Persian rugs, fine-art needlework, and beautiful jewelry could best be bought in the Ghetto.

During almost all of this time the Ghetto had renowned rabbis and communal leaders. Hezekiah Manoah Corcos, his grandson Tranquillo Vita (seventeenth century), Samuel Alatri (nineteenth century), and many others courageously fought for a change in the papal policy towards the Jews of the city. From time to time they were successful and obtained minor concessions for their brethren. But one great evil was never eliminated — the practice of kidnapping Jewish children and baptizing them against the will of their parents. With regard to this the popes remained unmoved, and the kidnapping tragedy continued to be the saddest aspect of Roman Jewish life during the three hundred years in the Ghetto.

The political and social emancipation of the Roman Jewish community came much later than elsewhere in Italy, because in the Eternal City the papal government survived until 1870. Only then did the walls of the Ghetto come down. The Jews gradually moved to other, more desirable parts of the capital. However, the neighborhood of the Ghetto has remained until now a Jewish section inhabited by families who date back a thousand years or more.

It is well known that in modern times the Jews of Italy have enjoyed a very large measure of equality. New favorable conditions developed which began to attract more and more

Jews to the big cities, and especially to the capital. The Roman Jewish community grew rapidly and its members began to rise on the ladder of society. Jewish cabinet members, ambassadors, generals, and professors were a familiar sight in the city. Luigi Luzzatti, a noted philosopher and economist, was appointed prime minister in 1910. Rome also had a Jewish mayor. Ernesto Nathan was born in London of Italian-Jewish parentage. In 1871, shortly after the liberation of the city, he moved to Rome and became one of its outstanding citizens. From 1907 to 1913 he served with distinction as the mayor of the Eternal City.

When Mussolini became Italy's dictator, the position of the Jews at first remained satisfactory. At that time about ten thousand Jews lived in Rome, comprising one quarter of Italy's Jewish population. The Collegio Rabbinico, the oldest modern rabbinical school in Europe, was moved from Florence to Rome. Once again the city had a flourishing Jewish kehillah which was conscious of its role as the oldest existing community of the European Diaspora.

However, shortly before the outbreak of the Second World War, when Mussolini became Hitler's ally, the fate of Roman Jewry became once more tragic. Jewish professors lost their positions and had to leave the country. The Chief Rabbi was compelled to resign and the position was given to a man who added much to the tragedy of the Roman Jews at the close of the war (see below).

In September 1943 the German army occupied Rome. Almost immediately it began to persecute the Jews in the same way as in Poland. On December 1 Mussolini ordered all the Jews of Rome to be placed in concentration camps and all Jewish property confiscated. Many found refuge in Christian homes and in several monasteries, but many were sent to the death camp in Auschwitz.

On Sunday, June 1, 1944, the Jews of Rome were liberated by the American Army. The survivors began to emerge from their hiding places and some of the refugees returned to the city. With the assistance of Jewish chaplains of the United States Army and the Jewish Brigade Group of the British Army, religious and cultural life began to reawaken. The unexpected conversion to Christianity of the Chief Rabbi Israel Zolli (Zoller), a friend of the Fascists, was a hard blow to Rome's Jewry. However, the community continued the work of reconstruction uninterruptedly. Professor David Prato, who had been banished by Mussolini, returned from Palestine and was reinstated as chief rabbi. True, Rome's Jewish community did not regain the brilliant status it had before the Second World War. But during the past twenty years it has been an active, Jewishly conscious community. It has rebuilt most of its religious and educational institutions. It is once again the eternal Jewish community in the Eternal City.

b

Apart from the historical path of the Jewish community of Rome, a mysterious link has existed through the ages between the Jewish people and the Eternal City. In the remote times of the Maccabean Revolution the city of Rome appeared for the first time on the horizon of the Jewish people. It was then the capital of a distant but friendly young republic, which was expected to aid in the struggle against the common Syrian enemy. In later times Rome became the symbol of the destruction of the Judean state and the Temple in Jerusalem. In the Middle Ages, Rome became the symbol of the endless dialogue and struggle between Judaism and Christianity. The capital of Christianity became a major topic of Jewish folklore. In its bitter plight during the Dark Ages, the Jewish people identified Rome with Edom-Esau. It was a sad but clear indictment of the religion that grew out of Judaism, and instead of being a brother to it became the arch-enemy Esau (Obadiah 1:10-14).

Yet, strangely enough, the deepest hope of the Jewish people for redemption was connected with Rome. "At the entrance of the City (Rome) . . . he (the Messiah) is sitting among the poor lepers" (Sanhedrin 98a). This would appear to

197

be an ironical comment suggesting that at the gates of the capital of the religion which claims that the Messiah had come, the true Messiah is still "waiting" for the day to come when he will reveal himself.

Of a much more practical nature was the significance of the Roman Jewish community because of its proximity to the papal court. Beginning with the sixth century, the influence of the popes on the Christian world was constantly growing, especially in matters of faith. Therefore, winning the favor of the pope became a major objective of Jewish "policy." Again and again Jews the world over asked the popes' help against excesses of the lower clergy. Often, indeed, effective help did come from Rome. When Portugal prepared to introduce the Inquisition, it was of great advantage to the Marranos that the matter was dependent on the pope. They sent an "ambassador" to Rome and succeeded to postpone for decades the establishment of the terrible institution. Similarly, effective protection was often given by the popes to the Jews in their defense against the blood libel. From the thirteenth to the seventeenth century a number of popes issued public statements *(bullae)* which cleared the Jews of that vicious accusation. When a wave of blood accusations flooded Poland in the eighteenth century, the Council of the Four Lands, the central communal organization of Polish Jewry, sent a messenger to Rome. There he succeeded to secure from Cardinal Ganganelli, later Pope Clement XIV, an extensive report on the blood libel which cleared the Jews of guilt. This report was utilized by the Jews during the Beilis trial (1913).

The Roman Jewish community played a significant role in all these events. When Jewish "ambassadors" came to Rome from distant countries, they found themselves in a strange metropolis. In addition, it was not easy to establish contacts with the papal court. It was in the Jewish community of Rome that the messengers found warmth, understanding, and willingness to help. This role of an intermediary between Jews the world over and the Vatican gave Roman Jewry a position of paramount importance. It established the community's unparalleled fame among Jews of the most distant countries.

There is still aother area in which Rome's attitude was of prime importance to the Jewish people. For hundreds of years the Jewish people looked on passively while "Seir and his father-in-law" (Esau and Ishmael, Genesis 28:9), Christians and Mohammedans, fought among themselves for the possession of the Holy Land. The feeling of deep sorrow because of Jewish passivity often found its expression in medieval Hebrew poetry. Such was the mood until David Reubeni, the mysterious Jew from the Orient, made an effort to regain the Holy Land for the Jews with papal agreement. The Reubeni episode has not yet been sufficiently clarified, and will remain a mystery until the Vatican will make accessible to historians the Reubeni papers which it probably keeps in its archives.

When in the spring of 1917 the negotiations on the Balfour Declaration entered their final stage, Nahum Sokolow went to see Pope Benedict XV on behalf of the World Zionist Organization. The Pope remarked to him: "How much has history changed! Nineteen hundred years ago Rome destroyed your country, and now you come to Rome to seek its restoration!" At present the Vatican is one of the spots to which the diplomats of the State of Israel direct careful attention.

c

The Jewish community of Rome also made an important contribution to Jewish communal life in general. We have seen that when Julius Caesar abolished all the *collegia* in Rome, he explicitly excluded the Jewish community. This was an act of major historical significance. It was tantamount to an official recognition, the first in history, of the Jewish community as the organizational framework of Jewish life in the Diaspora. In the Middle Ages the *kehillah* became the backbone of Jewish life, and Caesar's "recognition" provided a legal foundation for its existence.

Rome is also, perhaps, the only place in the world where a Jewish community has existed uninterruptedly for more than two thousand years. No expulsion of the Jews from Rome is recorded. Its Jewish community was spared even when a few popes of the Counter-Reformation times attempted to banish the Jews from all their territories.

This factual and "political" stability is responsible for the fact that Rome has had a Jewish population living in the same quarter for perhaps more than a thousand years. This stability made Roman Jewry remarkably regenerative. Whenever parts of the Italian peninsula became "Judenrein," Roman Jewry carried out to a considerable degree their recolonization by Jews. When in modern times Italian Jewry became rapidly urbanized and its numbers decreased, Roman Jewry made up for the losses through natural increase. During the few "philo-Semitic" years of Mussolini's regime, Roman Jewry was responsible for a slight increase in the total number of Jews in Italy.

The Roman community was also one of the first examples of a composite Jewish community, such as developed in our times in America and Israel. The Roman Ghetto harbored native Italian Jews, as well as Jews from Spain, Portugal, France, Germany, and the Orient. As early as the end of the thirteenth century, Italy had become a typical land of Jewish immigration. Jews came from all directions to the Eternal City. In Rome the first clashes between native and alien Jews occurred. It was also in Rome that a solution was found. The kehillah constitution, prepared by Daniel of Pisa, provided for equal representation of all Jewish groups in the city. On the basis of this constitution the different *nazioni* lived peacefully together until the "aliens" were no more aliens. Moreover, the heterogeneity of the population proved to be a great incentive towards positive Jewish living by provoking competition in good deeds. The charitable societies which in the period of the Ghetto numbered more than sixty can serve as a good illustration.

However, Roman Jewry's greatest contribution to the Jewish people is the concept of Jewish life which it created during the period of the Renaissance. This concept is still of major importance to the Jewish people. The Italian Renaissance was a period of great rapprochement between Jews and gentiles, unknown since the times of the old Roman Empire. Italian Jewry, therefore, faced a cultural challenge, equalled only by that of the Jews of the Hellenistic world. On the one hand the rediscovered general human culture lured them with all its beauty. On the other hand there was an immanent danger of losing their Jewish identity. Roman Jewry, and Italian Jewry in general, lived up to the challenge. They accepted the culture of the Renaissance willingly, but only in a "moderate" form. The Jews experienced along with the gentiles an "intoxication" with the new culture. Like the Christians they eagerly collected books, studied the classical languages, and taught their children music and dance. But, whenever they became aware of a real danger to their Jewishness they retreated to purely Jewish "grounds." Rome's Jewry emerged from the Renaissance with its Jewish and general human values strengthened. It was this strength which enabled the Jews of Rome to walk with dignity the long dark historical path in the period of the Ghetto, 1555-1870.

A great Italian-Jewish thinker of the nineteenth century once remarked that Italian Jewry was both pious and enlightened. Between the two extremes — the "Pious Man of Ashkenaz," alienated from the world, and the sophisticated Spanish Jew of the late Middle Ages — the Jews of Rome and Italy found a new path: to participate in general life as offered by the environment but not to forget their own Jewish roots.

IX

THE JEWISH COMMUNITY IN TURKEY—
A STORY OF GLORY AND DECLINE

Originally published in "The Chicago Jewish Forum," vol. 13 (1954), pp. 6-10

a

In the year 1453, that is five hundred years ago, there occurred one of the greatest historical events of the outgoing Middle Ages: the city of Constantinople, proud capital of the Byzantine Empire, was captured by the Turks. For a period of three hundred years the Empire had fought a losing battle against the young and forceful Asiatic nation. Generation after generation the Turks wrested from it pieces of its vast territory. The proud Empire called to its help the Christian nations of Western Europe. But this only delayed the catastrophe; it could not prevent the ultimate downfall of the doomed Empire. And so, the year 1453 witnessed the final act in the historic drama: Constantinople changed into Istanbul and became the capital of the mightiest Moslem ruler, the Sultan, and its famous Cathedral of Hagia Sophia became a Moslem mosque.

The fall of Constantinople was a political event of great significance. Suddenly Christian Europe realized that the Byzantine Empire, which, with all its weakness, had held up for centuries the Turks' march on Europe, no longer existed. Europe was open to a Turkish invasion. And the Turks, in fact, began driving towards the heart of Europe. They occupied the entire Balkan peninsula, parts of Hungary, and a large number of

Mediterranean islands. From time to time they tried to reach Vienna, the capital of the Holy Roman Empire.

Fear of the Turks became the central problem in European politics during the next 250 years. Everybody was afraid of them, and several Christian governments tried to come to terms with them by selling out the interests of other Christian nations.

The fall of Constantinople and the emergence of Turkey as the strongest power in Europe became a great event also in the history of the Jews. The Jubilee of the fall of Constantinople is in the fullest sense also a Jewish Jubilee.

b

During the thousand years of the existence of the Byzantine Empire a Jewish community lived within its territories. They were a separate Jewish group, known historically as the Romaniote Jews (because Byzantium considered itself the "true" Rome) or Gregos (i.e. Greek Jews). They spoke Greek and had a prayerbook, the Mahazor Romania, quite different from the other known orders of prayers. They were never very numerous and their fate was never too happy. The anti-Jewish laws enacted by the early emperors of Byzantium, Theodosius and Justinian, were in force for hundreds of years and never permitted the Jews to raise their head. Another group of laws imposed upon the Jews very insulting duties. Heavy taxes and recurring local expulsions added to make the empire a sort of a hell to its Jewish inhabitants. Under these hard conditions, also the cultural life of Byzantine Jewry remained poor, excelling only in the field of religious poetry, called Piyut, and in the Midrashim. In poetry and in the memory of the great past the Byzantian Jews sought comfort.

It was at the close of the thirteenth century that the situation began to improve. This was due to the influence of Jewish immigrants from Germany who, in the wake of their expansion, began to settle in the Balkan countries. German Jews were so cruelly treated at that time that settlement in the anti-Semitic Byzantine Empire looked attractive by comparison. The new immigrants imported a more active form of Jewish life and considerably strengthened the structure of the Jewish communal organization.

c

This was the situation when the Turks took the capital in 1453. The Turks ruled a great empire with a variety of ethnic and religious groups. They therefore necessarily developed a system of religious tolerance, in which the different groups could live peacefully side by side. In this system, there was space for a Jewish group striving for a better life. And so Jewish life in the Balkan countries began to change radically. The chief rabbi of Constantinople was recognized as the official representative of the Jews and enjoyed the status of a high dignitary.

The new situation deeply impressed a certain Joseph Zarfatti, an immigrant rabbi from Germany. So he sent to the Jews in the Western countries an enthusiastic call to settle en masse in Turkey, promising them complete religious freedom and manifold economic opportunities. The call came at a very critical moment. A wave of blood accusations was rolling over Southern Germany, costing many Jewish lives and holding in terror the entire Jewish population. Under these conditions Zarfatti's call encouraged Jewish immigration to Turkey, since we know that precisely then the German Jewish element in Turkey increased quickly, approaching in numbers the native Jewish community of the Gregos. Turkey was rapidly expanding. It needed qualified workers, merchants, financiers and physicians. The Jewish immigrants belonged in the majority to these economic categories and were received very heartily.

d

The full significance of the year 1453 in the history of the Jews became evident about forty years later, when a quarter of a million Jews were expelled from Spain. The majority of these Jews either succumbed to the ordeal of their wanderings or were baptized by force in Portugal, where they had hoped to find refuge. Only the eighty thousand who went to Turkey (except for an additional ten thousand who settled in Italy) were saved and could start a new life. If not for Turkey, the disaster of the expulsion would have been immensely increased.

This colossal force of Jewish immigrants poured into Turkey within the short period of about a year, forshadowing scenes of later times, when Jewish mass immigration reached this country or the State of Israel. They poured in like an avalanche, absorbed almost completely (though not without a dramatic struggle) the native Romaniote Jews and imposed an explicitly Sephardic character upon the Jewish community. A sort of a new "Golden Age" of Spanish Jewry set in in Turkey. Salonique, one of Turkey's foremost cities, came to be known as a Jewish "Republic," with its famous port closed for traffic on Sabbath; exporters, agents, merchants and longshoremen — all were Jews.

Especially significant became the Jewish community in the capital. It has been estimated that, in the year 1500, the Jewish population of Constantinople numbered about 30,000, a population large for that period. Jewish financiers, physicians and all kinds of experts were increasingly successful, and their standing gained importance with the growing expansion of the empire in Europe.

The Christian nations of Europe, which only a few decades earlier had looked with a mixture of bewilderment and pity at the refugees from Spain, were amazed to see how quickly they had become a leading factor in the political and economic growth of their new homeland. In fact, Jewish influence in Turkey was often exaggerated. The following event is very illustrative: In 1571 the Republic of Venice hitherto a haven of refuge for many Jews, decided to expel them. The Jews took energetic steps to have the decree revoked. The matter dragged on for about two years and the decree of expulsion was finally abolished. A contemporary Hebrew writer tells us how the expulsion came to be revoked. Many Jews, believing that the threat of expulsion would be carried out, decided to embark before the "rush" of the exodus started. They chartered a large number of vessels, which began to crowd the port of Venice. It so happened that the ambassador of the Republic in Constantinople returned home. When he noticed the unusual number of vessels and learned the purpose for which they had come, he hurried to the Doge and explained to him that once the Jews left the city, they would go to Turkey and add new strength to the Turks' might. Turkish strength — he said — was created by the skill and wealth imported by the Spanish Jews. This story is verified in a letter of an ambassador of another country, who was then also residing in Constantinople. It shows that the Venetian ambassador's assertion was an accepted opinion.

The belief that the Jewish immigrants made Turkey great was only strengthened by the activities of the controversial but brilliant personality of Don Joseph Nassi. It would lead us far astray to retell here the amazing and stormy career of this Portuguese marrano who became one of Europe's most outstanding statesmen in the sixteenth century. Suffice it to say that shortly after his arrival in Turkey Don Joseph became very close to the imperial court. He quickly acquired a thorough knowledge of the obscure pathways of Turkish politics and threw himself keenly into the turmoil of a fight between two pretenders to the crown. He probably contributed a great share to "his" candidate's victory and so became the leading man in Turkey's politics. Certain European monarchs, who had a guilty conscience in connection with the former marrano's sufferings, constantly suspected him of plotting to bring about their ruin.

How Don Joseph tried to avenge the evil done to his coreligionists is best illustrated by the most remarkable act of Jewish self-defense in the sixteenth century. In 1556, a number of marranos in the papal harbor city of Ancona were arrested by the Inquisition and subsequently burned alive. Among the victims were some of Don Joseph's friends and business associates, former marranos, who, like him, had escaped from Portugal and believed that in Italy they had reached a secure haven. Their tragic death caused great sorrow in Jewish circles,

206

unaccustomed to an auto da fé in enlightened Italy. The desperate wrath of the Jews found its expression in a large number of Hebrew poems in which the martyrs were eulogized for their steadfastness and courage. Don Joseph, however, was a type who did not know the meaning of despair. In the entanglements of Turkish politics, he had learned that a wrong is to be avenged. So he decided to strike back. At his initiative, Turkish Jewish merchants, who maintained business relations with Ancona, declared a boycott against its harbor. During the months that the boycott lasted, the Papal City was almost ruined economically. It was saved from a complete catastrophe only by Jewish disunity, which broke up the boycott after several months.

Don Joseph Nassi also made an attempt to foster Jewish settlement in Palestine. He obtained from the Sultan a permit to colonize Northern Palestine around the city of Tiberias. His plan was to build up industries by encouraging the immigration of Jewish artisans from the Papal States in which they were, as we have seen, cruelly oppressed.

Don Joseph's plan caused considerable commotion among the Jews in Italy, and entire communities prepared to embark for Palestine. Some of the groups actually reached Tiberias and began the work. However, at this point their benefactor suddenly dropped the project. There is no full explanation about these events. There is some evidence that the opposition of the neighboring Arabs made Don Joseph doubt the possibility of going through with his plans. But it also seems that his interest turned to some other, more selfish plans: namely, he hoped to become king of the island of Cyprus through the appointment of the Sultan. Be that as it may, the colonization plan of Tiberias remained a pre-Zionist episode, not yet sufficiently clarified as to its scope and the reasons for its failure.

Don Joseph's end was that of other sultanic "favorites." His numerous enemies succeeded, after years of intriguing, in undermining his position. The Jews as a community, however, remained unharmed. Other Jewish "favorites," men and women, took Nassi's place in the lobbies of the palace, and Constantinople's

Jewish community continued to flourish. Its strength, stability and wealth were a result of the basic fact that the Turkish empire, in its rapid expansion, found in its Jews the type of citizen it most urgently needed.

e

Against the background of political stability and economic prosperity, Constantinople's Jewry built up a magnificent structure of cultural and social activity. Famous rabbis stood at the head of its colleges, and brilliant scholars wrote significant works in the fields of Jewish jurisprudence and exegesis of the Bible. Simultaneously a network of Hebrew printing presses sprang up, which wrote a golden page in Jewish literary history. The importance of the Jewish printing presses lies in the fact that in Turkey Hebrew books could be printed without previously being censored. In the Christian countries they were subjected to censorship and correction by hostile clergymen or converts, who quite often completely deformed the text. In addition, Hebrew printing was completely prohibited in Italy in 1553 and thousands of Hebrew books were burned by order of the Pope.

In respect to Jewish charity also, Constantinople Jewry did much to help its brethren. The city became, along with Venice and Amsterdam, one of the three centers from which all financial assistance for the Jews in Palestine was directed. It held this position with distinction down to the eighteenth century. It was the wealthy and influential Jewish center which in those dark times gave to the Jews in Palestine that political and economic assistance without which it probably could not have survived.

Of utmost significance was the activity of Constantinople Jewry in favor of the victims of the Chmielnicki massacres in Ukraine in 1648. Not only were an estimated hundred thousand Jews murdered by the Cossacks, but additional tens of thousands, mainly women and children, were taken captives by the Tartar allies of Chmielnicki, and thrown on the slave markets of the Near East. At this point Constantinople Jewry stepped in. It quickly assigned large funds and redeemed about 20,000 of the captives. The chronicler of the events, Nathan Hanover, gives us in his famous book *Abyss of Despair* the following touching remark about Constantinople's Jewry: "Our brethren in Constantinople, the Lord preserve them, redeemed them together with other Polish captives, numbering approximately twenty thousand souls. They expended vast sums of money, all that was asked of them. They provided food and shelter for them to the present day (1653); they favored them with many services without limit. The entire land of Turkey manifested such generosity, especially the people of Salonica, may the Lord preserve them."

f

The Jewish tragedy of the Thirty Years War (1618-1648) which culminated in the massacres of Chmielnicki, together with a number of social, political, and religious causes, brought about in the year 1666 the most fascinating messianic episode in the history of our people. The movement was created by a Turkish Jew, Sabbatai Zevi, and the attempt was made to revive the Jewish State in the Holy Land. Failure was inevitable and disappointment, cruel. Modern Jewish historians know how to explain this strange movement which caused a shock to Jewry from which it did not recover for more than a hundred years. Despite all that, the movement was a mighty demonstration of the Jewish will to be redeemed and of the unquenchable belief that the Messiah would come. For the first time, all the world was shown that the connection of the Jewish people with its old homeland was a tangible historic factor. The Sabbatai Zevi movement reminded the non-Jewish world, in no uncertain terms, that there existed a claim of the Jews to their homeland. Who knows how important were the invisible strands which run from the strange messianic movement of the seventeenth century to the decision of the United Nations of November 29, 1947? This great demonstration of Jewish faith was made by Turkish Jewry. It was its last great share in an *active* Jewish history before it began to decline.

g

Constantinople's Jewry, and Turkish Jewry in general, began to lose importance along with the decline in power of the sultan's empire since the close of the seventeenth century. Its might began gradually to dwindle; it lost important provinces, and became more and more the "Sick Man of Europe." As a result, it lost most of its significance in international politics and its social degradation proceeded rapidly.

Together with the country as a whole, Turkish Jewry underwent an inevitable process of pauperization, degradation and levantinization. In the reawakened historical activism of the Jewish people in the nineteenth century, the voice of Constantinople's Jewry remained almost unheard. It was now a backward oriental community in the capital of a backward nation. But this cannot obscure the golden pages it wrote in Jewish history in the times of its greatness. The center of the Jewish people departed to other shores. But the memory of Constantinople's greatness and its social and cultural contributions to our people is alive. Indeed, Constantinople's Jubilee is a Jewish Jubilee.